why a catalog for Jewish kids?

Catalogs are great places to find things—whether for shopping, reading, learning, or just having fun. With the right catalog, you'll find just what you want.

This catalog is meant to be just right for Jewish kids. You don't have to start with page one and read it through to the end. You can flip through this book. Each time you open it, you'll find something to suit your mood or interest.

There will surely be times when you will want to learn more about yourself and your name, or more about the history of our people, both throughout the world and here in America. There'll be times when you'll want to meet new friends, learn about Hebrew and Yiddish (even how to blow your stack in Yiddish), or get some new facts about the Jewish holidays. This book can help you throw a holiday party, make holiday crafts, and cook Jewish delicacies. There are Jewish stories here from many times and places, a list of one hundred good books to look for in your bookstore or library, and a chapter with Jewish songs and music. And lots more. So start flipping, reading, learning, and enjoying.

the Jewish

Chaya M. Burstein

Designed by Adrianne Onderdonk Dudden

The Jewish Publication Society • Philadelphia • Jerusalem

kids catalog

Thank you to my daughters Dina and Bethy for their suggestions on the general content of this book; to David Adler, Sheila Segal, and Salena Rapp Kern, my hard-working editors; and to my husband, Mordy, who nudged and prodded me past many rough spots in the preparation of this book.

Thank you also to all the "friends" who appear in chapter 2; to Joyce Becker for writing chapter 8; to Ruchama and Shlomo Tamsut and Edith Donnenberg for their information on Sephardi cooking and customs; to Linda Shaffzin of *World Over* for her help in selecting material for chapter 12; to Betty Ann Ross for writing the introduction to chapter 13; and to Betty Ann Ross and Velvel Pasternak for their help in preparing the music for chapter 13.

Eighth Printing, 1993

© 1983 by Chaya M. Burstein
Bibliography © 1993 by Marcia Posner

Library of Congress Cataloging-in-Publication Data
Burstein, Chaya M.
    The Jewish kids catalog.
    Includes index.
    Summary: A miscellany of Jewish customs, history, language, holidays, crafts, recipes, beliefs, literature, music, folklore, and landmarks.
    1. Jews—Juvenile literature.   [1. Jews—Miscellanea.   2. Judaism—Miscellanea] I. Title.
DS118.B79 1982   909'.04924   82-13103
ISBN 0-8276-0215-4
Manufactured in the United States of America

The publisher gratefully acknowledges permission to reprint the following:
"The Garden" by Franta Bass from *I Never Saw Another Butterfly,* by permission of Artia Publishers.
"Clay Shabbat Candleholders," "Havdalah Candles," "Simple Havdalah Spice Boxes," "Sukkah in a Desert," "Simhat Torah Flags," "Simple Purim Masks," "Purim Puppets," "Liquid-embroidered Matzah Cover," and "Afikoman Holder," and "Paper Seder Plates" from pages 4, 19, 48, 62, 63, 108, 113, 119, 122, 127, and 155 of *Jewish Holiday Crafts,* copyright © 1977 by Joyce Becker, reprinted by permission of Hebrew Publishing Company.
"Easy-to-Make Holiday Cards," "Button People Card," "All Kinds of Dreidels," and "Hanukkah Menorot" from pages 132–133, 28, and 12 of *Hanukkah Crafts,* copyright 1978 © by Joyce Becker, reprinted by permission of Hebrew Publishing Company.
"Heavenly Hallah," "Grandma's Chicken Soup," "Pita Sandwiches," "Felafel," "Tehina Sauce," and "Hamantashen" from pages 4–5, 2, 90, 91, 92, and 66–67 of *A First Jewish Holiday Cookbook,* copyright © 1979 by Chaya M. Burstein, reprinted by permission of Hebrew Publishing Company.
"Nahalat Goldstein" from pages 4–5 of *World Over,* vol. 42, no. 5 (January 6, 1981).
"When Pruning Shears Shoot," by Sara Eshel, from pages 14–15 of *World Over,* vol. 42, no. 9 (May 5, 1981).
"Felicia to Felicia," by Terri Beverly Bernstein, from pages 10–11 of *World Over,* vol. 40, no. 12 (April 6, 1979).
"The Tallit," by Lois Ruby, from pages 8–9 of *World Over,* vol. 42, no. 2 (October 10, 1980).

*This book is dedicated
to the memory of my parents and teachers,
Benjamin and Rivka Malamud,
and to their great-grandchildren,
Jacob and Jesse.
May the apples fall close to the tree.*

Contents

Hebrew has a special sound not found in English, represented by the letters *het* ח or *khaf* כ. The *het* is written with a "ḥ" and the *khaf* is written with a "kh." Sometimes both are represented by "ch."

To make the sound, pretend you have a sore throat and are gargling with mouthwash. Try it out on **Ḥanukkah.**

6 AROUND THE JEWISH YEAR 88

7 HOLIDAY PARTIES 102

8 HOLIDAY CRAFTS 112

more

Some Jewish things about

You are a special person. Nobody exactly like you ever lived before. You have your own way of thinking, your own unique handwriting, and even your own way of drawing pictures. But you are also a member of a family and of a people. Your people's customs are part of what makes you special. This chapter tells about family roots, about Jewish customs for giving names, about your education and school, even about caring for your pets in a Jewish way. It's about some of the things that make you a special person.

WHAT'S IN YOUR NAME?

Jewish kids seem to have more given names (first names) than anybody else. They may have an English name that's used in school, a Hebrew name that's used in Hebrew school and in the synagogue, a funny nickname such as Pickles or Sweetie Pie, and sometimes a Yiddish name too.

Hebrew names have been used ever since the days of the Bible,

Girls' given names

אֲבִיגַיִל	**Abigail** God brings joy	אֶסְתֵּר	**Esther** a star	רָחֵל	**Rachel** a sheep
עָדָה	**Ada** ornament	אִתְיָה	**Etya** with God	רִבְקָה	**Rebecca** captivating beauty
עֲדִינָה	**Adina** dainty	חַוָּה	**Eve** life	רִנָּה	**Rina** song
אֲהוּבָה	**Ahuva** beloved	גִּילָה	**Gila** joy	רוּת	**Ruth** a friend
עֲלִיזָה	**Aliza** happy	הֲדַסָּה	**Hadassah** a myrtle (tree)	שָׂרָה	**Sarah** princess
אֲבִיטַל	**Avital** God protects	חַנָּה	**Hannah** grace	שָׁרוֹנָה	**Sharon** a level place, a plain
אֲבִיבָה	**Aviva** springtime	יְהוּדִית	**Judith** a Jew		
אַיָּלָה	**Ayala** deer	לֵאָה	**Leah** languid	שִׁירָה	**Shira** song
בַּת שֶׁבַע	**Bat Sheva** daughter of an oath	מַלְכָּה	**Malka** queen	שׁוֹשַׁנָּה	**Shoshanah** rose
		מַרְגָּלִית	**Margalit** jewel	שׁוּלַמִּית	**Shulamit** peaceful
בִּתְיָה	**Batya** daughter of God	מָרְתָה	**Martha** lady	שִׂמְחָה	**Simcha** joy
בְּעוּלָה	**Beulah** married	מִיכַל	**Michal** a brook	תָּמָר	**Tamar** palm tree
בִּלְהָה	**Bilhah** impetuous	מִרְיָם	**Miriam** rebel	תִּקְוָה	**Tikva** hope
בְּרָכָה	**Bracha** blessing	נָעֳמִי	**Naomi** pleasant	טוֹבָה	**Tova** good
חַיָּה	**Chaya** life	נֶחָמָה	**Nechamah** comfort	צִפּוֹרָה	**Tzippora** a little bird
דְּבוֹרָה	**Deborah** bee	נַעֲמָה	**Neimah** pleasant	וַרְדָּה	**Varda** a rose
דִּקְלָה	**Dikla** date palm	נִצָּה	**Nitza** blossom	יָעֵל	**Yael** mountain goat
דִּינָה	**Dina** justice	נוּרִית	**Nurit** a light	יָפָה	**Yaffa** pretty
עֶדְנָה	**Edna** a delight	עָפְרָה	**Ophrah** young deer	יוֹכֶבֶד	**Yocheved** glory of God
אִילָנָה	**Elana** a tree	אוֹרָה	**Ora** a light	זְהָבָה	**Zahava** gold
אֱלִישֶׁבַע	**Elisheva** oath of God	פְּנִינָה	**Penina** a pearl		

when the Jews lived in the Land of Israel. When they moved to other lands they often gave their children names that were popular in the new land. Even the name Moses is not Hebrew—it's Egyptian. But Jews always kept their Hebrew names too. Some people used them all the time, and some only used them in the synagogue and to keep records of weddings, births, and deaths.

If you have different Hebrew and English names, they may sound alike: Miriam in Hebrew can become Maryanne or Myra in English. Or they may sound very different: Aaron can turn into Andrew, Albert, or Abercrombie.

First names have interesting meanings. Many have Hebrew origins. Can you find yours in these lists?

Boys' given names

אַבְנֵר **Abner** father of light	עֶזְרָא **Ezra** a helper	מִיכָאֵל **Michael** who is like God?	
אַבְרָהָם **Abraham** father of many	גַבְרִיאֵל **Gabriel** man of God	מָרְדְכַי **Mordecai** taught by God	
אָדָם **Adam** of the earth	גַד **Gad** fortune	מֹשֶׁה **Moses** drawn from the water	
אַהֲרֹן **Aaron** mountainous	גֵרְשׁוֹן **Gershon** a stranger		
עַמִי **Ami** my people	חֲנַנְיָה **Hanan** graceful	נַחוּם **Nahum** comfort	
עָמוֹס **Amos** strong	הַלֵל **Hillel** praise	נָתָן **Nathan** God gave	
אֲרִי **Ari** lion	חִירָם **Hiram** noble	נֹעַם **Noam** pleasantness	
אָשֵׁר **Asher** happy	יִצְחָק **Isaac** he will laugh	נֹחַ **Noah** rest	
בָּרָק **Barak** lightning	יְשַׁעְיָה(וּ) **Isaiah** saved by God	עוֹבַדְיָה **Obadiah** servant of God	
בָּרוּךְ **Baruch** blessed	יִשְׁמָעֵאל **Ishmael** God hears	רַעֲנָן **Raanan** fertile, verdant	
בִּנְיָמִין **Benjamin** son of my right hand	יִרְמְיָהוּ **Jeremiah** raised high by God	רְאוּבֵן **Reuben** behold, a son	
חַיִים **Chaim** life	יוֹאֵל **Joel** the Lord is my God	שְׁמוּאֵל **Samuel** heard by God	
דָן **Dan** judge	יוֹחָנָן **Jochanan** God is gracious	שָׁאוּל **Saul** asked for	
דָנִיאֵל **Daniel** God is my judge	יוֹנָה **Jonah** a dove	שֵׁת **Seth** appointed	
דָוִד **David** beloved	יְהוֹנָתָן **Jonathan** God's gift	שָׁלוֹם **Shalom** peace	
דוֹב **Dov** a bear	יוֹסֵף **Joseph** he adds	שְׁלֹמֹה **Solomon** peaceful	
אֵהוּד **Ehud** praise	יְהוֹשֻׁעַ **Joshua** help belongs to God	שִׂמְחָה **Simcha** joy	
עֵלִי **Eli** majesty		טוֹבִיָה **Toviah** God is good	
אֱלִיעֶזֶר **Eliezer** help of God	יֹאשִׁיָהוּ **Josiah** God supports	צְבִי **Tzvi** deer	
אֵלִיָהוּ **Elijah** my strength is God	יְהוּדָה **Judah** God be praised, a Jew	אוּרִי **Uri** my light	
אֶפְרַיִם **Ephraim** fruitfulness		זְאֵב **Zev** wolf	
אֵיתָן **Ethan** strong	לֵוִי **Levi** companion		
יְחֶזְקֵאל **Ezekiel** God will strengthen	מֵאִיר **Meir** gives light		
	מְנַחֵם **Menachem** comforts		

Surnames

Jews in Europe did not use surnames (last names) until about two hundred years ago. They knew each other by their first names and their parents' names. Benjamin whose father's name was Eliahu would be known as Benjamin *ben* (son of) Eliahu. Rivka whose mother's name was Chaya would be called Rivka *bat* (daughter of) Chaya. People were also known by their work, such as Hannah the Seamstress and Moshe the Woodcutter. Later, when government officials told Jews to pick surnames, they chose names that told something about themselves.

Look for your last name and see what you can discover about your great-great-great-grandparents.

If your name is Cohen, Kahn, Cahan, or Katz, your ancestors were probably priests in the Holy Temple in Jerusalem 2,000 years ago.

If your name is Levy, Levine, LaVine, or Segal (from the Hebrew *segan levi*, meaning "head of the tribe of Levi"), your ancestors may have sung songs to God during services at the Temple.

But most of our ancestors were not Temple bigwigs. They were just plain folks called Yisraelim who came to the Temple at holiday time to pray and bring gifts to God. They chose surnames that answered questions like these:

What work did they do?

Abulafia   father of medicine
Ackerman   owner of a field or farm
Aptheker   druggist
Baumgartner   tree gardener
Becker   baker
Cantor, Chazzan   synagogue cantor
Dayan   judge
Farber   dyer of cloth
Feldman   owner of a field
Fiedler   fiddle player
Fishman, Fisher   fish sellers
Gabbai   synagogue official
Holtzman   woodsman
Kaplan   religious leader
Kaufman   merchant

Kunstler   artist or craftsman
Lederer   leather worker
Lehrer, Malamud   teacher
Mocatta   mason
Nagel   carpenter
Parness   synagogue president
Rader   wheel maker
Saltzman   miner or seller of salt
Schechter, Schachter   butcher
Schneider   tailor
Schuster   shoemaker
Spivak   singer of songs for nobility
Wechsler, Wexler   money changer
Ziegler   tile maker
Zimmerman   carpenter

Where did they come from?

Ashkenazi, Deutsch   from Germany
Berliner   from Berlin
Blumenfeld   from a field of flowers
Blumenthal   from a valley of flowers
Cordoba   from the city of Córdoba, Spain
Danzig   from Danzig (Gdańsk), Poland
Eisenberg   from a mountain of iron
Galil   from the Galilee
Hollander   from Holland
Litvak   from Lithuania
Lubavich   from Lubavich, Russia

Lucca   from the town of Lucca, Italy
Mizrachi   from the east
Osterman   from the east
Pollack   from Poland
Rothenberg   from Rothenberg, Germany
Speyer   from the town of Speyer, Germany
Strassberg   from Strasbourg, France
Weinberg   from a hill of grape vines
Wiener   from the city of Vienna
Yerushalmi   from Jerusalem

How would their neighbors describe them?

Asher   happy
Altman   wise, old man
Baruch   blessed
Dreyfus   man with a cane, three-footed
Ehrlich   honest
Fried   peaceful
Geller   blond-haired
Gottlieb   God-loving
Graubart   gray-bearded
Gross   large or fat
Klein   small
Mandel   young and happy

Mazal   lucky
Mazliah   prosperous
Nissim   miracles
Rahamim   merciful
Saadiah   helped by God
Sasson   joyous
Schwartz   dark hair or complexion
Seligman   happy
Stiller   quiet
Weinik   wine-loving
Weiss   pale or fair
Zadok   fair or righteous

Who were their parents?

Names that end with *itz, sky, ov,* and *son* mean "son of" or "descendant of." An *es* ending means "child of." Here are some examples:

Abramson   son of Abraham
Aronowitz   son of Aaron
Antonofsky   son of Anton
Jacobson   son of Jacob

Zeilicovitch   son of Zelig
Perles   child of Pearl
Zeldes   child of Zelda

The Talmud says:

"A good name is more desirable than riches."

"Beauty fades but a name lasts."

"Every person has three names: one his father and mother gave him, one others call him, and one he earns for himself."

Stein (German for "stone") is part of many names such as Goldstein, Silverstein, Rothstein (red stone), Steinberg (stone mountain), and Burstein (amber). Baum (German for "tree") is found in names like Waldbaum (forest tree), Mandelbaum (almond tree), and Cedarbaum.

Before there were street addresses in Europe people used to hang a wooden sign with a picture over their front doors. Many Jews chose surnames to match their painted signs. A family with a red shield *(roth schild)* on their sign chose Rothschild. A family with the picture of a goose became Gans (German for goose); a fox, Fuchs;

European Jews did not name children after a living relative. They were afraid it might confuse the Angel of Death. If there were two Jacobs, for instance, the Angel might accidentally whisk away the wrong one. But sometimes they tried to confuse the busy angel. If a child was sick they would change its name. Jacob might become Eliezer. When the Angel of Death came looking for little Jacob and found only little Eliezer he would give up (they hoped) and go away empty-handed.

a ship, Schiff; a bear, Baer; a rooster, Hahn; an eagle, Adler; and an ox, Ochs. What kind of sign and picture would you make to hang in front of your room or house?

Some families name children after relatives who have died. It helps them to remember and honor those who are gone. Are you named after someone? Ask your parents why they chose that person and what he or she was like.

Boy babies are given their Hebrew names at the time of their *brit milah* (ritual circumcision). The names of girl babies are announced during the Torah reading at the synagogue. Some parents name their baby girls at a *simḥat bat* (celebration for a daughter) ceremony with special readings and prayers. When a baby becomes an official member of the community, everybody celebrates with wine and cake.

Sometimes immigration officials changed or shortened the names of new immigrants. A story is told about a Jewish immigrant who was given a very Irish name when he arrived. He was so nervous as he answered the official's questions that he completely forgot his name. "Oy!" he cried, "shoyn fargesen!"—which means in Yiddish "I forgot already." The official nodded and wrote "Shawn Ferguson" on the immigration papers.

WHERE DO YOU COME FROM?

Was your great-great-grandfather a famous rabbi or a horse thief? Did he come to North America before the Boston Tea Party or just last month? There's a lot of history in your family, and it's your own history too. Here's how you can do some detective work to uncover it.

Start out with the family photograph album. Are there pictures of people you don't know? Funny, faded pictures of women with gigantic hats and wide, long skirts; of men with black coats, canes, and long beards; and of little boys in knee pants and girls in braids and frilly dresses? Ask your parents who they are. Find out where and when they lived and how you are related to them.

Another place to look is on the first page of the family Bible or *siddur* (prayer book). Some families record births and deaths there.

Ask your grandparents, aunts, uncles, and old family friends to tell you about close relatives. Then ask them for this information about each person:

1. person's name
2. date of birth
3. place of birth
4. date of marriage
5. place of marriage
6. date of death
7. place of death

Write down all the information. To save space use these abbreviations:

b. date of birth
m. date of marriage
d. date of death
p. place

PEDIGREE CHART

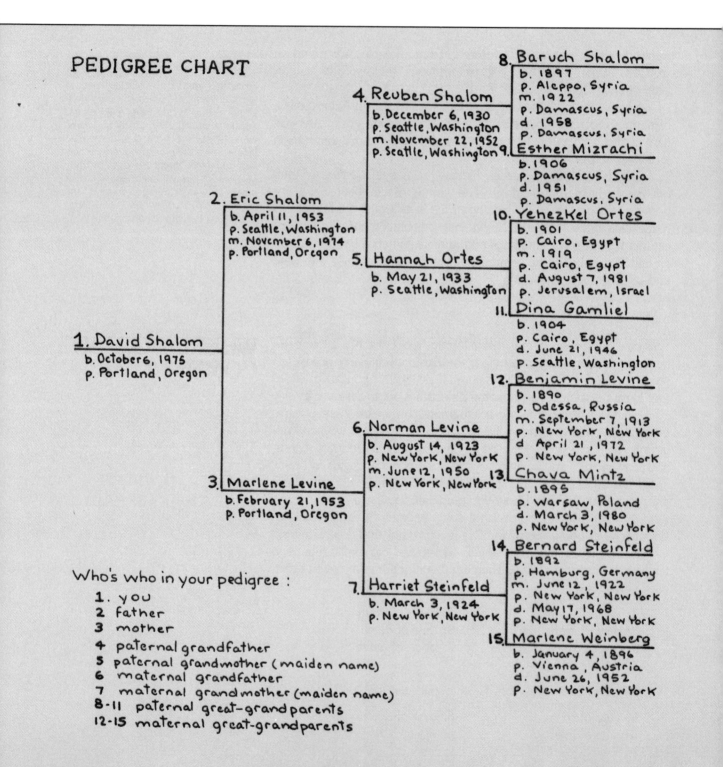

8. Baruch Shalom
b. 1897
p. Aleppo, Syria
m. 1922
p. Damascus, Syria
d. 1958
p. Damascus, Syria

4. Reuben Shalom
b. December 6, 1930
p. Seattle, Washington
m. November 22, 1952
p. Seattle, Washington

9. Esther Mizrachi
b. 1906
p. Damascus, Syria
d. 1951
p. Damascus, Syria

2. Eric Shalom
b. April 11, 1953
p. Seattle, Washington
m. November 6, 1974
p. Portland, Oregon

10. Yehezkel Ortes
b. 1901
p. Cairo, Egypt
m. 1919
p. Cairo, Egypt
d. August 7, 1981
p. Jerusalem, Israel

5. Hannah Ortes
b. May 21, 1933
p. Seattle, Washington

11. Dina Gamliel
b. 1904
p. Cairo, Egypt
d. June 21, 1946
p. Seattle, Washington

1. David Shalom
b. October 6, 1975
p. Portland, Oregon

12. Benjamin Levine
b. 1890
p. Odessa, Russia
m. September 7, 1913
p. New York, New York
d. April 21, 1972
p. New York, New York

6. Norman Levine
b. August 14, 1923
p. New York, New York
m. June 12, 1950
p. New York, New York

13. Chava Mintz
b. 1895
p. Warsaw, Poland
d. March 3, 1980
p. New York, New York

3. Marlene Levine
b. February 21, 1953
p. Portland, Oregon

14. Bernard Steinfeld
b. 1892
p. Hamburg, Germany
m. June 12, 1922
p. New York, New York
d. May 17, 1968
p. New York, New York

7. Harriet Steinfeld
b. March 3, 1924
p. New York, New York

15. Marlene Weinberg
b. January 4, 1896
p. Vienna, Austria
d. June 26, 1952
p. New York, New York

Who's who in your pedigree:
1. you
2. father
3. mother
4. paternal grandfather
5. paternal grandmother (maiden name)
6. maternal grandfather
7. maternal grandmother (maiden name)
8-11 paternal great-grandparents
12-15 maternal great-grandparents

The Bible tells that all of us share one ancestor, Adam. Why only one? The Talmud explains: God created only one person so that nobody should be able to say, "My father (ancestor) is better than your father."

Now get a large piece of paper for a chart. You can make two kinds of charts. One is called a pedigree chart. It starts with you and traces your line back through your parents, grandparents, great-grandparents, and so on.

The second kind is a family tree. Start with one of your great-grandmothers and great-grandfathers. Write their names and other information on the tree trunk. Make a branch for each of their children and write the name and other information on it. Then divide each branch, adding a new twig for each child. You may discover lots of long-lost aunts, uncles, and cousins when you are making this chart.

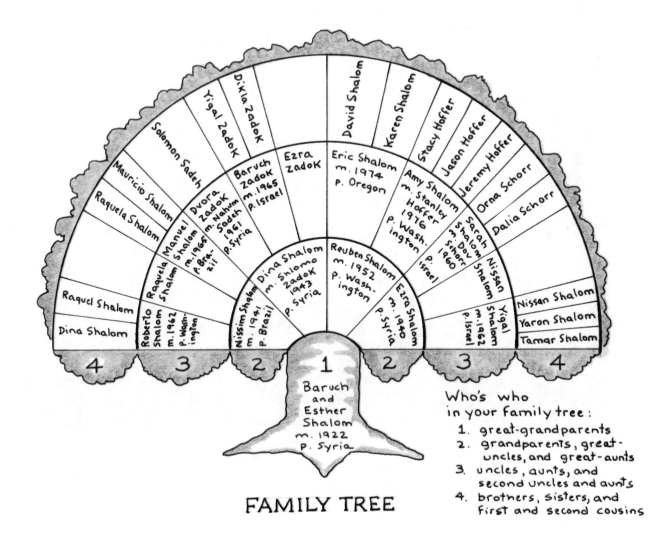

FAMILY TREE

Who's who in your family tree:

1. great-grandparents
2. grandparents, great-uncles, and great-aunts
3. uncles, aunts, and second uncles and aunts
4. brothers, sisters, and first and second cousins

*There's a tiny museum of immigration inside the **Statue of Liberty** in the middle of New York harbor. It has pictures and exhibits about the people who came to settle in the United States. Visitors can listen to tape recordings that immigrants made, telling about the old country and about their first adventures in this new land.*

When your chart is done, get a map and find the countries and towns where members of your family once lived. Trace the journeys they made across continents and seas to reach the United States or other countries.

This is just the beginning. Tracing family roots can be like solving a mystery that has a hundred suspects. Some people check the lists of names on old ship registers to find out when their ancestors came to this country. Others hunt through graveyards and read tombstones.

The Zelicovitch family took this picture in 1908 in Russia. Then the family scattered all over the world. Tracing their travels is like watching history happen.

Mama and **Papa Zelicovitch** were killed in a pogrom in Russia in 1921.

Pinyeh, the oldest son, and his wife and four children stayed in Russia. The family has not heard from them since the Holocaust during the 1940s.

Chaim, the middle son, went to Argentina with his wife. Two of his children settled in Israel.

Velvel, the younger son, and his wife and little boy came to the United States.

Bobbeh, the older daughter, went to Argentina.

Rivka, the younger daughter, came to the United States. Her granddaughter lives in Israel.

There are many ways to trace your own history. If you and your parents want to be detectives, these books will help you:

- *My Jewish Roots,* by David Kranzler, New York: Sepher-Hermon Press, 1979.
- *From Generation to Generation,* by Arthur Kurzweil, New York: Morrow Junior Books, 1980.

"When a teacher fights with his wife it's hard on the students."—Yiddish proverb

"Bad-tempered people can't teach."—Talmud

HEBREW SCHOOL DAYS

Hillel and Shammai were teachers in Israel long ago. One day a non-Jew came to Shammai and said, "If you can teach me the whole Torah while I stand on one foot I'll become a Jew."

This man is either stupid or insulting, thought Shammai. How can a book like the Torah be taught in a few minutes? He chased the man out of his house.

The man went straight to Hillel and repeated his offer. Hillel smiled and answered, "What is hateful to you, do not do to somebody else. That is the whole Torah. The rest is commentary. Now go and study."

The man studied Torah and became a Jew.—adapted from the Talmud.

"Do not move to a town where there is no Hebrew teacher for your children," the rabbis warned many years ago. Jewish parents listened to that advice and made sure to set up a *heder,* a one room school, in each new hometown. Soon the voices of little boys chanting Torah echoed into the street. Maybe they gave the neighbors a headache, but they made their parents and rabbis happy.

The school wing is still the busiest, noisiest part of most synagogues. Bible, prayer, and the Hebrew language are taught, as they were in the *heder,* but with a few changes. Compare the following description of a *heder* in Europe a hundred years ago, with your own Hebrew school.

At the age of three or four, when he was hardly out of diapers, a boy was wrapped in his father's prayer shawl and carried off to *heder.* He was set down on a bench at a long table with many other boys. The teacher opened a book, pointed to each letter and read, "Aleph, bet, gimel . . ."

"Aleph, bet, gimel . . ." repeated the little boy. Suddenly, to his surprise, a shower of candies fell onto the pages of the book. The teacher had dropped them from above his head.

"You see," the teacher said with a smile, "the angels in heaven are throwing candy down to show you that Torah study is sweet."

The teacher, or *rebbe,* had his hands full. His pupils were all ages, from three to thirteen. Each one seemed to be studying on a different page in a different book. From early morning until dark a hubbub of voices sang out with different melodies and words. When things got too noisy, or when the *rebbe* caught boys secretly playing games with coins or buttons, he whacked them with a *kantshik,* a three-tailed whip. And only heaven could help the boy who was caught with a storybook tucked inside his Bible. Only books of religion were allowed in *heder.*

The best students, the *rebbe's* favorites, could recite page after page of Torah from memory. Some knew each page so well that when the *rebbe* pushed a needle through several pages they could name the word that the needle had pierced on each page.

There were never enough books in the *heder.* In Yemen books were so scarce that little boys sat in a circle around each book when they learned to read. Some could read only sideways or upside down from that time on.

Girls did not go to *heder.* A few studied with private teachers. But most parents thought a girl should learn to bake and sew and

"Some scholars are like donkeys; they only carry a lot of books."—Bahya ibn Pakuda

"I have learned much from my teachers, more from my coworkers, but most of all from my students."—Talmud

take care of her little brothers and sisters rather than learn Torah. When a girl was stubborn and studied and did well, people would marvel and say, "She has a man's head."

Religious education has changed since *ḥeder* days. Both girls and boys go to Hebrew school today. It's still important to memorize words and prayers, but there's time to ask questions and discuss history, prayers, Bible, and current events. Workbooks with games and puzzles make learning easier. Some religious schools also have crafts rooms, gyms, baseball fields, choirs, drama groups, and swimming pools. Does all that make today's schools better than the *ḥeder*? The old-time *rebbe* would probably answer with a loud "no!" and a shake of his *kantshik*. After all, if a needle was pushed through the pages of a Talmud, how many of you could name each word that the needle pierced?

Oyfn Pripitshek

("On the Hearth")
a Yiddish folksong about the ḥeder

On the hearth a tiny fire burns
And the house is warm.
And the *rebbe*
teaches little children
To say the *aleph-bet*.
Remember children,
remember dear ones,
What you study here.
Repeat again, and then
once again,
Kometz, aleph, oh.

Autographs

א ב ג ד ה ו ז

ח ט י כ ל

Abba, Imah, Sabta too
All wonder how you made it through

Hebrew goes from right to left
Chinese up and down
If you want to read my wish
Good luck!
You'll have to turn it around

Yours till the Messiah comes

God made the rivers
God made the lakes
God made you
We all make mistakes

Yours till Niagara falls
the hallah loafs
the ear locks
the candle sticks
and the Torah rolls

Abraham, Isaac, and Jacob
Would all agree
You're the only boy(girl) for me

I love you once
I love you twice
I love you more
Than chicken soup with rice

938-6665

Godzilla, Frankenstein, and the Golem agree
Your face is scarier than all three

Graduation day at Hebrew school is a sad and happy time. It may be the last time that you'll see some of your teachers and classmates. Collect their autographs in a book and then you'll never forget them— even if you want to.

Here are some poems from an autograph book from a Hebrew school in Brooklyn, New York:

Here's advice that can't be beat
Never mix your milk and meat
And don't forget that friends like me
Aren't found under every tree

There's mystery in the Bible
There's mystery in dikdook [grammar]
But how you graduated
Is a mystery in any book

Ashes to ashes
And dust to dust
You're the kind of friend
That I can trust

Faster than a speeding bullet
Higher than a chimney flue
What can it be?
It's you—Super Jew!

And these came from the teachers:

Taller than a house
Wider than a tree
Torah is up there
As high as can be—
Reach for it!

It's better to be a tail among lions
Than a head among foxes

Talmud

The most important thing for you
Is not to study but to do
Talmud

Your future lies before you
Like freshly fallen snow
Be careful where you walk
For every step will show

Imagine having a bar mitzvah in the shadow of King Solomon's Temple Mount! Some families fly to Israel to celebrate this milestone beside the Mount, at the Western Wall in Jerusalem.

THE BIG BIRTHDAY

Thirteen candles on a birthday cake.

A prickly new haircut or a stylish hairdo.

Hugs and kisses from relatives and family friends. Cries of "My, my, my, how big you've gotten" and "How time flies!"

Something also seems to be fluttering around in the birthday girl or boy's stomach—jittery butterflies—because the BIG birthday, the day of the *bar* or *bat mitzvah*, is even more challenging than a final exam at school. It is the first time that a Jewish boy or girl stands before the members of the synagogue and takes part in the service as an adult. After years of studying Judaism, the Hebrew language, the *siddur,* and the Bible, the young Jew has finished one stage of religious training. Now it is time to become a full partner in the responsibilities of the Jewish religion.

Each of the three branches of Judaism—Orthodox, Conservative, and Reform—sees this milestone in a somewhat different way.

Orthodox Jews follow the laws of the Torah and Talmud with

Here's a rabbinic saying to cool a hot discussion between adults and kids: "Don't limit your child to your own learning. He was born in another time."

Bar mitzvah can be a wild time. The Midrash tells that when the patriarch Abraham was thirteen years old he smashed his father's idols and became the first Jew.

few changes. Both boys and girls study Jewish traditions. But a boy also learns to place *tefillin* (phylacteries) on his forehead and arm and to prepare for the responsibility of becoming part of a *minyan,* the group of ten adult males needed for prayer in the synagogue. On his bar mitzvah day the boy puts on a *tallit* (prayer shawl) and is called up for an *aliyah* to the Torah. He often reads all or part of the week's reading from the Torah scroll. Then he may chant the *haftarah,* a section from a later book of the Bible. Sometimes the bar mitzvah also leads part of the *tefilot* (prayer service).

Some Conservative and Reform Jews have made changes from Orthodox religious practice. In some congregations the bat mitzvah leads the Friday evening service. In others, the bat mitzvah as well as the bar mitzvah is called up to the Torah, and the bat mitzvah may be considered a member of the minyan.

Whatever the type of synagogue, the bar or bat mitzvah also may give a *drashah,* an explanation of the Torah reading or of some other aspect of Jewish life. It's a great time to speak out while your rabbi, parents, and everybody else are listening. But then get ready to duck—some congregations shower the new adult with raisins, nuts, and candy.

The BIG birthday ends with more hugs and kisses, lots of food and presents, maybe a birthday cake. What an accomplishment—the first stage is done! The bar or bat mitzvah is an adult member of the Jewish community. It's time now to finish the birthday cake, clean up the gift wrappings, and move on. There's a lifetime of Jewish learning and living ahead.

Many Reform and Conservative congregations add another "growing-up" celebration to Jewish life. A few years after the bar and bat mitzvah they have a confirmation ceremony for their students marking the added years of Jewish study after the BIG birthday.

In the small towns of Eastern Europe, bar mitzvah parties were not fancy, catered affairs. The guests often ate pickled herring, chick-peas, and sponge cake instead of roast chicken and gooey layer cake. But when the bar mitzvah boy stood up and delivered a well thought-out *drashah,* the guests smacked their lips. With such entertainment, even cold chick-peas became a royal feast.

After the bar mitzvah many boys ended their formal schooling and went out to work. But they didn't stop studying. Groups of men would meet in the synagogues in the evening to read and discuss Torah and Talmud. Learned women told Bible stories or read aloud to their neighbors on peaceful Sabbath afternoons. The *drashah* was part of *shtetl* life from childhood to old age.

YOU AND YOUR PETS

Pets know more about you than your best friend does. They know if you're loving or not, careful or careless, gentle or mean. If your pet could talk, what would he say about you?

The rabbis said that animals are God's creatures, just as people are. They must be treated kindly and responsibly. Here are some rules they gave for care of animals:

- On the Sabbath, when people rest from work, they must allow their work animals to rest also.
- Nobody should buy an animal or a bird until he has provided for it.
- First you must feed your animals, then you may eat.
- Drive your horse with oats, not with a whip (with rewards instead of punishment).
- Do not harness a horse and an ox to work together.
- Don't muzzle the ox while he threshes the grain (he has a right to nosh too).

Most people don't have work animals any more. But many of us have pets in our homes. Here are some important rules for taking care of them.

- If your pet is allowed out, attach a name and address tag to his (or her) collar.
- Feed him at a regular feeding time, and always keep his water bowl filled.
- Don't pick a dog or cat up by the legs. Put one hand under his chest and one behind his rear legs to lift him.
- Use one simple word to give him an order. Use the same word for the same order each time. He gets mixed up when you use long sentences and different words.
- Keep his cage or basket or tank clean

Animal Proverbs
(They tell us about ourselves too.)

*A goat has a beard, but that doesn't
    make him a rabbi.
If a horse had anything to say he'd
    speak up.
You can tell a donkey by his long
    ears and a fool by his long tongue.
A meowing cat won't catch a mouse.*

Stories of beasts, bugs, and birds *from the Midrash and folklore*

What's Fair Is Fair

a story told by Hasidim

HANANIAH the peddler was a cruel master to his horse. After a hard, hungry life, the horse died and went to heaven. Many years later Hananiah also died and flew up to heaven. The horse was waiting for him at the gate and dragged him right before the heavenly court.

"This man doesn't deserve to be in heaven," the horse complained. "He beat me and drove me without pity. He never gave me enough to eat, and he never once patted my head or said a kind word."

"Tch, tch, tch," the angels clucked. "You're right."

"Just a minute," Hananiah interrupted. "I was a poor man. I couldn't feed the horse more food. I hardly had food for myself. Maybe I made him work hard, but I worked hard too. Besides, he's nothing but a horse. What more did he deserve?"

"You're right too," said the angels.

From the heavenly throne God's voice boomed down: "Since the horse is right and Hananiah the peddler is right, there's only one fair solution. They will both go back to earth. But this time Hananiah will become the horse, and the horse will become Hananiah."

When the Ten Commandments were given at Mount Sinai, the whole universe stood still and listened. Fish stopped swimming, birds stopped flying, cows stopped mooing, and even the waves of the ocean stopped tossing.

Midrash

The Soft-Hearted Spider

DAVID might not have lived to become king of Israel if it were not for a little spider. David was being chased through the mountains by King Saul and his soldiers. Saul was jealous of David and wanted to kill him. At last David grew so tired that he couldn't run anymore and crawled into a cave to hide. The spider who lived in the cave looked down at the hunted man and felt sorry for him. Soon the spider heard Saul and his men coming up the mountainside. He quickly swung himself back and forth across the cave opening and spun a perfect web. King Saul reached the cave, saw the web, and called to his men, "David can't be in here. The web isn't broken. Let's move on."

David's life was saved.

Balaam's Donkey

BALAK, the king of Edom, was afraid that Moses and his army of Jews would attack Edom. He ordered a powerful magician called Balaam to curse and destroy the Jews.

Balaam jumped onto his donkey and rode off to follow the king's order. Suddenly the donkey stopped short in the middle of the path. She could see an angel blocking the way. But Balaam saw nothing. "Move!" he yelled and hit the donkey with his stick. She just shook her head and lay down on the path.

"Get up, you rotten ass! If I had a sword I'd kill you," shouted Balaam.

"Hee, haw," snorted the donkey. "If you can't kill me without a sword, how do you expect to kill the Jews with no more than your curse?"

She was a smart donkey. Balaam never did curse the Jews. God made him bless them instead.

2 Friends around the world

Adam from Missouri likes bicycle racing. Jeff from Oregon likes video games. Sivan from Jerusalem digs carrots and radishes in her garden. Efrom from Moscow paints Hebrew words on his T-shirt.

In this chapter you'll meet them and other Jewish girls and boys from all over the United States and from other countries too. Do you think they'll be like you and your friends—or very different? Read their letters and see.

Shannon Alyce Wollman, age 12
Baltimore, Maryland
"Reading, playing piano, ballet, and backgammon are things I like to do. I like to gossip with my friends too. My beautiful scenic temple and the prayers and hymns make me proud to be a Jew. But I am sad that so many of my ancestors were killed in the Holocaust."

Rachel Menahem, age 9
Jerusalem, Israel
"My parents came from Iraq, and I was born in Jerusalem in an old part of the city. I love the city. There are such special things in it, like the Wall. I have a flute and I like to play it, and I like to do ballet dancing. After my flute lesson I go walking with my friends, and sometimes I buy things for my brothers and myself. A girl in my class is an Arab. She invited the whole class to her house. It was very nice."

Sivan Sarlin, age 11½
Kibbutz Sasa, Israel
"I love reading. When I get into a book I don't know what's going on around me. With my friends I like to do projects and share secrets. And I love to talk with my mother about her childhood in Austria. In class my favorite subject is creative dramatics. We make up wild, silly plays. Anti-Semitism worries me. We hear about it on the radio and TV."

Ralph Seltzer, age 7
Sydney, Australia
"I love summer because I love to swim. I also like to play tee-ball with my friends and to do jigsaw puzzles and play Othello. Math is my favorite subject at King David School and I like learning Hebrew songs and stories from the Bible. What I like best about being Jewish is eating matzo ball soup! My grandparents came from Russia and Poland and my father was born in Shanghai, China."

Jeff Caplan, age 11
Portland, Oregon
"I was born in Portland and so were my parents. Three of my grandparents came from Europe. Video games are my favorite toys. They're challenging and fun. I like to watch TV and collect rocks and write comic strips. The thing I like about being Jewish is showing Jewish things to your friends of other religions."

Michael Adler, age 4

Woodmere, New York

"Duck, duck, goose is my favorite game. I like Shabbat because we have a Shabbat party at school and I can spend the whole day with my mother and father. When I grow up I want to be a big boy."

Livnat Kalina, age 11

Kibbutz Ga'ash, Israel

"My parents are from Peru and Mexico. I love to collect dolls from all different countries with different costumes. Nothing bothers me about being Jewish because here in Israel there is no difference between people like there is in other countries."

Lloyd and Ruth Dean, ages 13 and 11

Leeds, England

"We love to go on holiday with our parents. We've been to Grossinger's in New York and to Yugoslavia."

Lloyd: "I like golfing and athletics. This summer I went waterskiing for the first time. Though I fell down and got a bit bruised I will try it again. This year I was bar mitzvahed. I enjoyed studying for it and wasn't nervous at all. I go to an all-boys' school and plan to be a lawyer."

Ruth: "I like to read, swim, get dressed up. I am starting a scrapbook on the new prince, William, our king-to-be. And I think Princess Diana is lovable. I used to go to a co-ed school but now I'm in an all-girls' school and I think it's much better this way. I like history and want to be a chemist when I grow up."

Sharon Perry, age 12

Ramat Hasharon, Israel

"Basketball is my favorite game. I also like to dance ballet. With my friends I like to chat, with my parents to play cards and chess. I like the holidays because of the unique atmosphere and the family gathering. At school I like history and Bible. By them we know the history of mankind and specially the history of the Jewish people."

Michael Pikus, age 8

Moscow, U.S.S.R. (Russia), and Brooklyn, New York

"I came to America one year ago. I like it better here than in Moscow. In school I am learning to read English. Mathematics is my best subject because I learned it in Russia. I play with little cars and I play basketball with my friends. In Russia I played the piano but here I have no piano. I like to eat out with my parents and to visit relatives."

Want to find a new friend in Brooklyn or Hollywood or Natchez? It's easy. Become a pen-pal. World Over, a magazine for Jewish kids, has a pen-pal P.O.B. club. They'll find a pal for you if you send them this information:

Iliana Pressman, age 10
Kitchener, Ontario, Canada
"Stuffed animals, ping-pong, skiing, swimming, and reading are all my favorites. I like going out to eat and seeing movies with my parents too. Hebrew school is good because it's interesting to learn about being Jewish. But it bothers me when there's a holiday and I'm not at school—the kids ask me where I was and what I did and things like that."

Parham Soroudi, age 11
Tehran, Iran, and Los Angeles, California
"The year I came to the United States was 1977. In Iran I lived in Tehran. It's real different here than Iran, and it's better here because in Iran there aren't a lot of good games or hobbies. I go to sixth grade in Akiba Academy. I like to eat spaghetti and tacos and hot food and hamburgers. But I can't eat any more meat in restaurants because I decided to be kosher. When I grow up I want to be an archaeologist or own a store."

Rena Dorph, age 10¾
Los Angeles, California
"I have two sisters, one older and one younger. I love my whole family!!! I like being Jewish very much! I like having a rest on Saturday and I like going to Jewish day school and I like more things but there's no room to write them. What I don't like is not being able to write on Saturday, and sometimes I don't like keeping kosher. And I like to swim, roller-skate, and things like that."

Emanuel Zvi Pressman, age 10
Kitchener, Ontario, Canada
"I like a lot of things—skiing, ping-pong, sailing, space, Star Wars toys, drawing, future movies. With my parents I like to go to restaurants, shopping, traveling, sports, staying at home, and having a loving time. I like Shabbat and lighting candles, but I don't always like praying and reading about Jewish life."

Susan Katz, age 11
Largo, Florida
"I like reading or swimming at the beach, taking walks, or just talking. I think it's an honor to be Jewish and Hebrew school is fun, but it's easy as pie!"

Yaniv Miller, age 11
Kibbutz Sasa, Israel
"I like basketball because it's a game where everybody plays together and it's fun. In school I like the independent study time. We can choose what we are interested to study about, and then I'm not bored. My parents and grandparents are from the United States."

Shalom Adari, age 13
Tel Aviv, Israel
"This picture is from a few years ago. My brother and I are on the balcony of our house. Bicycle riding is my favorite sport, and my hobby is to collect stamps. At school I like biology and handiwork (shop or crafts) best. I like to use my hands and work with metal. And I like to go to synagogue and put on tefillin every morning."

Shimon Adari, age 11
Tel Aviv, Israel
"Painting and gymnastics are my favorite subjects. I like to work with clay and mold things too. In these subjects I can express everything I wish. In sports I like to ride a bicycle and skate board. My parents and grandparents came here from Morocco."

Enan Francis, age 7
New York City
"I go to a Sephardic Temple every Shabbat and I enjoy singing there. I may be a rabbi someday. I like games and speedcars, but my favorite place is summer camp where I can be with all my Jewish friends and sing Hebrew songs every day."

Danny Stern, age 10
Morristown, New Jersey
"Baseball and soccer are my favorite sports because they're running and active. I like radio control cars and models too. About being Jewish—I like some of the holidays and learning about the people who never gave up, like when they were escaping from Egypt, and the people who fought the wars, like Moshe Dayan. I was in Israel when I was 4. I don't remember much, except I remember 12 Kfir jets flying in formation over my head."

Tapharah Francis, age 8
New York City
"I enjoy going to Temple in the morning on Shabbat and returning for Havdalah. I like to sit with my rabbi's daughters. I enjoy riding a bicycle, going to camp, writing stories, and acting in plays. Best of all I like making and painting things for all the Jewish holidays."

Billy Furman, age 9
Levittown, New York
"Being Jewish makes me feel special because there are not many Jews where I live. Sometimes people call me names like "Jew-bagel" and that bothers me. I like all sports, especially baseball. I collect sport cards. I think Israel is the most beautiful place in the world. I'd love to go there."

1. ***Jewish sleep-away camps*** Some have campers and counselors from all over the United States as well as from Israel and other countries. Get information from your synagogue, Hebrew school, or from a camp association such as:

Association of Jewish Sponsored Camps
130 East 59th Street
New York, New York 10022

Some great places to meet more Jewish friends:

Sandi Fine, age 14
Syosset, New York
"I love to go shopping (for myself), go to shows, just sit around and talk. My favorite school subject is biology. We learn about ourselves, how we came to be, why we're exactly the way we are, and other mind-blowing facts. As a Jew I like the feeling that I'm original and that other religions are based on our Bible. I'm kosher, and sometimes that puts a damper on my social life. Also, I wonder about God, but I like religious customs. I want to go to Israel to see the place I've learned about for so long and to trace my roots."

Zafrir Elkin, age 9
Kibbutz Yad Mordecai, Israel
"My grandparents and my father came to Israel from Poland. My mother was born here. I like to read, play basketball, ride a bicycle, and see television. In school math is my favorite subject because I like to solve problems."

Mayah Querida Morgenstern, age 11
Nice, France
"When I see another kid with a Jewish Star or a Chai I feel close to him. My grandfather told us all about Auschwitz, where he spent a few years during the war. My father was hidden by nuns and it was a bad time for Jews. Whenever Pepe (grandfather) came to eat in our house he said 'This is better than at Auschwitz.' But even though he made a joke of it, he got a strange and sad look in his eyes when he thought about it."

Aliyah Ester Morgenstern, age 15
Nice, France
"I'm happy to be a Jew because of the richness of the Jewish past and the link I have with other Jews all over the world. I hope I will meet the right Jewish man and we will continue a long tradition together. Every year from about second to eighth grade we had to write a composition about Christmas in December, and each year I wrote about Hanukkah. Some teachers were interested, others didn't take it well. How stupid people can be!"

Iris Cohen, age 7½
Tel Aviv, Israel
"I like being Jewish because I was born Jewish. I don't know how it is to be Arab or Christian. My grandparents came from India and Lebanon. I like to play with dolls because I like father-mother play. I also like to dance ballet because it's a combination of sport and dance. Bible is my best subject at school. I want to learn all the sayings and fulfill them."

Scott Greenfield, age 12
Staten Island, New York
"I like to play hockey because I play it well. Also, I like to travel around the United States with my parents. Science and experiments are my best school subjects. I enjoy learning about Jewish history and holidays. What bothers me is that gentile children make fun of a person wearing a yarmulka."

2. **Jewish clubs** Look them up under Organizations, American Jewish Youth, in the Mini-Encyclopedia (chapter 15), and consult the most recent *American Jewish Year Book,* published by The Jewish Publication Society of America and the American Jewish Committee.

Ari Burstein, age 11½
Plainview, New York
"I go to Solomon Schechter Day School where I attend classes in both Hebrew and English. I like Hebrew better because it gives you a good feeling to learn about the history of the Jews. We are supposed to be God's chosen people so I guess it's an honor. Some things I like are: soccer, lifting weights, most sports, and reading. I read *The Black Stallion* and all the sequels. In school my favorite subject is Prophets. It's interesting to learn how our ancestors lived. I'm hoping I can go to Israel for my bar mitzvah."

Shira Burstein, age 8
Plainview, New York
"The thing I love most is to hug my parents and spend time with them. I like to play with Smurfs because you can make different adventures with them. I have little blue lady and men Smurfs, a hockey Smurf, and an out-of-space Smurf. What bothers me about being Jewish is that some people are against Jews. My class went on a trip to the U.N. One of the kids asked the guide why they were thinking of putting Israel out of the U.N. She said they weren't. Math is my favorite subject at school because I'm very, very, very, very, etc., good at it!"

Andy Rapkin, age 12
Baltimore, Maryland
"Baseball, football, golf, and collecting baseball cards and coins are my favorite hobbies. I like science and labs at school. My Hebrew school is not that good, but I like Jewish traditions. My favorite is going to my grandparents' house on Friday night for the Sabbath meal. What's hard about being Jewish is that I have to take the tragedies and tormenting of my fellow Jews around the world."

Ruthie Shimron, age 9
Jerusalem, Israel
"I built a puppet theater and I like to make puppet shows and ride my bike and read. I think it's a kind of honor that I was born in the holy city of Jerusalem. I like to go to the Wall and to walk in the Old City. My father lived in Canada and then came to Israel and married my mother. I think if I was an American I would not have as many friends."

Elizabeth Katz, age 10
Largo, Florida
"Skating is my favorite sport. It's fun and the tricks are neat. I like Jewish holidays and the stories about the Jews. Hebrew school is okay too, but my teacher is from Israel and it's hard to understand her."

Sarah, Adam, and **Jesse Pope,** ages 7, 6, and 4
Columbia, Missouri
Sarah: "I like dolls because I like playing mother."
Adam: "I like bicycle racing with Sarah."
Jesse: "I like baseball."
"We all like to go to the park and fly kites, and we like Jewish songs and latkes and holidays like Shabbat and Hanukkah and Pesach. Sometimes we wish we could have the Easter bunny come and bring candy too. And we love each other and our parents and ourselves."

Debby Straus, age 16
Amsterdam, Holland
"Hi. I'm in twelfth grade in a Jewish high school called 'Joodse Scholengemeenschop Maimonides' in which boys and girls study together. I study algebra, chemistry, biology, Dutch, English, German, and history. The school has about 700 pupils, which is quite nice because you know everybody and everybody knows you. You're not just a number to the teacher but a person. The disadvantage though is that you don't meet any gentiles."

Roneete Levy, age 11
Portland, Oregon
"My parents and grandparents were all born in Bulgaria and then went to Israel, and then my parents came here. I like to draw and go to the beach and the movies. I like Hebrew school too, but going right after school is no fun."

Ivan Wolnek, age 13
Port Washington, New York
"This picture was taken at my bar mitzvah. That's me—Ivan—on the right. My brother Seth is on the left. I like to talk and fool around, and I like to build model trains and rockets and watch them work. In school, science is my favorite subject because we're always learning something new. I go to Hebrew day school and I think it's great."

Seth Wolnek, age 12
Port Washington, New York
"Microvision, strato-matic, baseball, hockey, and sport cards are my favorite sports and hobbies. I like these things because they take a lot of skill and they're fun. I like to study Torah in school (Hebrew day school) because it is very interesting. Being Jewish makes me feel good because it's like being singled out from everybody else, but sometimes I feel like I have to hide it."

Sivan Almog, age 11½
Seoul, Korea, and Jerusalem, Israel
"I love to read, and I collect bottles of different shapes and colors. I have a vegetable garden with radishes, carrots, and other vegetables. Best of all I love to dance classic ballet and folk dancing. What I like in Israel is that I live with my people and everybody shares the holidays and celebrations, except there are some Arabs who are jealous of us. But I have an Arab girl friend and I like to visit her. Her family is exactly like mine. I was born in Korea. I am adopted. My parents and grandparents came from Bulgaria and Lithuania."

Liat Ofek, age 9
Kibbutz Hatzor, Israel
"Acting in plays is my favorite hobby because I'm good at it. I like dance and crafts and studying English too. Two things that worry me are the government in Israel today, and also that many people in the world don't like Jews."

Ariela, Naomi, and **Ilana Wiener,** age 9

Woodmere, New York
(You must've guessed that their picture was taken a few years ago and that they are triplets.)

Ariela: "I like piano, baseball, softball, gymnastics, and swimming because they're all fun and you usually don't get hurt in them. A good thing about Hebrew school is that if I learn Hebrew and go to Israel I'll be able to talk their language."

Naomi: "My hobbies are playing the accordion and reading. Hebrew school is good because I learn Jewish history and I feel it's partly my job to help my people. Sometimes it bothers me when there's a meeting or a party on Shabbos and I can't go."

Ilana: "I like learning Chumash and history at Hebrew school. We have contests about doing mitzvot too. My favorite games are electronic and swimming. I like the noise and sport of the electronic games and the strokes and hard work of swimming."

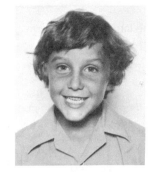

Gregory Jordan, age 7
Sydney, Australia
"My parents and I were born in Australia but my grandparents came here from Europe and Israel. I have a collie dog called 'Kimmi.' Snoopy, a stuffed dog without much stuffing, is my favorite toy. I follow the Parramatta Rugby League football team and I play tennis and tee-ball and have lots of good friends. My favorite movies are adventure movies like *Star Wars* and cartoons. I go to a terrific school called King David School. I like math because I like doing sums, and I like Mrs. Siderowitz's prayer class. I am the chazan."

Ellie Schaffzin, age 10
Philadelphia, Pennsylvania
"Two things I like are baseball and reading. Baseball: I love the way the players can just get under the ball or just swing and hit that ball. Reading: I love books because they take me away to far-off places without a plane or a car. I like going to a Jewish school because I can be with people all like me and learn about what I am and what it means to be me. I love studying Torah and the way the rabbis have something to say about everything and they tell me why we do this or that."

Bertha (Bertie) Coralie Ferdman, age 7
Guaynabo, Puerto Rico
"Swimming and skating are my favorite sports. I like to go to the movies with my parents. Hebrew school is not so much fun but I like to learn about Jewish history. Art is my best subject at school and we make nice things."

3 The great history trip

DATE	EVENTS	IMPORTANT PEOPLE
1900 B.C.E.	Abraham of Ur turned away from the gods of his family and began to worship *one* God. "I will make of you a great nation," promised God. He led Abraham and his family to the Land of Israel and told him, "Unto your seed have I given this land."	**Abraham** **Sarah** **Isaac** **Rebekah**
1750 B.C.E.	In a time of famine Abraham's great-grandchildren left Israel and went south to live in Egypt. Many years later the pharaoh (king) of Egypt enslaved them.	**Jacob** **Rachel** **Leah** **Joseph**
1450 B.C.E.	God forced the pharaoh to free Abraham's descendants, the Jews. Moses led them into the desert, where they received the Torah. After years of wandering they reached the Land of Israel.	**Moses** **Miriam** **Aaron**
1410–1050 B.C.E.	The Jews conquered the land and settled down in separate tribes led by judges.	**Joshua** **Deborah** **Samson**
1050–933 B.C.E.	Saul unified all the tribes and became the first king of Israel. David, the next king, made the kingdom larger and stronger. David's son Solomon built the Holy Temple in Jerusalem.	**Samuel** **Saul** **David** **Solomon** **Nathan**

B.C.E. (before the common era)
corresponds to the Christian B.C.
C.E. (common era) corresponds
to the Christian A.D.

A timeline of Jewish history from Abraham to you

DATE	EVENTS	IMPORTANT PEOPLE
928 B.C.E.	After Solomon's death some of the people revolted against the harsh rule of his son. The kingdom split into two: Israel (also called Samaria) in the north and Judah (also called Judea) in the south. For the next 400 years the prophets taught the people to be honest and kind with each other and to obey God.	**Elijah** **Amos** **Micah**
722 B.C.E.	Assyria conquered Israel, the northern kingdom, and took away its people as captives. Only the Jews of Judah remained in the land.	**Isaiah**
586 B.C.E.	The Babylonians conquered Judah (Judea), destroyed the Temple, and carried many Jews off to Babylonia. The captives refused to forget their religion. They built synagogues for prayer and study in the new land.	**Jeremiah** **Ezekiel**
538 B.C.E.	A new Babylonian king allowed the Jews to return to Judea and rebuild the Temple. Prayer and study continued in the synagogues of Babylonia.	**Esther** **Ezra** **Nehemiah**
332 B.C.E.	Judea was swallowed by the Greek Empire. Hellenistic (Greek) sports, religion, and customs spread among some Jews.	
168–164 B.C.E.	The Greek-Syrian king Antiochus wanted all his subjects to be Hellenists. He would not let the Jews follow their religion. They revolted and drove Antiochus out. For a short time Judea was free again.	**Hannah** **Mattathias** **Judah Maccabee** **Salome Alexandra**

When Judea was conquered and the Jews were taken away to Babylonia, their masters demanded that they sing and play their harps. The Jews refused, with these words:

*How shall we sing the Lord's song
In a strange land?
If I forget thee, Oh Jerusalem,
Let my right hand forget her skill.
Let my tongue cleave to the roof of
   my mouth
If I do not remember thee,
If I do not set Jerusalem above my
   greatest joy.*

Psalm 137

DATE	EVENTS	IMPORTANT PEOPLE
63 B.C.E.	The growing Roman Empire took over the rule of Judea.	**Herod**
30 C.E.	The Romans executed Jesus, the leader of a small Jewish sect. His followers left Judaism and began to spread their new Christian religion throughout the Roman Empire.	**Hillel** **Shammai** **Philo**
66–73	The Jews rebelled against Roman rule. The huge Roman army defeated them, burned the Temple, and carried off many prisoners. The last of the Jewish rebels died at Masada.	**Simeon bar Giora** **Johanan ben Zakkai**
132–135	Again the Jews revolted and fought to be free. The Romans drove them out of Jerusalem and forbade the practice of Judaism. But the Jews prayed and studied in secret.	**Akiva ben Joseph** **Simeon bar Kokhba** **Meir** **Beruriah** **Simeon bar Yoḥai**
210	Study was dangerous under Roman rule. The rabbis were afraid that the laws based on the Torah would be forgotten. They wrote them down in the Mishnah. The center of study began to shift to Babylonia, where the Jews had more freedom.	**Judah Ha-Nasi** **Abba Arikha** **Samuel**
400s	Babylonian Jews built academies and were led by a Jewish ruler called the "exilarch." In approximately 495 C.E. the Babylonian Talmud was written down. It has guided Jews ever since.	**Ashi** **Rabina**

The Kol Nidrei prayer on Yom Kippur eve asks God to forgive us if during the year we break some of the promises we make to Him. It gave special comfort to Jews during the Crusades, and later in Spain, who were forced to leave their religion to save their lives.

DATE	EVENTS	IMPORTANT PEOPLE
622	Muhammad founded the religion of Islam in Arabia. It spread through the Mediterranean world. Under Islam Jews often had more freedom than under other religions.	
740–970	Judaism spread as far as Russia, where the kingdom of the Khazars became Jewish.	**Saadiah (ben Joseph) Gaon** **Hasdai ibn Shaprut**
950–1391	Babylonia declined, and a new center of Jewish life grew in Spain. Jews became doctors, poets, scientists, and statesmen under liberal Christian and Muslim (Islamic) rulers.	**Samuel ha-Nagid** **Solomon ibn Gabirol** **Judah Halevi** **Abraham ibn Ezra** **Moses ibn Ezra**
950–1100	Other Jews settled in England, France, and Germany, where Gershom, Rashi, and their followers studied and taught Jewish law. In Egypt, Maimonides modernized Bible and Mishnah study. The rabbis sent responsa (letters of advice and judgments on Jewish law) to communities all over the world.	**Gershom ben Judah** **Rashi** **Maimonides**
1096–1320	Armies of Christian Crusaders marched across Europe to Palestine to drive out the Muslims. Along the way they destroyed hundreds of Jewish communities. Some Jewish survivors escaped eastward into Poland.	**Meir of Rothenberg**

The First to Know
Through the centuries Jews waited eagerly for the Messiah to come. A Yemenite Jewish legend tells of a woman who every night tied herself to the foot of the donkey standing by her door so that she would be awakened when it heard the footsteps of the Messiah.

DATE	EVENTS	IMPORTANT PEOPLE
1200–1400	Persecution of Jews increased in Western Europe. They were forced to wear special badges or hats, were forbidden to work at most jobs, and were heavily taxed. In 1290, when the Jews of England became too poor to pay taxes, they were expelled.	
1348–1349	The Black Plague killed thousands throughout Europe. "The Jews caused the plague—they poisoned the wells!" cried many people. They attacked Jews and expelled them. More Jews moved to Poland.	Jacob ben Moses Halevi
1300–1492	Oppression grew in Spain. In 1492 all Jews were ordered to leave. Some decided to remain and practice their religion in secret. They were called Marranos. Many Marranos were discovered and killed.	Moses de Leon Solomon ibn Adret Joseph Albo
1500–1600	Spanish and Portuguese Jews fled to Italy, North Africa, and the New World. They were welcomed in the Turkish Empire, including Palestine, which became a center of religious study.	Gracia Mendes Joseph Nasi Isaac Luria Joseph Caro
1400–1648	In Poland, Jews lived peacefully as merchants, inn keepers, and artisans. The Jewish Council of Four Lands governed them.	Shalom Shakhna Moses Isserles Solomon Luria
1648–58	Cossacks in Poland revolted against their rulers. Then they turned on the Jews and destroyed 700 communities. War and expulsion ruined many more.	

DATE	EVENTS	IMPORTANT PEOPLE
1665–76	False messiah Shabbetai Zevi brought hope of redemption to the desperate Jews of Poland and other lands. But the hope died when he was imprisoned and forced to become a Muslim.	**Shabbetai Zevi**
1500–1700	Marranos moved north to Holland and France, where they began to live openly as Jews again. Jews began to return to England.	**Manasseh ben Israel** **Glueckel of Hameln**
1654	In the New World, twenty-three Jews escaped the Inquisition (the church court) in Brazil and came to New Amsterdam.	**Asser Levy** **Jacob Barsimson**
1750s	A joyous religious revolution called Hasidism cheered the Jews of Eastern Europe. In Western Europe commerce and industry were growing. Jews found new freedom to work and do business.	**Israel Ba'al Shem Tov** **Shneur Zalman of Lyady** **Gaon of Vilna** **Moses Mendelssohn**
1787	The constitution of the United States promised religious freedom to all. Four years later France gave equal rights to Jews. Centuries of persecution seemed to be ending.	**Haym Salomon** **Aaron Lopez** **Rebecca Gratz**
1800–1900	Equal rights spread in Western Europe. Many Jews became important merchants, writers, and politicians. In Eastern Europe there were attacks (pogroms) on Jews, yet Hebrew and Yiddish culture flowered.	**Moses Montefiore** **Mayer Rothschild** **Samuel Oppenheimer** **Judah Leib Gordon** **Isaac Leib Peretz** **Sholom Aleichem**

DATE	EVENTS	IMPORTANT PEOPLE
1881	More violent pogroms burst out across Russia. Jews began to leave for Western Europe and America: The first modern Zionists went to Palestine, bought land from the Arabs, and settled there.	**Maurice de Hirsch** **Edmond de Rothschild** **Moses Hess**
1894	In democratic France a Jewish captain named Dreyfus was falsely accused of treason. Anti-Jewish feelings flared up again. Some Jews declared, "We will only be free in our own land, in the Land of Israel." In 1897 the First Zionist Congress took place.	**Leon Pinsker** **Theodore Herzl** **Max Nordau**
1900–14	Revolution and pogroms drove more Russian Jews to Western Europe, America, and Palestine.	**Emma Lazarus** **Lillian Wald**
1917	During World War I, Great Britain issued the Balfour Declaration. It said that the British government "views with favor" the building of a Jewish homeland in Palestine. Many Jews came, bought land, and built new villages and towns in Palestine.	**Ahad Ha-Am** **Louis D. Brandeis**
1933	After World War I, Germany and many other countries were very poor. People had no jobs and no money. The Nazi party took power in 1933 and blamed all Germany's troubles on the Jews. They attacked Jews and imprisoned them in concentration camps. Some escaped, but many others could find no place to go.	**Leo Baeck** **Stephen S. Wise** **Abba Hillel Silver** **Henrietta Szold** **Recha Freier**

During their wanderings Jews became negotiators rather than warriors. This story is told of a Jew in the Russian army.

Russian and German armies faced each other across a no-man's-land. The Russian officer shouted to his troops, "Get ready men. We're going to attack. It will be man against man in hand-to-hand combat!"

"Please, sir," called the Jewish recruit, "would you show me my man? Maybe I can come to an understanding with him."

DATE	EVENTS	IMPORTANT PEOPLE
1939–45	World War II raged. The Nazis conquered most of Europe. In each country they destroyed the Jewish population. By 1945, when Germany was defeated, 6 million Jews had been killed in the Holocaust.	**Mordecai Anielewicz** **Janusz Korczak** **Tzivia Lubetkin**
1948	The State of Israel was established. Nineteen hundred years of Jewish homelessness ended. Survivors of the Holocaust and all other Jews could finally come home.	**David Ben-Gurion** **Chaim Weizmann**
1967	Israel fought the Six-Day War against her Arab neighbors, reunified Jerusalem, and freed the Temple Mount where the Western Wall stands.	**Moshe Dayan** **Yigal Allon**
1973	The Yom Kippur War broke out. Israel fought off attack by three Arab countries.	**Golda Meir** **Arik Sharon**
1979	Egypt and Israel signed the Camp David agreement and made plans for peace in the Middle East. Peace talks continued off and on with other Arab countries.	**Menahem Begin**
19??	YOU WERE BORN!	**YOU**
1990	After a long struggle, the gates of the Soviet Union were opened. Jews left to live in Israel, the United States, and Western Europe.	**Natan Sharansky** **Ida Nudel**

YEARS AND YEARS OF COSTUMES

What's a Jewish costume? A beaded deerskin shirt? A sari? A big fur hat? You can take your pick of these and hundreds more because throughout the centuries Jews have lived in many countries and have adopted the clothing of each new home.

A few garments haven't changed over the years. One is the *tallit*, the prayer shawl with fringes *(tzitzit)* that people wear in the synagogue. It is like the draped cloth that the first Jews wore in Israel.

Another traditional garment is the head covering. Since biblical times Jewish women, especially married women, have covered their heads as a sign of modesty. Very Orthodox women still cover their heads all the time with hats, scarves, and wigs. Many women still cover their heads for services. For centuries a head covering—a hat or a skullcap—has been the sign of a traditional Jewish man, especially in synagogue services.

Dress up like Abraham

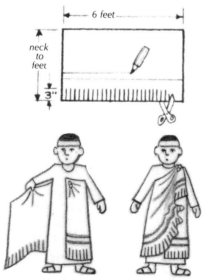

Abraham's wife Sarah can wear the same costume, but don't give her a beard! Instead of the headband, she should wear a long scarf or a cloth about 36 inches long and 18 inches wide. She also would enjoy a bracelet for her wrist and one for her ankle.

You will need:

an old light-colored sheet, tablecloth, or curtain
a long-sleeved nightshirt or nightgown
brown construction paper, 8 inches by 10 inches
sandals
a hairband or tennis headband
a staff (a thick branch or a cut-down broomstick)

1. Cut the cloth so that it is 6 feet long and as wide as your measurement from your neck to your feet.

2. Cut fringes 3 inches deep along one of the long edges. Above the fringes draw 2 stripes with a blue marking pen.

3. Put on your nightshirt.

4. Hold the sheet with the fringed edge down, parallel to the ground, and pin one of the top corners to the middle of your nightshirt. Wrap the rest of the sheet under your left arm, around your back, under your right arm, and across your chest. Pin it to the left shoulder of your nightshirt and let the end hang down.

5. To make a beard, cut both long edges of the brown paper in a curve to leave room for your mouth and to shape the beard. Cut deep fringes up from the bottom edge. Curl the fringes gently using the side of a pencil.

6. Put a piece of tape at the top corner of each side and fasten under your ears.

You will need:

construction paper	sandals
foil	lots of bracelets and necklaces
a sheer scarf	a wide-sleeved blouse
pajama bottoms (the bigger the better)	a brightly colored scarf or tie
rubber bands	light-colored crepe paper, 4 feet by 20 inches

Dress up like Queen Esther

1. To make a crown, take a piece of construction paper 9 inches wide and 12 inches long and fold it in half with the long ends together. Fold it again with the short ends together. Measure 2 inches up from the fold on the short open end and make a mark. Measure 3½ inches up from the fold on the short folded end and make a mark. Draw a line between the marks and cut on the line. Open the first fold. This will be the front of the crown.

2. To make the back of the crown, cut a strip of construction paper 4 inches wide and 12 inches long. Fold it in half with the long ends together.

3. Overlap an end of the front and an end of the back parts of the crown and staple. Fit the crown around your forehead about an inch above your eyebrows, overlapping the two open ends. Hold them together, take off the crown and staple the ends together.

4. Cover the crown with strips of aluminum foil. Tape them in place. Cut jewels out of brightly colored paper and glue them onto the foil.

5. Put the sheer scarf over your head and set the crown on it.

6. Pin the pajamas at the waist to keep them up. Gather the bottoms at your ankles with elastic or wide rubber bands.

7. To make a tunic, fold the crepe paper in half with the short ends together. Fold again with the long ends together. Measure 2 inches along the short fold and make a mark. Measure 2 inches down along the long fold and make a mark. Draw a line between the marks and cut through all four layers of paper. This will be the neck opening.

8. Measure from the edge of the neck opening 4 inches along the short fold and make a mark. Draw a line connecting the mark to the bottom corner on the unfolded side. Cut along the line through all four layers of paper.

9. Open the tunic. Decorate the bottom edge with paper jewels or other cut-out designs. Slip it on and tie the brightly colored scarf around your waist.

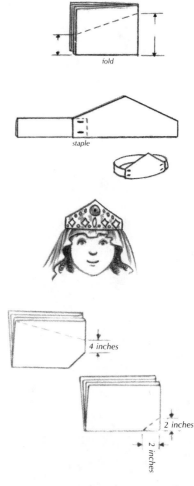

Esther's uncle Mordecai can wear the same costume, but he won't need as much jewelry. He should have a beard (see Abraham), and he should wear a skullcap instead of a crown.

HISTORY
PAPER DOLLS

JOSH
U.S.A.

Joseph Nasi
Turkey 1550

Haym Salomon
U.S.A. 1770

Yigal
Israeli Boy Scout
today

ALISA
U.S.A.

Yael
Israeli Girl Scout
today

Rebecca Gratz
U.S.A. 1800

Doña Gracia Mendes
Italy 1550

TO TRACE AND DRESS:

1. Place tracing paper on this page and trace the dolls and costumes.

2. Place carbon paper on a sheet of drawing paper. Put the tracing paper with the traced dolls and costumes on the carbon paper. Tape it down. Draw over the traced lines. The line will come out on the drawing paper underneath.

3. Remove the tracing paper and carbon paper. Color the dolls and clothing on the drawing paper. Cut them out. Glue the dolls onto cardboard.

IN GOLDEN AMERICA

All of Dutch New Amsterdam seemed to be running to the Battery on the first day of September 1654. Children with their yellow hair flying and wooden shoes clacking on the cobblestones, women untying their aprons as they hurried, men with their tools in their hands . . . and ahead of everybody stomped peg-legged Peter Stuyvesant. The sailing ship *Saint Charles* had just tied up at the dock, and everybody wanted to see her strange cargo.

The townspeople crowded close as twenty-three tattered men, women, and children came down the gangplank. Strange indeed. They were not rosy and fair like the Dutch, but slim and pale with large dark eyes and black hair. They were carrying pitifully small bundles. As the ship's captain stood arguing with Peter Stuyvesant, the news raced through the crowd: The strangers were Jews from Spain—secret Jews, known as Marranos, who had been forced to convert to Catholicism. They had left Spain and crossed the ocean to Brazil, where they had hoped to live as Jews again. But the Jesuit priests of Spain followed them, and the Jews barely escaped from Brazil in time. If the Jesuits had caught them, they would have been burned to death.

"Tch, tch," some of the citizens clucked sympathetically. "Let them stay here."

But Stuyvesant was pounding his thick cane on the dock. No, no, no, he did not want strange people with a strange religion to live in his little town. As the governor appointed by the West India Company, he would decide who could stay, and these twenty-three people had to leave!

Luckily for the Jews, the captain of the *Saint Charles* was a stubborn man. He refused to take them back aboard until their passage money was paid. And the Jews had no money.

After weeks of arguing, a letter arrived from the West India Company in Holland. Let the Jews stay, said the letter, as long as they "shall not become a burden to the company or to the community, but be supported by their own nation."

There was still trouble ahead for the little group of Sephardi (Spanish) Jews. Jacob Barsimson and Asser Levy had to fight the town council for the right to carry guns and stand guard against attacking British or Indians, just as all the other citizens did. Joseph d'Acosta and others had to argue that they be allowed to own a house and do business. It took a year before the Jews were given permission to buy ground for a cemetery, and it was seventy-five years before they could build a synagogue. But these were small problems compared to the terrors of Catholic Spain. Here in New Amsterdam, Mistress Mercado and the other Jewish women could scrub their brick floors on Friday afternoon and light the Sabbath candles at sunset; the tiny community could pray and fast on Yom Kippur; little David Faro could practice his *haftarah* in a loud, squeaky voice—and nobody would drag them off to jail.

Asser Levy soon opened a butcher shop and a tavern. Abraham de Lucena took his rifle and snowshoes and crossed the river to trade with the Indians for fur pelts. His son stayed home, studied hard, and became a rabbi of the first Jewish congregation in North America, Shearith Israel, which still exists today in New York City.

Dutch New Amsterdam became British New York in 1664, and old Peter Stuyvesant sailed sadly home to Holland. More Sephardi Jews arrived and a few German Jews too. They settled in Newport, Charleston, New Orleans, and other cities, as well as in New York.

The Jews of Newport built a handsome synagogue in 1763. It is still standing today and looks as solid and safe as the White House. But there are hidden steps built into the reading platform that lead to a secret passage in the basement. In spite of their fine synagogue, the Jews of Newport could not forget the terrors of Spain, so they made sure that they could escape at a moment's notice.

Hadassah

Bong, bong, bong—the Liberty Bell rang as the Declaration of Independence was signed in 1776. Inscribed on the bell were these words from the Bible (Torah): "Proclaim liberty throughout the land, unto all the inhabitants thereof."

As the colonies grew larger and more independent, people got tired of taking orders from faraway England. In 1776 the American Revolution against the British broke out. Patriot Americans and loyalist Americans fought each other. There were American Jews on both sides.

Haym Salomon, a Jew from Poland, helped raise the money that kept George Washington's Revolutionary army going. The story is told that on Yom Kippur eve in 1779 he was called out of the synagogue by a desperate messenger from General Washington. The army had not been paid, and the soldiers were about to mutiny. Salomon folded his *tallit* and rushed around Philadelphia begging, borrowing, and persuading until he raised the money and sent it off.

The British were driven out. The colonies became the United States of America, and the founding fathers wrote a great new constitution. It was the first national constitution ever to promise religious freedom to *all* its citizens. President Washington made the message even clearer when he wrote to the Jews of Newport: "May the children of . . . Abraham who dwell in this land continue to merit and enjoy the good will of the other inhabitants, while everyone shall sit in safety under his own vine and fig tree, and there shall be none to make him afraid."

American Jewish Historical Society

Uriah Levy was a hot-tempered little man who took the U.S. Constitution very seriously. When he joined the navy in 1812, he would take no "put-downs" and no insults to his Jewish religion. The "terrible-tempered Lieutenant Levy" fought one duel and was court-martialed six times. But he ended up with the important job of commodore and was able to force the navy to stop the cruel practice of flogging. The navy never forgot "terrible Uriah." A century later a new destroyer was named the U.S.S. *Levy.*

Biblical place names are found all over the United States. The Jordan River feeds the Great Salt Lake in Utah. Jericho, Bethpage, and Babylon are all crowded onto Long Island in New York. And there are Bethlehems in New Hampshire, Pennsylvania, and many other states.

People were fighting for democratic rights in Europe too in the early 1800s. Their revolutions were crushed, and many disappointed revolutionaries, Jews and non-Jews, came across to the young United States. Some of the German Jewish immigrants brought a new kind of worship, Reform Judaism. The Sephardi Jews didn't think much of their Ashkenazi (German) cousins with their different religious customs. But many German Jews didn't stay around to be snubbed. They loaded their children, their feather quilts, and their pots and pans into wagons and headed west to Ohio, Kentucky, Illinois, and Missouri, where they built new communities. Jewish horse-and-buggy peddlers were soon carrying everything from hair grease to axe heads to small towns and farms all over the Midwest and the South. Years later the wagons and tiny general stores of German Jewish immigrants grew into giant department stores such as Macy's and Gimbels.

Gold was struck in California in 1849, and Americans stampeded west to get rich. Levi Strauss, a Jewish manufacturer, never found a single gold nugget, but he got rich anyway by making the strongest pants in the gold fields. Levi used heavy canvas and fastened the seam corners with metal rivets. Miners crowded into his shop to buy Levi's untearable pants. People are still buying them.

The country was busy adding new states to the Union, fighting the Indians and sending covered wagons overland. But at the same time a terrible question was tearing it apart: Should slavery be allowed? Most Southerners, including Jews, thought slavery was right and proper. But others, such as the Jewish brothers Isaiah and Joseph Freedman, risked imprisonment to help slaves escape through the

Hadassah

The *Statue of Liberty* in the harbor of New York City has greeted new immigrants since 1886. Ms. Liberty is so big that forty people can stand inside her head. The last stanza of the poem "The New Colossus," by the Jewish poet Emma Lazarus, is inscribed on the base of the statue:

> Give me your tired, your poor,
> Your huddled masses yearning
> to breathe free,
> The wretched refuse of your
> teeming shore.
> Send these, the homeless,
> tempest-tost to me.
> I lift my lamp beside the golden
> door!

Underground Railroad. Rabbi David Einhorn of Baltimore narrowly escaped being tarred and feathered because he warned that slavery was a danger to the democratic rights of all Americans.

The slavery question exploded into the Civil War in 1861. Judah Benjamin, a Jewish lawyer who had been a U.S. senator from Louisiana, become the Confederate secretary of state. Twelve hundred Southern Jews fought in the Confederate army and navy. On the Union side there were 6,000 Jews, including nine gold-braided generals. A banker called Seligman, who had been a poor Jewish peddler thirty years before, raised $200 million in loans for the Union.

When the war ended the country leaped ahead again. Railroads spread across the country. Farms and factories sprang up and began to ship everything—blue jeans, sewing machines, cornflakes, potatoes—on the new "Iron Horse." There were 200,000 Jews in the United States at the end of the Civil War. They helped develop such industries as textile manufacture, railroads, department stores, and even mining. Meyer Guggenheim, a German Jewish immigrant, saved enough from his peddling to invest in a lead mine in Colorado. His business grew until it became a great empire of copper and silver mining.

Stories about "rich America where the streets are paved with gold" reached Europe. Poor people scraped their pennies together and bought tickets to sail across the ocean. In Russia and Poland the Jews were not only poor, they were also being robbed and beaten by the police and by their neighbors. After bloody attacks in 1881, many Jews packed their bundles and started for the "golden land." Between 1880 and 1914, 2 million Jewish immigrants and 20 million other immigrants reached the United States.

The newcomers didn't find gold in the streets. They found crowded apartments and dark, hot sweatshops (small factories). Men, women, and children worked from early morning till dark for between two and eight dollars a week.

The older American Jews were embarrassed by their Russian cousins. Their Yiddish language sounded funny. Their black coats and beards, kerchiefs and earlocks, looked strange. But, after all, they were fellow Jews. So settlement houses and schools were set up to help the newcomers learn to read and write English, to use handkerchiefs, and to cook American style.

The Russian Jews were fast learners. Soon they were organizing unions, building their own synagogues, publishing Yiddish newspapers, and baking the best bagels and knishes in the world.

Horse-drawn wagons, pushcarts, and new immigrants crowded together on the streets of the Lower East Side of New York. Before World War I, this was the first stop in the "golden land" for many Jewish immigrants. These immigrant children found play space on a rooftop.

Museum of the City of New York

In 1914 World War I began, and immigration was stopped. Some 225,000 American Jews fought in the American forces. When the war ended after four years, Congress decided to close the door to immigrants.

American Jews were cut off from Europe, but they still cared about the Jews across the ocean. They sent money and helped set up schools and job-training programs in Europe. At the League of Nations (an early United Nations) they fought for a Jewish homeland in Palestine.

At home in America, many Jews worked to make life better for all citizens. They formed labor unions to get fair treatment for workers. They fought for women's right to vote and for the rights of black Americans. Jewish philanthropists helped to build hospitals, colleges, and museums.

But soon money began to run out. The Great Depression started in 1929. It was a hungry, jobless time in the United States and Europe. Anti-Semites blamed the depression on the Jews, and organizations

These children are on their way from Germany to Palestine. They were saved by Youth Aliyah, a project supported by American Jews that began its work in 1934. It brought thousands of children to Palestine, cared for them, and educated them in children's villages.

Hadassah

Kibbutz Sasa in northern Israel was settled by American Jews in 1949. The best apples in Israel are grown here, and some very pretty babies, too.

Ben Zion Dorfman

such as the Anti-Defamation League of B'nai B'rith worked to disprove the lies. In the 1930s anti-Semitism also was growing in Germany, where the Nazis were beginning to ruin and drive out the Jews. Some German Jews escaped to the countries of Western Europe and to the United States. Others reached Palestine.

In 1939 German tanks rumbled into Poland. World War II had begun. As the Nazis advanced, they sent Europe's Jews to death camps. Two years later the United States entered the war, and 550,000 American Jews served in the armed forces. The Nazis were finally beaten. But when the camps were freed only a small number of survivors were found. Six million Jews had been killed.

World Jewry was horrified. Some American Jews felt that European Jews had died because there was no homeland to which they could escape when the Nazis threatened them. They urged the United Nations and the U.S. Congress to support establishment of a Jewish country. At last, in 1948, the State of Israel was born. After almost

Each spring, rain or shine, American Jews parade and celebrate in honor of the State of Israel's birthday.

Irving Weiner

1,900 years, there was a Jewish homeland again. Since then many American Jews have helped Israel with money and political support. Some have gone there to live.

After World War II, Americans began to move from the cities to the suburbs and from coast to coast. More than half of all American Jews still live in the East, but Jewish communities in the South and along the Pacific coast are growing. Synagogues, Hebrew schools, and day schools are being built in new neighborhoods. There's a Hadassah group in Nome, Alaska, a B'nai B'rith chapter in Honolulu, a Lubavicher student center in Seattle—all places where Jewish people now live, pray, and work.

Way back in 1654 there were twenty-three Jews in what was to become the United States. In 1980 there were nearly 6 million. Jewish communities have changed a bit since New Amsterdam. They have cemeteries, synagogues, swimming pools, bowling leagues, and nursery schools. But in one way they haven't changed at all: Jews still believe that it is their responsibility to help each other and to support the nation of Israel.

One Step Ahead of Columbus

Luis de Torres, a Jew and the interpreter for Columbus's fleet, was the first crewman to splash ashore in the New World. Columbus thought the American Indians might be Jewish, members of the Ten Lost Tribes, so he sent de Torres ahead to greet them with a *"shalom aleikhem."*

Almost 200 years before Columbus, Rabbi Moses de Leon wrote in the Zohar, a book of religious thought, that the earth is round and that it revolves.

AMERICAN JEWISH SPORTS FIGURES

Mark Spitz, born in 1950, won seven gold medals in swimming at the 1972 Munich Olympics. He was the first athlete to win so many medals in any Olympic sporting event.

Sylvia Wene, born in 1928, is the only woman to have bowled three perfect games in professional competition. She was Women's Bowler of the Year in 1955 and a member of the All-America teams in 1955 and 1959–62.

Harold Solomon, born in 1952, is small for a tennis player, but he plays a tireless game that wears down his opponents. He is famous for his "moonball," a high, floating ball that slows the pace of the game. He once played a moonball marathon in France that lasted more than five hours.

Abraham Hollandersky (alias Abe the Newsboy) had 1,309 boxing matches in the thirteen years from 1905 to 1918. That's almost two fights each week. They don't make fighters like that anymore.

Sandy Koufax, born in 1935, became a pitcher for the Brooklyn Dodgers when he was only twenty. It took him six years to get going, and he considered quitting. But in the following six years he won many awards and pitched what was at the time a record number of strike-outs in a single game—eighteen. On Yom Kippur in 1961, Koufax shocked his manager when he refused to pitch in a crucial game and went to synagogue instead. In 1972 he became the youngest player ever elected to the Baseball Hall of Fame.

Allie Sherman, born in 1923, was too small (125 pounds) to play football in high school. He got his chance at Brooklyn College and later with the Philadelphia Eagles. Sherman became a coach for the New York Giants, drilled them in the T-formation, and led them to three Eastern Conference titles.

Max (Slapsie Maxie) Rosenbloom, 1904–56, never got past third grade in school and spent time in reform school. But he became world light-heavyweight champion, fighting 300 bouts in sixteen years. Slapsie Maxie got his nickname because he fought with his gloves open, slapping his opponents down.

Lillian Copeland, 1904–64, set world records in three events—shotput, discus, and javelin. In the 1932 Olympics she captured the gold medal, and set Olympic and world records, for her discus throw. In 1935 she paid her own way to the Maccabiah Games and won three gold medals.

Alice Green, born in 1951, was a three-time member of the United States National Table-Tennis Team. She took part in "ping-pong diplomacy," playing the mainland Chinese team in 1972 and 1979.

Rod Carew, born in 1945, holds the American League record for stealing home plate the most times in one season: seven steals in 1969.

Max (Slats) Zaslovsky, born in 1925, was an expert at long-range set shots in basketball. He played in 540 National Basketball Association games in ten years, scoring 7,990 points for his teams.

Hank Greenberg, born in 1911, was the first Jew elected to the Baseball Hall of Fame. "Hammering Hank" almost topped Babe Ruth's record for most homeruns in a single year in 1938. He later became part owner of the Chicago White Sox.

Sid Gillman, born in 1911, was a star end for Ohio State's football team. He coached many teams during a forty-year coaching career, with a record of 115 pro victories.

Dick Savitt, born in 1927, won the Australian tennis singles tournament in 1951, at a time when Australian players dominated the game. He also won the Wimbledon tournament and then became U.S. indoor singles champion in 1952, 1958, and 1961. Savitt was voted into the International Tennis Hall of Fame in 1976.

Sid Luckman, born in 1916, was an outstanding T-formation quarterback for the Chicago Bears, completing 52 percent of his passes and helping his team to win four championships. Luckman was voted into the Football Hall of Fame.

Art Shamsky, born in 1941, played baseball for the Cincinnati Reds, New York Mets, and other teams. He hit .538 in the 1969 championship series, helping the Mets into the World Series.

Marty Hogan, born in 1958, is an Orthodox Jew and is considered "King of Swing" in the world of professional racquetball. He is the only person to win the national championship for five years straight.

Brian Gottfried, born in 1952, a tennis star from Florida, is most successful at playing doubles. He and Raul Ramirez won the Italian Open doubles for four consecutive years.

Barry Silberg, a Milwaukee rabbi, broke all the records for a very unusual sport. In the summer of 1978, he jumped rope 50,180 times in six hours without a break.

Abe Saperstein, 1902–66, founded and coached the funniest, fastest, and most popular basketball team in sports history, the Harlem Globetrotters. For forty years they have clowned and competed before millions of fans in eighty-seven countries, and they have starred in two full-length movies. Saperstein and the Globetrotters helped make basketball an international sport.

THE HOLOCAUST

In 1933 Jewish children in Germany felt as safe as you and your friends feel today. They played soccer, went on hikes, took piano lessons, and worried about tests at school. They knew Germany had lots of troubles since adults were always talking about high prices and unemployment and the ineffective government. But the children didn't pay much attention. Those were adult problems.

When Adolf Hitler and his Nazi party took over the government, some of the adults thought things might get better. Hitler seemed like a strong leader. He was certainly a noisy leader. He shouted his speeches in a loud, hoarse voice, and his followers raised their arms and shouted back so loudly that the houses shook—*"Sieg heil, sieg heil, sieg heil!"*

"Germany was once a great country," yelled Hitler, "and we will make her great again. All Germany's troubles are caused by the Jews and the Communists. We must get rid of them. Then Germany will rise up and rule the world!"

People listened. It felt good to blame their troubles on somebody. "Jews are not really Germans anyhow—they're different," they said to each other. "Maybe Hitler is right."

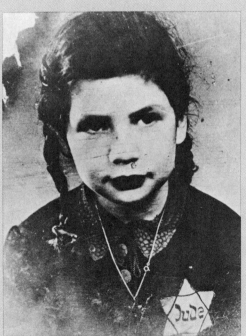

This girl wears her yellow star, marked *"Jude"* (Jew), sewn onto her jacket.

Zionist Archives

German boys and girls stopped playing with their Jewish friends. Jewish children were asked to leave their soccer teams and their scout groups. At school they had to move to the back of the room.

"Be patient," said their parents. "Soon Hitler will find out what fine, useful citizens we German Jews are, and then things will get better."

But things got worse.

"Jews are a lower species. They're not the same as our great, pure German people. We must stamp them out," Hitler shouted.

"Sieg heil!" thundered his followers. The crowds of people listening and shouting grew larger and larger.

Jewish children were forced out of school. Stores and factories owned by Jews were shut down. Jewish doctors, scientists, and teachers were fired from their jobs. All Jews were ordered to wear armbands with a yellow star. Jewish boys and girls, men and women, were stopped on the streets and insulted, beaten up, or dragged off to jail. They were outcasts in their own land.

Some Jewish families sadly began to pack their suitcases and leave. They took passage to Palestine, England, the United States— to any country that would let them in. Jews who lived in the countries near Germany got worried and tried to leave also. But doors all over the world were beginning to close.

"We're so sorry," said the polite British rulers of Palestine, "but there are already too many Jews here."

From country after country the same answers came:

"We'd like to help, but . . ."

"You have our sympathy, however . . ."

"There's no room . . ."

"We regret . . ."

"No!"

Some German Jewish children were rescued by Youth Aliyah, a program supported by the World Zionist Organization, and brought to Palestine, leaving their parents behind. But soon it was too late even for the children. Hitler's tanks and guns had begun to rumble across the borders. He was leading Germans out to conquer the world. The German army marched into Austria in 1938, then into Czechoslovakia, Poland, France . . . on and on.

Though he was busy conquering Europe, Hitler did not forget his second goal: the destruction of the Jews. When German soldiers captured a town, they ordered all the Jewish families to come to the town square. People quickly took clothing and food, dressed the children warmly (nobody knew where the Germans would take them—it might be a long trip), and hurried to the square. Sometimes Hitler's deadly work was done immediately. German guns swept the square and cut down the shocked families before they knew what was happening. At other times the Jews were marched off or taken by train to walled-in parts of town called ghettos, where they worked in factories making supplies for the German army.

A very few people escaped from the guns and the trains and reached the forests. There they joined anti-Nazi fighters (partisans) or hid with peasants.

Some non-Jews tried to help. When the Germans invaded Denmark in 1940 and began to arrest Danish Jews, hundreds of Danish fishermen carried 7,000 Jews to safety in Sweden in small boats.

In the ghettos people worked long hours and were crowded tightly together. There was never enough food. Children grew pale and thin. Many died.

Hungry children in the Warsaw Ghetto in 1942.

Yad Vashem

This statue of Mordecai Anie-lewicz, the leader of the Warsaw Ghetto Revolt, stands in Kibbutz Yad Mordecai in Israel. This farm settlement is named after the hero who died fighting the Nazis when he was twenty-four years old. Anielewicz had been a free partisan fighter in the forest, but he made his way back to the ghetto to organize the resistance. In the last days of the Warsaw Ghetto, Mordecai wrote: "I am proud that I came to this moment, that my eyes see a grenade and a pistol in the hands of a Jew. I am ready to die. To this task I grew up. . . . With the end of this battle I must end."

In spite of everything the Jews had hope. How can things get any worse, they thought. But things got worse, much worse than anybody could imagine.

World War II had begun. England and the United States were fighting against Germany. Soon the Nazis would be defeated. We must be brave, they decided. We must not let the Nazis turn us into animals. So they ran schools for their children in the ghettos, and they organized their own choirs, orchestras, and art classes.

From time to time the Germans asked for volunteers to go to a different work place. They promised that there would be better food and more space. People climbed into the waiting trains hopefully. But they were not carried to new places. The train doors were locked, and they were taken to death camps—to Treblinka, Auschwitz, and Bergen-Belsen—where huge gas chambers worked day and night killing Jews.

News of the death camps reached the ghettos. Frightened whispers raced from family to family: "Hitler is slaughtering our people. Soon he'll kill us too!"

Most people refused to believe the terrible news. They couldn't

If a friend of yours was very sick or if one of your classmates was hurt in a school-bus accident, you would be really upset. But what can you feel when 1½ million children are hurt or killed? How can anybody imagine so many children? And yet 1½ million Jewish children died in the Holocaust.

One of them, twelve-year-old Franta Bass, wrote this poem when she was a prisoner in the Terezin concentration camp:

The Garden

A little garden,
Fragrant and full of roses.
The path is narrow
And a little boy walks along it.
A little boy, a sweet boy,
Like that growing blossom.
When the blossom comes to
   bloom,
The little boy will be no more.

imagine that even a madman like Hitler would murder thousands of people in cold blood—and for no reason. Only a few of the young people accepted the truth. They knew they could not wait for the war to end. There was no time for hope. They had to fight the Nazis now!

Resistance groups were formed in the ghettos of Vilna, Bialystok, Warsaw, and other cities. In Warsaw young men and women crept through the dark sewers under the walls of the ghetto. They bought guns and bullets from the Polish resistance outside and carried them back. Fighters were posted on rooftops and in basements all through the ghetto.

Before Passover in 1943, German soldiers marched in to "clear out" the Warsaw Ghetto. Bullets suddenly whistled around them and forced them back. They called in flame throwers and tanks. The ghetto fighters tossed hand grenades to destroy the tanks and vanished into the buildings. For days the fighting went on. At last the Germans backed out beyond the walls to safety and began to smash the ghetto to pieces with long-range guns and bombs.

Thousands of Jews were killed in the bombing. Those left alive fought from under the rubble, from the cellars and the sewers, for forty-two days. In the end, a few escaped through the sewers to join the partisans (resistance fighters) in the forests.

There were more revolts against the Nazis in the ghettos and even in the death camps. Some Jews cut through the barbed wire or jumped from trains and escaped to the forests. Partisans ripped at the Germans with fierce hit-and-run attacks. But the Nazi murder machine could not be stopped. One after another, the ghettos were emptied. Between lines of German soldiers, naked Jewish children, women, and men were forced into the gas chambers to be killed. Then great brick ovens burned their bodies to ash.

In early 1945 the Allied armies finally began to push the Germans back. Hitler was losing the war, and he would never rule the world. He had failed. But he had also succeeded, for 6 million Jews from every country in Europe had been destroyed in the Holocaust he created.

The story of the Holocaust is told in Yad Vashem, a memorial and library on a quiet, sunny hilltop in Jerusalem, Israel. Records and names of the dead and of their lost villages and towns are kept here, and a light burns in their memory. Yad Vashem also pays tribute to the many brave Christians who risked their lives trying to save Jews during the Holocaust.

Orphan children from the ghetto of Lodz boarding a train that will take them to a death camp (September 1942).

ISRAEL, LAND OF THE STIFF-NECKED PEOPLE

When the prophet Jeremiah got really angry at the Jews for disobeying God, he called them a stubborn, stiff-necked people. That was 2,000 years ago, when the Jews were living in Judea, the Land of Israel. Ever since Jeremiah's time, stubbornness has been getting Jews into trouble and out of trouble. It was one of the reasons they were driven from their homeland in 70 C.E. And it is one of the reasons they came back to build the State of Israel in 1948.

Way back in 70 C.E., the Land of Israel (Judea) and most of its neighbors were ruled by the powerful Roman Empire. The Jews hated being told how to run their country and their Holy Temple in Jerusalem. They left their villages and farms, gathered an army, and attacked the Romans, trying to drive them out and make Judea free again. After a long, hard fight the Romans smashed the revolt. They killed the Jewish leaders and destroyed the Temple. But the stiff-necked Jews would not give up. They revolted again and again. Finally the Romans burned Jerusalem to the ground, shipped off all the Jews they could catch to become slaves in faraway lands, and changed the name of the country from Judea to Palestine.

That might have been the end of the story. But the Jews stubbornly refused to let it end. Over the centuries they kept coming back to the Land of Israel. Pious, bearded rabbis came from France, a homesick poet from Spain, a bejeweled minister from Turkey, Kabbalists from Italy, and others who wanted to cry and pray at the ruins of the Temple in Jerusalem. The Jews who were scattered around the world turned toward Jerusalem each day when they prayed. At

Theodore Herzl on board a ship sailing to Palestine. Herzl was a strong leader and a farsighted man. After the First Zionist Congress he wrote in his diary: "In Basle I established a Jewish state. If I were to say that aloud today universal laughter would be the response. Maybe in five years, certainly in fifty, everybody will recognize it." Fifty-one years later the State of Israel was born.

Zionist Archives

If you will it, it is no dream.
Theodore Herzl

Passover they sang, "To the next year in Jerusalem," and they waited for the Messiah, God's chosen messenger, to come and lead them home.

In 1882 some young Jews in Russia got impatient with just waiting and praying. They wanted to go home to Israel and be free and independent again. They formed a group called Bilu, packed their knapsacks, and headed over the mountains and across the sea to Palestine.

The Bilu idea—to build a homeland again after centuries of wandering—thrilled people all over the world. They named it "Zionism," since "Zion" was the biblical name for the Land of Israel. When Theodore Herzl, an Austrian writer, called the First Zionist Congress in Basle, Switzerland, in 1897, hundreds of excited Jews came together to make plans for rebuilding the Jewish homeland. More impatient young people kissed their parents goodbye and started walking and sailing to Palestine to become *halutzim* ("pioneers").

Lunchtime for early *halutzim* in a rocky field in Palestine.

Zionist Archives

The Bible describes the Land of Israel as a land of milk and honey, but when the *halutzim* got there they found a blazing sun and gray fields full of rocks and giant mosquitoes. "It doesn't matter," they said, "the land needs us and we need the land." They dug, planted, and built. They got blisters and aching muscles. Some of them died of fever. But they were as stubborn as the Jews of Roman times—they would not give up. Slowly the bare hills grew fuzzy with young forests, and fields turned green and fruitful.

As the Zionist movement grew, the countries of the world started to take notice. In 1917 England issued the Balfour Declaration approving the idea of a Jewish homeland. Five years later the League of Nations agreed to a plan for a Jewish state. Since most of the people of the Middle East are Arabs, the League of Nations also set up four Arab states. But many Arabs were against the idea of a Jewish homeland. They attacked Jewish towns and burned Jewish farms and forests. The *ḥalutzim* would not be scared off. They learned to shoot rifles and ride horses to patrol their settlements. They built tall lookout towers to guard against attacks and kept right on working.

Lights of a lookout tower brighten the dark fields of a kibbutz in southern Israel. The border kibbutzim and villages are always on guard against attack.

Israel Consulate General Library

While the Jews of Palestine were rebuilding their homeland, the terrible Nazi danger was growing for those who remained in Europe. The Nazis came into power in Germany in 1933 and began to force Jews out of their jobs and homes and to throw them into prison. Some escaped to Palestine and to other countries. But the British who governed Palestine soon closed the ports and would admit only a few refugees. Other countries closed their doors too. The Nazis reached out to destroy the Jews of Austria, Poland, Hungary, and Czechoslovakia. They boasted that they would make all Europe "clean" of Jews. Europe's Jews waited helplessly. There was no place to which they could escape.

Off the coast of Italy a boat loaded with Jewish refugees is pushed out toward a small waiting ship. Before and after the war these "illegal" ships slipped past British patrol boats to reach Palestine. The refugees splashed ashore and were quickly hidden in the Jewish villages and kibbutzim.

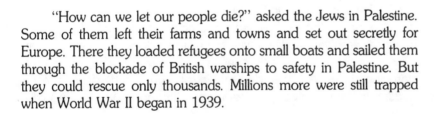

"How can we let our people die?" asked the Jews in Palestine. Some of them left their farms and towns and set out secretly for Europe. There they loaded refugees onto small boats and sailed them through the blockade of British warships to safety in Palestine. But they could rescue only thousands. Millions more were still trapped when World War II began in 1939.

Hanna Senesch left her kibbutz in Palestine to try to save Jews in Europe. She was caught and killed by the Nazis in 1944, when she was twenty-three years old. This poem is her "goodbye" to the world:

Blessed is the match that is burned up in its own flame.
Blessed is the flame that burns deep inside the heart.
Blessed is the heart strong enough to stop beating to save its honor.
Blessed is the match that is burned up in its own flame.

"Home is the place where, when you have to go there, they have to take you in."—Robert Frost

During World War II, Palestinian Jews fought beside the British to defeat Nazi Germany. Such courageous Jews as Hanna Senesch and Enzo Sereni still tried desperately to reach the Jews of Europe. They parachuted behind the German lines to help rescue Jews who were locked in death camps. But this time Jewish courage and stubbornness could not win. By the end of the war the Nazis had killed 6 million Jews, more than half the Jews of Europe. Just about every Jew in the world had lost a member of his or her family.

After the war the United Nations divided Palestine into a tiny Jewish state and an Arab state. The Arabs refused to accept the plan. They would not agree to any Jewish state, no matter how small. But the Jews knew there had to be a Jewish state. Never again would Jews die because no door was open for them. Israel's door would always be open! They accepted the United Nations plan, and on May 14, 1948, David Ben-Gurion, the first prime minister, declared the establishment of the State of Israel. It was the first free and independent Jewish state in nearly 2,000 years!

Sounds of the *shofar* were heard across the land. Girls and boys in shorts, yeshivah students with bouncing earlocks, housewives, taxi drivers, soldiers—everybody danced and sang in the streets in great stamping circles. And bearded rabbis carrying Torahs danced in the middle. In New York and London and all over the world Jews celebrated.

But it was a short celebration. The very next day seven Arab states attacked Israel. The Israelis had few weapons and were greatly outnumbered, but they had plenty of stubbornness and imagination. They nailed sheets of metal onto taxis to make tanks. They stuffed rags into soda bottles filled with gasoline to make bombs. They fought with old Turkish bayonets, Czech rifles, and anything else they could find until, at last, they drove their attackers out. Many Palestinian Arabs ran away too and became refugees.

A great, happy, homecoming celebration began for the Jewish people. From more than seventy countries they returned to the Land of Israel. Operation Magic Carpet brought the Jews of Yemen. Operation Ali Baba brought the Jews of Iraq. The streets were like a costume party with people wearing turbans and veils and khaki shorts and striped robes and bright kerchiefs. Everybody seemed to speak a different language. On the buses people asked for directions in dozens of languages and lots of them got lost.

**Too Many Chiefs—
Not Enough Indians**
President Truman of the United States and President Weizmann of Israel were comparing their jobs one day.

"My job is very tough," said Truman. "There are 180 million people in the United States and as president, I am responsible to each one of them."

"Mine is tougher," Weizmann said. "There are only one million Jews in Israel, but as president of Israel I preside over one million presidents."

Israeli girls from Yemen are teaching a dance to their new European neighbors. Israelis began to learn each other's customs, songs, and dances and tasted each other's strange new foods. The country was becoming more than a melting pot of peoples—it was a pressure cooker!

Zionist Archives

Most of the newcomers lived in tents and tin shacks. They squooshed through ankle-deep mud to go from place to place. But they laughed at their problems and said, *"Yihiyeh tov"*—"It will be good."

In the next ten years almost a million new immigrants came to Israel. Soon most of them were speaking Hebrew, the language of Israel. And slowly the tents and shacks and mud were replaced by solid houses and sidewalks.

"Oy vay! How are we all going to fit in there?" the mother of this immigrant family seems to be thinking as she arrives at her new home in Israel in 1950. The houses and apartments built in the early years were small. But at least the roofs didn't leak and there was indoor plumbing. It was a good beginning.

Israel Consulate General Library

The name "Jerusalem" means "City of Peace" in Hebrew. But over the centuries at least fifteen different peoples have fought to win the not-so-peaceful city. Though the bosses at Jerusalem's city hall kept changing, Jewish people were always part of its population.

There was plenty of work to do. A giant pipeline was laid to bring water to new towns and farms in the thirsty south. New ports and ships were built. Oranges, chocolate, fresh flowers, and other products were carried across the sea to be sold in other countries, and machinery and raw materials were carried back. Huge blue and white Israeli planes brought tourists to visit the fast-growing country.

But there was no peace between Israel and her Arab neighbors. There was a war in 1956 and another in 1967 that lasted only six days. When the 1967 war was over, Israel had taken the Old City of Jerusalem and the site of the ancient Temple. Jerusalem was whole again.

Jews blow the *shofar* and pray again at the Western Wall, the remaining outside wall of the Holy Temple in Jerusalem. Before the Six-Days War, the Wall and the Old City were controlled by Jordan, Israel's western neighbor. Israelis were not allowed to cross the border and pray there.

Romanian and Russian Jews began to arrive after the Six-Day War. As the country grew stronger, Israelis found time to have fun and develop all kinds of interests. Orchestras and rock groups played to sell-out crowds. Book fairs, hiking trails, soccer stadiums, and even archaeological digs were bustling. New museums and universities were built. And Israelis became great "noshers"—felafel sandwiches, sunflower seeds, and soda were sold on almost every corner.

War came again on Yom Kippur in 1973. Then, six years later, there was a first tiny, hopeful step toward peace. Egypt, Israel's neighbor to the south, signed the Camp David Accords with Israel.

"An insincere peace is better than a sincere war."—the Rabbi of Lublin

Boys play on one of the grim leftovers of the 1973 war, a ruined Syrian tank on Israel's northern border.

George Holz

In 1982 Israeli forces fought in Lebanon with guerrilla forces of the Palestine Liberation Organization. As before, after the war was over, Israelis and Jews all over the world were hopeful that this would be the last time Israel would be forced to defend herself.

By 1991 more than 4,000,000 Jews shared the small Land of Israel with 874,000 Muslims, Christians, Druze, and people of other religions. They are all Israelis, and they are all represented in the Knesset, Israel's parliament, where they talk, argue, and sometimes even yell while trying to solve problems together.

It's not easy. There is so much that Israelis disagree about— religion, taxes, soccer, land ownership, how to raise kids, and more. But everybody agrees on one thing: the need for peace. All Israelis hope that peace (*salaam* in Arabic, *shalom* in Hebrew) will come quickly now.

It won't be easy to make peace. But it wasn't easy to fight the Romans, or to hold onto Judaism through the years of wandering, or to build the Jewish homeland, or to fight four wars in Israel. Only a stubborn, stiff-necked people could have done it.

Yihiyeh tov!

Talking Jewish

MAMA HEBREW'S FAMILY

Jewish languages are like a big family with children of different ages, shapes, and sizes, all sharing the same mother. Hebrew, the first and oldest language of the Jewish people, is the "mother tongue." The Jews of the Land of Israel spoke Hebrew 4,000 years ago, and the Bible is written in Hebrew.

When the Jewish people were forced to leave their homeland they carried the Bible and their Hebrew language with them. They scattered all over the world and learned new languages wherever they settled. When they spoke to each other, they used a mixture of Hebrew and the new language. And when they wrote letters or did business with Jews in faraway lands, they wrote in Hebrew, or they used the words of their new language but wrote them with Hebrew letters.

As the years passed, Hebrew began to be used mostly for praying and studying the Bible and for other books of religion. Jews in

Secret Languages

The Rothschilds are a very rich, widespread family of Jewish bankers. In the 1800s they built a coach with a false floor so that they could send secret messages to each other. To be even more sure of secrecy, they wrote the messages in Hebrew or Yiddish.

Another widespread family of business people, the Sassoons of India and China, also knew how to keep a secret. They sent messages in Chinese, written in the Hebrew alphabet.

Sometimes grandparents or parents speak Yiddish or Hebrew to each other to tell secrets right in front of their kids. Very unfair! The only way to stop them is to learn the language as fast as possible.

Europe called it *"lashon ha-kodesh,"* the holy language. Everyday business such as cooking, flirting, selling in the marketplace, or yelling at the kids was done in the Jewish language of the area. But Hebrew continued to hold all Jews together. A Jew from Poland and a Jew from Morocco might not understand each other's Yiddish or Judeo-Arabic, but since all Jews studied and prayed in Hebrew, they could understand each other in that language.

It's still true today. If you find yourself in a strange land where you don't speak the language, just walk into the nearest synagogue and say the Hebrew greeting *"Shalom aleikhem,"* "peace be unto you." The Jews will welcome you with *"Aleikhem shalom,"* and you'll feel right at home.

Rabbi Isaac Luria used to pray to God with all his heart and soul. One day an angel flew by and whispered to him that his poor neighbor Abraham the carpenter prayed even more earnestly than he. This Abraham must be a very learned man, thought Rabbi Isaac. I must speak to him. He hurried down the street and found Abraham sawing wood in front of his small house.

"Excuse me for interrupting you," said Rabbi Isaac, "I see you are a carpenter."

"That I am," said Abraham.

"Aha. Are you also a scholar?" asked the rabbi.

"No," Abraham answered sadly. "I don't even know all the letters of the *aleph-bet*. I know only from *aleph* to *yod*."

Rabbi Isaac was puzzled. Could the angel have made a mistake? "If you don't know the *aleph-bet*, how do you say your prayers?" he asked.

"I just repeat the letters that I know over and over again," said Abraham, "and I ask God to put them together into a prayer."

After Hebrew, the most widespread of the Jewish languages is Yiddish. In the 1920s two-thirds of all the Jews in the world understood Yiddish. The language began when Jews settled in Germany in the twelfth and thirteenth centuries. They mixed Hebrew and French with German and used their own Hebrew alphabet to write it down. When Yiddish-speaking Jews moved on to Eastern Europe, Polish and Russian words were added to Yiddish, and the language became even more special. But it was a Cinderella language, beloved by simple people and snubbed by the Hebrew scholars. At last, in the 1800s, writers began to publish songs, plays, poems, and novels in Yiddish. There were also scores of Yiddish newspapers and journals. Yiddish blossomed for a hundred years until World War II. Then, when most of the Jews of Eastern Europe were destroyed in the Holocaust, Yiddish became a language without a home.

The Jews who settled in Spain began to speak a language that was mostly Castilian Spanish blended with a little Hebrew and Arabic. They called it Ladino. Like the Yiddish-speaking Jews, they wrote their language in Hebrew letters. When the Jews were expelled from Spain in 1492, they found their way to Italy, North Africa, Turkey, and even across the ocean to the New World. The first Jews in Brazil, and later in New Amsterdam (New York), spoke Ladino.

Judeo-Arabic grew up around the Mediterranean Sea and throughout the Middle East, wherever Jews lived with Arabic-speaking people. Great Jewish scientists, poets, and religious thinkers such as Maimonides and Saadiah Gaon, wrote in the Arabic language using the letters of the Hebrew alphabet.

Many other languages have been children of Mother Hebrew, but only Yiddish, Ladino, and Judeo-Arabic are still being spoken.

Language Firsts

The first Ladino book was printed in 1510 in Constantinople. And a Judeo-Arabic newspaper printed in 1856 was the first newspaper in all of India.

Ashkenazim and Sephardim

Germany is called Ashkenaz *in Hebrew. Spain is called* Sepharad. *Yiddish-speaking Jews, usually from Central or Eastern Europe, are called "Ashkenazim." Ladino- or Arabic-speaking Jews, some of whose families had come from Spain long before, are called "Sephardim."*

LASHON HA-KODESH GOES MODERN

Eliezer Ben-Yehuda came to Palestine in 1881 with a great plan: He would work to rebuild the Jewish homeland, and he would make Hebrew the language of the new country. All newspapers and books must be printed in Hebrew. All school children must be taught in Hebrew. Even at home people must speak only Hebrew.

This was very hard on Eliezer's wife and little son, who didn't know any Hebrew at all. But Eliezer would not speak to them until they learned the language. Even after Mrs. Ben-Yehuda learned a little Hebrew, her troubles were not over. There simply were not enough words for people to use every day. Hebrew was a language of prayer. It had lots of words to describe God, but very few words for ordinary things like brooms, boots, gloves, trains, or ice cream.

Eliezer Ben-Yehuda and other scholars formed a language council (Va'ad ha-Lashon) to make up new Hebrew words for the new land. He also wrote a big, thick Hebrew dictionary so that everybody could learn the old words and look up the new ones.

Israelis are very grateful to the "father of modern Hebrew." Two main streets are named after Eliezer Ben-Yehuda in Israel's two biggest cities, Jerusalem and Tel Aviv. Some people think the streets should have been named after the long-suffering Mrs. Ben-Yehuda.

When the State of Israel was born in 1948, Jews came from every land in a great, happy rush. They spoke Yiddish, Ladino, Judeo-Arabic, Judeo-Persian, Russian, English, Hindustani, Amharic, Arabic, and more. The taxi drivers and bus drivers and the policemen and policewomen of Israel had to talk in sign language. School teachers drew pictures on the board to explain lessons. The streets were filled with a babble of languages.

Babble in Israel

Some of the immigrants knew Hebrew from their religious studies. But how could they buy groceries or find out which bus went where or fix a flat tire with the words from the prayer book?

So the government of Israel set up special language schools called *ulpanim*. Grandparents, parents, and children all went to school to learn modern Hebrew. The children often learned faster than the grownups and had to help their parents with their homework.

New words When the Va'ad ha-Lashon started work the Hebrew language had about 8,000 basic words. Today there are 80,000. The scholars tried to base their words on earlier Hebrew words. Here are some examples:

ENGLISH	HEBREW		HEBREW SOURCE
nuclear energy	כֹּחַ גַּרְעִינִי	ko'aḥ garini	ko'aḥ strength garin seed or nucleus
telegram	מִבְרָק	mivrak	barak lightning
strike	שְׁבִיתָה	shevitah	shavot rest
computer	חַשְׁבָּן	ḥashban	ḥashov to think

Words from other languages crept into Hebrew too, in spite of the hard-working Va'ad ha-Lashon.

ENGLISH MEANING	HEBREW WORD		SOURCE
flat tire	פּוּנְטְשֶׁר	poncher	*English* puncture
red-headed person	גִּ׳ינגִ׳י	jinjy	*English* ginger
little doll, cute girl	בּוּבֶּלֶה	bubeleh	*Yiddish and Hebrew* doll
friendly get together	קוּמְזִיץ	kumsitz	*Yiddish* come and sit
may God be willing	אִינְשַׁלַה	inshallah	*Arabic* may God be willing

COMMON PHRASES

English	Hebrew		Yiddish	
Happy birthday	יוֹם הֻלֶּדֶת שָׂמֵחַ	yom holedet sameiakh	אַ פֿרײלעכן געבורטסטאָג	a freylekhen geburstog
I love you	אֲנִי אוֹהֵב אוֹתָךְ	ani ohev otakh	איך האָב דיך ליב	ikh hob dikh lib
How are you?	מַה שְׁלוֹמְךָ	mah shelomkha?	וואָס מאַכסטו	vos makhst du?
What time is it?	מַה הַשָׁעָה	ma ha-sha'ah?	וויפֿיל איז דער זײגער	vifil azeyger?
Good morning	בֹּקֶר טוֹב	boker tov	גוט מאָרגן	a gut morgen
Good night	לַיְלָה טוֹב	layelah tov	אַ גוטע נאַכט	a gute nakht
Hello	שָׁלוֹם	shalom	שלום	sholem
Everything is O.K.	הַכֹּל בְּסֵדֶר	ha-kol be-seder	אַלץ איז אין אָרדענונג	alles iz in ordnung
Happy holiday	חַג שָׂמֵחַ	ḥag sameiaḥ	גוט יום־טוב	gut yontif
Have a good Sabbath	שַׁבָּת שָׁלוֹם	Shabbat shalom	אַ גוטן שבת	a guten shabes
Be seeing you	לְהִתְרָאוֹת	le-hitra'ot	זײַ געזונט	zay gezunt
Really?	בֶּאֱמֶת	be-emet?	טאַקע	takeh?
Please	בְּבַקָּשָׁה	be-vakashah	זײַ אַזוי גוט	zay azoy gut
Thank you	תּוֹדָה	todah	אַ דאַנק	a dank
Let's eat	זְמַן לֶאֱכוֹל	zeman le-ekhol	לאָמיר עסן	lomir esen

SOME SPECIAL THINGS ABOUT HEBREW

1. Hebrew is written from right to left............... SIHT EKIL. Yiddish and other languages using the Hebrew alphabet are written from right to left also.

2. Hebrew is usually written without vowels. For beginning readers the vowels are added underneath the letters. If reading without vowels sounds easy, try to figure out this sentence:

NBDY CN RD WTHT VWLS EXCPT TH ISRLS.

3. Hebrew has two sounds not found in English, represented by the letters *het* ח or *khaf* כ and *ayin* ע .

To make the *het* or *khaf* sound, pretend you have a sore throat and are gargling with mouthwash. To learn the *ayin* sound, find a Sephardi Jew from Yemen or Morocco and ask him or her to teach it to you. Most Ashkenazim can't do it right. In English the *het* sound is written "ḥ," the letter "h" with a dot underneath. The *khaf* sound is written with a "kh." Sometimes both are represented by "ch."

HEBREW MINI-DICTIONARY

tree
עֵץ
etz

house
בַּיִת
bayit

father
אַבָּא
abba

baby
תִּינוֹק
tinok

mother
אִמָּא
ima

boy
יֶלֶד
yeled

girl
יַלְדָּה
yaldah

grandmother
סָבְתָא
sabta

grandfather
סָבָא
saba

hand
יָד
yad

head
רֹאשׁ
rosh

eye
עַיִן
ayin

knee
בֶּרֶךְ
berekh

foot
רֶגֶל
regel

tail
זָנָב
zanav

family
מִשְׁפָּחָה
mishpaḥah

milk
חָלָב
ḥalav

bread
לֶחֶם
leḥem

fish
דָּג
dag

store
חָנוּת
ḥanut

synagogue
בֵּית־כְּנֶסֶת
bet keneset

park
גַּן
gan

day
יוֹם
yom

night
לַיְלָה
laylah

dog
כֶּלֶב
kelev

cat
חָתוּל
ḥatul

lion
אֲרִי
ari

bear
דֹב
dov

elephant
פִּיל
pil

bicycle
אוֹפָנַיִם
ofenayim

ice cream
גְּלִידָה
gelidah

fruit
פֵּרוֹת
peirot

automobile
מְכוֹנִית
mekhonit

hat
כּוֹבַע
kova

shirt
חוּלְצָה
ḥultzah

skirt
חֲצָאִית
ḥatza'it

socks
גַּרְבַּיִם
garbayim

shoes
נַעֲלַיִם
na'alayim

pants
מִכְנָסַיִם
mikhnasayim

school
בֵּית־סֵפֶר
bet sefer

teacher
מוֹרָה
morah

A Hebrew-English mishmash

What is ma.
And me is who.
And who is he
And he is she.
So what is what?
What is ma.

YINGLISH

Many Yiddish words jumped into the melting pot of American English and became "Yinglish." How many of these do you know?

Oy vay! How awful! or Oh no!

nudnik a nuisance, a boring person

nudjeh to annoy or bother somebody

chutzpa nervy; sassy; like the man who killed his mother and father and pleaded for mercy because he was an orphan

shamus detective

kibitz to criticize, tease, or make comments

gonif thief

nosher one who loves to eat between meals

tushy buttocks

knish a thin sheet of dough wrapped around cheese or potato and baked

kosher okay, proper, or in order; literally, according to Jewish dietary laws

shlemiel a foolish person who does everything wrong

shnook a timid, shy shlemiel

shlep to drag or lug; a long trip

shlepper a slow or sloppy person

JEWISH FOLK SAYINGS

Ladino

- Each rooster crows in his own chicken coop.
- He who sleeps with dogs gets up with fleas.
- When people call you a jackass, look to see if you have a tail.
- A fly can't get into a closed mouth, so keep your mouth shut.

Yiddish

- After a thief kisses you, count your teeth.
- A pimple is no problem on someone else's bottom.
- An ignoramus is lucky—he doesn't know that he doesn't know.
- The whole world is one town.
- If things aren't the way you like, you've got to like them the way they are.
- Little children won't let you sleep. Big children won't let you live.

GETTING MAD IN JEWISH

Can you match the drawings to the curses? Answers on page 107

In Yiddish

A You should grow like an onion with your head in the ground and your feet in the air.

B A trolley car should grow in your belly and all day you should spit out transfers.

C Go hit your head against the wall.

D Pieces should fall off you.

E If you had twice as much sense, you would be an idiot.

F May all your teeth fall out except one, and with that one you should have a toothache.

In Hebrew

G May your name be erased.

H Go to Azazel. (Azazel is the name of a huge rock from which a goat was thrown on Yom Kippur in ancient times.)

In Judeo-Arabic

I May the sweat of a thousand camels infest your armpits.

J May your right ear dry up and fall into your left pocket.

K You are some smart donkey!

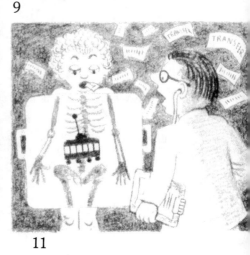

Around the Jewish year

THE HEBREW CALENDAR

All Jewish holidays are dated by the Hebrew calendar, and so are the most important happenings in each person's life—birth, marriage, and death. If you compare your birth date on the Hebrew calendar and on the general calendar, you'll find that the calendars are very different from each other.

The general calendar is based on the sun. Each year is 365 days long because it takes the earth 365 days to move around the sun.

The Hebrew calendar is based on the moon. Each month begins with the appearance of the new moon, and it takes 354 days for the moon to circle the earth twelve times.

There is a difference of eleven days between the solar (sun) year and the lunar (moon) year. The Hebrew calendar makes up the difference by adding an extra month every few years.

The date of each year of the Hebrew calendar seems to be much further ahead of the general calendar. That's because Jews start counting their calendar years with the day the world was created, as described in the Bible. That was 3,760 years before the general calendar began. To figure out the present year of the Jewish calendar, add 3,760 to the general year between January 1 and Rosh Ha-Shanah, and add 3,761 to the general year between Rosh Ha-Shanah and January 1. For example:

1985 (general calendar) + 3760 = 5745 (Hebrew calendar)
Now see if you can figure out your Jewish birth date.

This chart shows how the Hebrew months and holidays relate to the general months and to the seasons of the year.

General month	September October November	December January February	March April May	June July August
Hebrew month	Elul Tishri Ḥeshvan	Kislev Tevet Shevat	Adar Nisan Iyyar	Sivan Tammuz Av
Holiday	Rosh Ha-Shanah Yom Kippur Sukkot Simḥat Torah	Hanukkah Tu Bi-Shevat	Purim Passover Lag Ba-Omer Yom Ha-Atzma'ut	Shavuot Tisha Be-Av

Legends tell that a huge book containing every person's name is opened in heaven during the New Year holidays. Our past deeds are judged and our fate for the next year is decided and written down in the book. That's why, when people send greeting cards to each other before Rosh Ha-Shanah, the card often says, "Le-shanah tovah tikatevu," which means, "May you be inscribed (written down in the huge book) for a good year."

A YEAR FULL OF HOLIDAYS

Rosh Ha-Shanah

The first and second days of Tishri

Right at the beginning of the school year, when you're just starting to doodle in your new notebooks, the first holiday of the Jewish calendar comes along. It is the Jewish New Year, Rosh Ha-Shanah.

This isn't a sleeping-late, pancakes-and-eggs-for-breakfast holiday. It's a hurry-up-and-get-into-your-dress-up-clothes-and-go-to-synagogue holiday. On Rosh Ha-Shanah, Jews gather in the synagogue to do some hard thinking about how they spent the past year and how they could do better in the next one. All morning the large room is filled with people swaying back and forth and praying. During the service the sharp cry of the *shofar,* the ram's horn, cuts through, calling out to everyone: "Obey God's laws. Work to be a better, kinder person during this new year!"

At home, even before lunch, the family dips slices of apple or round ḥallah (holiday bread) into honey. "May it be a good, sweet year—*shanah tovah u-metukah*" we say to each other, and we exchange sweet, sticky kisses.

Sometimes we get disgusted with ourselves. We feel stupid or ugly or shy or too scared or too pushy. We may think that someone else is perfect and that we can never be like that.

A rabbi called Zusya of Hanipoli thought about this problem and said:

"When I am judged by the heavenly court, they will not ask, why weren't you Abraham or Moses? They will ask why weren't you Zusya?"

So you don't have to be as great as some hero—just try to make the very most of yourself.

The Ten Days of Repentance

The ten days from Rosh Ha-Shanah to the next holiday, Yom Kippur, are called the Days of Repentance *(teshuvah)*. You go back to school after Rosh Ha-Shanah, but between math and gym and recess you can do some remembering. Did you break your brother's or sister's toy during the year, or call your friend a fat slob, or do something else that you know was wrong? It is not enough to feel sorry. These ten days are the time to *tell* people that you are sorry and to think about how you can do better in the year ahead.

THE TZADDIK

adapted from a story by I. L. Peretz

Yom Kippur was nearly over. The fate of the little congregation would soon be decided. Everybody waited restlessly as the rabbi read the final prayers. Suddenly his voice was choked—he stood silent. Minutes passed, half an hour, an hour. Still the rabbi stood like a stone.

People grew worried. What was wrong? They could not know that the rabbi stood silent because he had received a terrible answer to his prayers. God had told him that the congregation would be punished for its sins and would suffer in the new year.

Only one person was not worried, a little boy who stood waiting in the doorway for his father. The silent rabbi and the white Torahs gleaming in the dark room filled the boy with awe and joy. He wanted to pray, to speak to God, but he was a farm boy who had not gone to school, so he knew no Hebrew and no prayers. The only way he could express his joy and excitement was by whistling.

His piercing whistle filled the quiet room. "Who did that? Who dares to whistle in the synagogue?" people cried out angrily.

But the rabbi raised his hand. He turned to face the congregation with a happy smile. "Where is the *tzaddik* (great and good person) who whistled a prayer from deep in his heart?" he asked. "That earnest whistle convinced God to forgive us for our sins!"

Everybody searched, but nobody found a *tzaddik*. Who could guess that the *tzaddik* was a little farm boy?

What's Good About Fasting?
Being hungry makes us think of people who don't have enough food to eat and makes us want to help them. The Talmud says that after a person eats and drinks he has but one heart, for himself alone. Before a person eats and drinks (when he is fasting) he has two hearts, one for himself and one for all hungry people.

Yom Kippur
The tenth day of Tishri

Yom Kippur, the last of the ten days of *teshuvah,* is a day of fasting (no eating). People go to the synagogue with empty, growling stomachs and spend the whole day thinking and praying. Legend tells us that during Yom Kippur the gates of heaven are wide open and all our thoughts and prayers fly right to God's ears.

Slowly the sun begins to sink. Its rays poke through the windows and shine across the tired congregation. As the last prayers are said, the sky is already dark and stars are twinkling in the window.

The *shofar* blasts a great, loud call. Yom Kippur is over. A happy New Year to everyone. Let's eat!

Sukkot
The fifteenth to the twenty-second of Tishri

By the time it's Sukkot, the harvest holiday, the stores are selling crisp apples and sweet corn, fresh from the field. If you have a garden, you're doubly lucky. First, you can grow and harvest your own vegetables. Second, you have a perfect spot for building your *sukkah,* a small shed covered with leaves and branches.

The Pilgrims got the idea for their first Thanksgiving feast from reading about Sukkot in their Bibles.

For the next seven days the family and their guests eat dinner in the *sukkah.* Some people even sleep in it. The moon and stars peek through the open roof, the squirrels scurry across, and a sudden rain may chase everybody into the house.

The *sukkah* was used by farmers in Israel during harvest time. They would work in the fields all day and then, instead of coming home, they would sleep in small *sukkot* beside their crops. Earlier, when Moses led the Jews through the desert, they slept in *sukkot.*

On the eve of Sukkot we stand in the sukkah *with the fruit bobbing overhead and invite our biblical ancestors to come and join us. Abraham, Sarah, Isaac, Rebekah, Jacob, Moses . . . please share our* sukkah *and our holiday.*

We bring greens into the synagogue for the Sukkot holiday—a *lulav* made of willow, palm, and myrtle branches—and a lemon-like fruit called an *etrog.* The willow, palm, and myrtle branches and the *etrog* are called the *arba minim* (four species). When each person shakes the *lulav,* the synagogue sounds like a field of rustling, ripe corn.

Even if it's pouring cats and dogs outside and messing up the sukkah decorations, we say a prayer for rain for the farmers in Israel who are planting their winter crops.

At Simhat Torah, even young children can say the blessing for reading the Torah. They all stand under a tent made of a large tallit *(prayer shawl) and say the blessing together.*

Simhat Torah

The twenty-third of Tishri

The Torah is divided into fifty-four sections. Each section is called a parashah. A new parashah (sometimes two) is read each Sabbath from one Simhat Torah to the next.

On Simhat Torah you can run and skip up and down the synagogue aisles waving a flag with an apple on top. You can sing and giggle and laugh out loud—and even your Hebrew teacher won't yell at you. Simhat Torah is more like a party than a synagogue service. It's a party for the Torah.

All year long we have read the Torah in the synagogue, section by section. At Simhat Torah the last section is read. Then all the Torah scrolls are carried around and around the room in a clapping, singing, dancing parade. And when the parade is over, we roll the Torah to the very first section and begin another year of reading from *Bereshit,* "In the beginning . . ."

Hanukkah

The twenty-fifth of Kislev to the second of Tevet

A dreidel is a small spinning top with four sides. Each side has a Hebrew letter: נ *(nun),* ג *(gimel),* ה *(heh),* ש *(shin). They stand for "Nes Gadol Hayah Sham," which means "A great miracle happened there." An Israeli dreidel has a* פ *(pey) instead of a* ש *(shin), for "Nes Gadol Hayah Po," which means "A great miracle happened here." To find out how to play dreidel, look in the Hanukkah party section on page 104.*

In the middle of the winter the sky is dark when you get up in the morning, and it is almost dark again when you come home from school. Just then, when you need it most, the Holiday of Lights arrives. For eight days Hanukkah candles shine on the window sill and brighten the night. Grandparents, aunts, uncles, and friends come to help light the candles in the Hanukkah menorah *(hanukiyah)* and to sing and eat sizzling *latkes.* We exchange presents and play games of *dreidel* and tell the story of brave, stubborn Judah Maccabee.

More than 2,000 years ago, a Syrian king named Antiochus, tried to force the Jews to give up their religion. Judah Maccabee led his people in a fight to drive the Syrians out of Israel. The Jews finally won back the Holy Temple in Jerusalem. They scrubbed and cleaned it and polished the huge menorah. But when the priests were ready to begin services they could only find a tiny jar of pure oil to burn in the menorah, only enough for one day. By a miracle, the oil burned on and on for eight days.

During Hanukkah in Israel young people gather at Modin, where Judah Maccabee and his brothers lived. They light torches at a huge bonfire, and runners carry them to cities and villages all over the country.

Torches, bonfires, and candles light up the winter nights in honor of the miracle of the oil. *Latkes* (pancakes) or *sufganiyot* (doughnuts) are special Hanukkah treats because they're made with oil and remind us of the miraculous jar of oil in the Temple. Some people insist that we make *latkes* because the Jewish villagers would quickly fry batches of them to feed the Maccabees when they came racing through town to do battle with the Syrian enemy.

For Ḥanukkah
    Hayyim Nahman Bialik

Father lighted candles for me;
Like a torch the shamash *shone.*
In whose honor, for whose glory?
For Ḥanukkah alone.

Teacher brought a dreidel *for me,*
Solid lead, the finest known—
In whose honor, for whose glory?
For Ḥanukkah alone.

Mother made a pancake for me
Hot and sweet and sugar-strewn.
In whose honor, for whose glory?
For Ḥanukkah alone.

Uncle had a present for me,
A shiny penny for my own.
In whose honor, for whose glory?
For Ḥanukkah alone.

SOME MENORAH RULES:

1. A Ḥanukkah menorah has nine candleholders, one for the *shamash* (the server) and eight more for the eight nights of the holiday. The eight candleholders should all be the same height. Light the *shamash* first and use it to light the others.

2. Add the candles to the *ḥanukiyah* from right to left, but light the candles from left to right.

3. Put the *ḥanukiyah* on the window sill where it will shine into the street and everybody will see it.

Trees have a shivery midwinter birthday, Tu Bi-Shevat. The wind howls through their branches. Soon the sap will start to move up from their roots way out to the tips of their branches—but not yet. They have a few more weeks to sleep.

It's still chilly and rainy in Israel on Tu Bi-Shevat, but the almond tree is covered with white flowers. Israeli school children put on their boots and raincoats and climb into the hills to plant trees for the holiday.

We celebrate Tu Bi-Shevat in the United States by eating fruits and nuts that grow in Israel—grapes, oranges, figs, dates, carobs, pomegranates, almonds, and more. Some people plant orange seeds, avocado pits, and other seeds indoors. And we buy Jewish National Fund tree certificates so that somebody in Israel will plant a tree for us.

Tu Bi-Shevat
The fifteenth of Shevat

Some parents in Israel plant a tree for each newborn baby. When the baby grows up and gets married the tree's branches are used to make the poles for the wedding canopy.

Trees were always very important in Israel. Rabbi Johanan ben Zakkai told his students: "If you're planting a tree and someone runs up and tells you that the Messiah has come . . . finish planting the tree first, then go and greet the Messiah."

Do you want to plant a tree in Israel for your mother for Mother's Day? Or for your father, your grandma, your best friend, or just because trees are nice? Write or call your local Jewish National Fund or the Jewish National Fund, Inc., at 42 East 69th Street, New York, N.Y. 10021. They'll let you know how much to pay and how to get your tree certificate.

In Europe at Purim time children would dress in costumes and go door to door singing:

> Today is Purim
> Tomorrow no more
> Give me a penny
> And throw me out the door!

The gala Purim carnival in Israel is called Adloyada *because, according to Jewish tradition, each person should drink and make merry until he or she doesn't know* (ad lo yada *in Hebrew) the difference between wicked Mordecai and good Haman—or, wait a minute, is it the other way around?*

Purim

The fourteenth of Adar

The noisiest, funniest holiday of the year is Purim. Everybody comes to the synagogue carrying noisemakers *(groggers)* and listens carefully as the *megillah* (scroll) of the Book of Esther is read. It tells the story of Mordecai and his niece Esther, a Jewish girl who married King Ahasuerus of Shushan in Persia. When the king's prime minister Haman plotted to kill all the Jews, Esther risked her life to turn the king against Haman and to save her people.

Each time the reader of the Purim *megillah* mentions "Haman," the listeners twirl their *groggers*, stamp their feet, and hiss and boo. By the end of the reading everybody needs a pick-me-up, and there usually are sweets and drinks for all. On Purim day we feast on a huge meal, a Purim *se'udah*, with wine and lots of *hamentashen*, filled pastries that are shaped like Haman's three-cornered hat.

Purim is a time for masquerades. In Israel the streets and buses are filled with gypsies, spacemen, Indians, and skeletons hurrying to costume parties. Jews everywhere celebrate with parties, puppet shows, carnivals, and silly skits. There is also a Purim custom of *mishlo'ah manot*, carrying gift dishes of sweet treats to friends and neighbors, and money is collected for funds that help the poor.

Passover

From the fifteenth to the twenty-second of Nisan

Matzah *has always been flat and hard like the bread our forefathers took into the desert. Years ago in Europe it was rolled by hand and was round in shape and very thick, thicker than a bagel.* Matzah shemurah *(specially watched) is often still made by hand today, but it's almost as thin and crisp as machine-made supermarket* matzah. *The lines of little holes keep the* matzah *from curling or getting bumpy in the oven.*

There's a fresh new feeling out of doors. The frost has melted. Grass is turning green and seedlings are pushing up. Spring is exactly the right time for Passover, the great holiday of freedom and renewal.

The vacuum cleaner zooms around the house, the floor waxer swishes, kitchen closets are emptied, empty boxes are filled. All dishes and pots and foods (like bread) that are not kosher for Passover are put away. Watch out—hide your baseball cards and your raggedy blue jeans—it's pre-Passover cleanup time! The house must be clean and shiny as new in time for the *seder*—the special meal where the story of Passover is told.

When everybody gathers around the table for the *seder* on the first night of Passover the youngest child asks the Four Questions, beginning with, *"Mah nishtanah . . .* Why is this night different from all other nights?" Everybody answers by reading aloud from a small book called the *Haggadah*. It tells how we Jews were slaves in Egypt and how God helped us to become free.

We taste bitter herbs and, as our mouths pucker, we think, "this

After eight days it's time to fry up the last batch of matzah brei, *put away the special pots and dishes, and say good-bye to Passover. But many Moroccan Jews are not ready. They make the holiday last a day longer with a feast called the maimuna. In Jerusalem the feasters dress in traditional brightly colored beaded vests and robes and meet in the park for singing, dancing, and picnicking.*

is how bitter it was to be a slave.'' We crunch the *matzah* and remember how our people grabbed their bread before it could rise and ran out of Egypt to find freedom. It's special to be free. We're lucky. For the whole week of Passover we eat special food on special dishes to celebrate the time when Jews went forth from slavery to freedom.

On the *seder* table there's a tall cup of wine that nobody drinks. It's for the prophet Elijah. According to tradition Elijah visits each *seder* and takes a sip. When the wonderful moment comes for the Messiah to bring peace to the world, it is Elijah who will come first and tell us the good news.

The most welcome *seder* guest is of course Elijah. But a *seder* is open to everybody who is far from home—students, tourists, and other travelers are all welcome.

Kids have two important jobs at the *seder*. They have to ask the Four Questions (you'll find them in the first few pages of your *Haggadah*), and they have to try to find the *afikoman*, a special, wrapped piece of *matzah*. Watch to see where the *seder* leader hides the *afikoman*. If you get it, hold it for ransom. The *seder* can't be finished without the *afikoman*.

For the first meal after Passover Morrocan Jews prepare platters of thin pancakes. Each person fills his or her pancake with jelly, cheese, honey, and nuts, or other tasty fillings.

Counting the Omer

The forty-nine days between the second day of Passover and Shavuot are called the days of counting the *Omer*. This is an anxious time for farmers in Israel. Their plants are young and tender. They need just enough rain and sun—not too much, not too little—or the summer crop may die.

In ancient Israel farmers would bring a bundle *(omer)* of barley to the Holy Temple at Passover, and prayers for rain would be said. Each day after that would be counted until Shavuot.

During the counting of the *Omer* no weddings or happy celebrations are held because the students of Rabbi Akiva died in a plague during this period. One exception is the thirty-third day, the one day on which no student died. The day is called Lag Ba-Omer. In 1948 another exception was made—Israel Independence Day, on the twentieth day of the *Omer*.

Israel Independence Day
The fifth of Iyyar

The nation of Israel is very, very old—more than 3,000 years old. But the State of Israel is very young. It has been an independent country only since 1948. How can anybody or any country be old and young at the same time? Here's how it happened.

Many years ago the Jewish people lived in their own Land of Israel. The Romans conquered the land and drove most of the Jews out. For hundreds of years they were scattered all over the world. Finally they began to return to the Land of Israel, to build cities and

Israel is about as big as the state of New Jersey. For a whole country that's pretty small, but the land is full of variety. There's warm, blue water for skin-diving and thick, salty water for mining minerals. There are wooded hills where goats and sheep graze and rocky deserts where Bedouins and camels roam. There are busy, noisy cities and busy, quiet farms. It's a small, exciting country!

plant forests and farms. In 1948 the United Nations recognized the new State of Israel in its old-new land.

On that first Independence Day people blew the *shofar*, hugged and kissed, and danced and sang in the streets. Now there are giant parades in the cities of Israel on Independence Day, which is known as Yom Ha-Atzma'ut.

We have parades here too, and parties, and birthday cakes with lots of candles in honor of the State of Israel.

*If Jews move to Brooklyn or Los Angeles or Paris, it's just a move. But if they go to Israel to live, it's a special move called **aliyah** (meaning "going up" in Hebrew). Since 1948 Jews have "gone up" to Israel from more than seventy countries.*

Here's a holiday especially for school kids, a scholars' holiday. The best place to celebrate is *not* the synagogue or classroom, but on a hike in the woods.

The scholars' holiday began in the days when the Romans ruled the land of Israel and forbade the study of the Torah. One Lag Ba-Omer story tells about a teacher named Simeon bar Yoḥai who hid in a cave in the mountains. His students would climb up and study with him in secret. To fool the watching Romans, they carried bows and arrows and pretended that they were just going hunting.

Children in Jewish schools put away their books and go on hikes and picnics at Lag Ba-Omer. In Israel huge bonfires are lit on the mountainside where Simeon bar Yoḥai is buried. Some Israelis bring little boys to that place and give them their first haircut on Lag Ba-Omer day.

Lag Ba-Omer
The eighteenth of Iyyar

Rabbi Akiva and Simeon bar Kokhba are remembered at Lag Ba-Omer too. They were both killed fighting for freedom against the Roman armies. Many other freedom fighters and their families hid in caves and refused to surrender. Archaeologists have explored caves in Israel and found letters, clothing, and even women's makeup kits left more than 1,800 years ago.

The word shavuot *means "weeks" in Hebrew, and the holiday comes seven weeks after Passover.*

Shavuot
The sixth and seventh of Sivan

The green, flower-filled holiday of Shavuot arrives on the fiftieth day of counting the *Omer*. School is almost over, roses are blooming, and the Japanese beetles haven't landed yet. It's a wonderful time.

On the first Shavuot, many years ago, the Jewish people stood in the hot, stony Sinai desert and received the Ten Commandments from God. They carried them to the Land of Israel and built a Temple, a House of God, in Jerusalem. Each Shavuot, when the first wheat and fruits were ripe, the people brought some of their crop to the Holy Temple. This offering was a "thank you" to God for the Ten Commandments, for the Bible that guided them, and for the fruitful land that fed them.

On Shavuot we decorate our homes and synagogues with flowers and leafy branches. At the synagogue we read the Ten Commandments aloud. Then we go home and eat blintzes, berries,

On Shavuot we read the Book of Ruth, a story of harvest time and love with a happy ending. Some people stay up all of Shavuot night studying Torah and other books of religion. Legends tell that the heavens open up at midnight on Shavuot eve—for an instant. Stop reading and stare straight up, and if you don't blink or fall asleep, you might see angels, the heavenly throne, or the whole universe.

In Europe little children would begin to study Torah on Shavuot because that was the time the Torah was first given to the Jewish people. In some synagogues confirmation ceremonies are held for students on Shavuot.

99

Around the Jewish year

cheesecake, and other dairy dishes. Why dairy? According to Jewish folklore, the people were too tired to cook after their long wait to receive the Torah. They trudged back to their tents and feasted on milk and cheese and other easy-to-fix foods.

Who Understands Rich People?

Mendl the pauper got a mouth-watering whiff of frying blintzes as he passed a rich family's window on Shavuot. He could hardly wait to get home.

"Bayleh," he called to his wife, "you must make blintzes. For once let's enjoy like the rich people do."

"But Mendl, for blintzes we need cheese and eggs, and we haven't any," said Bayleh.

"So leave out the cheese and eggs."

"And a little sugar and butter," she went on.

"Don't bother me with details," he said impatiently. "Just make the blintzes."

Bayleh shrugged. She mixed flour, water, and oil, fried the batter carefully, and served it to Mendl.

He took one bite and slammed his fork down. "Feh!" he exclaimed. "I don't understand rich people. How can they enjoy such stuff?"

Many bad things have happened to the Jewish people during their long history. During the year there are fast days and memorial days when we think about those events and try to learn from them.

In the middle of each summer we observe the fast day of Tisha Be-Av. The Holy Temple in Jerusalem was destroyed by the Babylonians on this day in 586 B.C.E. The Jews rebuilt the Temple, but on another Tisha Be-Av, 656 years later, the Romans destroyed it. Then they drove all the Jews out of the holy city of Jerusalem. On Tisha Be-Av in 1492 the Jews were expelled from Spain.

But the sadness of Tisha Be-Av is mixed with hope. The Jewish people have a home again. We have come back to the Land of Israel and to Jerusalem. We can pray at the Western Wall of the Temple and plant crops in the fields of Israel.

There is a happy legend about Tisha Be-Av. It tells that the Messiah, who will come to bring peace to the world, will be born on the ninth of Av. The saddest holy day of the Jewish year may one day be the beginning of friendship and peace for all people.

Tisha Be-Av
The ninth of Av

We could make a long list of sad things to remember. One of the saddest of all would be the death of 6 million Jews in the Holocaust during World War II. On Holocaust Remembrance Day, Yom Ha-Sho'ah, we say the **Yizkor** prayer in their memory. This observance is on the twenty-seventh of Nisan.

People come to Jerusalem to pray at the last remaining wall of the Holy Temple, this is the Kotel Ma'aravi or Western Wall. Some write their worries and prayers on bits of paper and push them into the cracks between the great stones of the wall. They hope God will pay special attention to prayers from the wall of His ancient house.

A good angel and a bad angel follow people home from the synagogue on Friday eve, says the Talmud. They peek in the window of the house. If the candles are lit, the table is set, and the children are clean and smiling, the good angel says, "May it be God's will that next *Shabbat* should be just like this one."

"Amen," mutters the bad angel, scowling and gritting his teeth.

But if the house is a mess and everybody is nasty and quarreling, the bad angel twirls his mustache and grins and says, "May it be God's will that next *Shabbat* should be just like this one."

The good angel, with tears in his eyes, must nod and whisper, "Amen."

The Sabbath

The seventh day of each week

Shabbat *gets a special honor—it's the only holiday mentioned in the Ten Commandments. The fourth commandment tells us "Remember the Sabbath to keep it holy."*

We don't have to wait all year for the Sabbath *(Shabbat)* because it comes at the end of each week. On Friday afternoon there's a rush of running errands and cleaning up. Brush the cat, empty the garbage, polish the candlesticks, lick the cake batter from the mixing bowl—a million jobs to do. But by sundown smells of good food fill the house. The golden ḥallah, the candlesticks, and wine for the *Kiddush* blessing are ready on the table. After the candles are lit, we say *"Shabbat shalom"* to each other and sing *Shalom Aleikhem* to welcome the Sabbath angels and to greet the best day of the week.

The Sabbath is our day of rest. The Torah tells that God worked to create the world for six days, and on the seventh day He rested. So every week, from Friday at sundown until it's dark on Saturday

"Quick, Mama, add some water to the chicken soup! Papa is bringing a guest home for Shabbat."

Jewish housewives often got this warning in the small towns of Europe on Friday evening. Travelers would come to the synagogue for services and townspeople would invite them home for supper. To invite a guest for Shabbat is a mitzvah (a good deed or commandment).

night, there's time for going to synagogue services, singing, storytelling, reading, talking, and just loafing. Legend tells us that when we put away our daily work we also put away our daily souls, and a more loving and happy *Shabbat* soul enters each person to spend the peaceful day.

Too quickly the sun goes down and the sky darkens. We light the braided candle for *Havdalah* and say goodbye to the Sabbath and our Shabbat souls. The fussy weekday soul is back, with its weekday worries—homework, report cards, ice cream money. But, remember, even if you have a hard week, *Shabbat* will be back in just six days.

Rosh Hodesh
The first day of each month

When the first silver sliver of moon appears in the sky, the holiday of Rosh Hodesh is celebrated and the new Hebrew month begins. Many years ago people would sit on the mountaintops near Jerusalem at the end of the month and watch the sky. At the first sight of the new moon they would race down to tell the priests. Trumpets would be blown and torches waved. People watching on other hills would light torches too, and the news of the new moon would race from mountain to mountain across Israel.

The people would count the days carefully from that first night so that all important dates and each holiday could be observed right on time.

When Jews moved away from Israel and couldn't see the waving torches anymore, a new custom began. Most holidays were celebrated for two days instead of one. Even if people were a day late or a day early in their reckoning, they would still share the holiday with Jews all over the world for one day.

In Eastern Europe Rosh Hodesh was a half-holiday from school for Jewish children and a holiday from work for women. And in Tunis gifts were sent to Jewish girls on the "Rosh Hodesh for girls," which fell on the sixth day of Hanukkah.

Special prayers are read in the synagogue at Rosh Hodesh.

Holiday parties

Holidays are the most fun and most meaningful when they are shared with family and friends. On holidays like Passover, Sukkot, and the Sabbath we are expected to invite company, even strangers, to share our meal. So do a *mitzvah* and have fun too—make a holiday party!

There are all kinds of parties: noisy, game-playing parties; eating till you're stuffed parties; and quiet, feeling good together parties. Each of our holidays has its own stories, customs, and foods, so each holiday party can have a special quality.

Here are some ideas.

ONEG SHABBAT

Now and then our family has a quiet *Oneg Shabbat* (pleasure of *Shabbat*) party. After dinner we take our desserts into the living room and settle down. We sing *Shabbat* songs for a while, and then each of us tells about something that's interesting or important to him or her. Sometimes we read a play together, with each person taking a different part. Bethy, who can't read yet, and Shushy the cat do all the sound effects. Once we sat in the dim candlelight and told the eery, dramatic story of the Golem of Prague. You'll find it on page 166.

Your family may have different ideas for an *Oneg Shabbat*. Try it, you'll love it.

SUKKOT PARTY

If you can, have a Sukkot party in a *sukkah*. If you don't have a *sukkah,* you could have the party in the living room, the playroom, the den, anywhere. Sukkot is such a happy, friendly holiday that it deserves a celebration.

You can start out by asking all your guests to help you decorate. Have cranberries and popcorn ready to string into chains with needle and thread. Or use strips of construction paper and glue them into paper chains. Tape Rosh Ha-Shanah cards or paper cut-outs to the chains or to a string. Hang the chains across the *sukkah* or the room. Then hang fruits and vegetables (real, plastic, or paper-cuts) by string from the ceiling.

Games

Chinning This is a pass-the-apple race. Divide into two teams. The first person on each team tucks the apple under his or her chin and passes it to the next person, chin to chin, without using hands. If the apple drops, pick it up and start again, but no hands while passing.

Chomping One person from each team stands before an apple hanging by a string and tries to take a bite out of it. Have a time limit on this because there will be a lot of teeth gnashing.

Moshe Omeir *("Moses Says")* Sukkot tells of the years when Moses led the Jews through the desert. They whined and complained a lot, and Moses had to be a tough leader to keep them going. Play *Moshe Omeir* just like "Simon Says," and see how many of you would have made it through the desert.

Invitations At Sukkot it's customary to invite the spirits of our ancestors into the *sukkah*. Have all the players sit in a circle. Begin by saying, "At Sukkot time I invite Father Abraham into the *sukkah*." The next person must repeat what you said and add another name: "At Sukkot time I invite Father Abraham and Mother Sarah into the *sukkah*." As the list of names gets longer and longer, people forget names and drop out, until only one person, the one with the best memory, is left.

Food

For this sweet harvest holiday, use lots of fruit, apple cider, honey, and sponge cake, stuffed dates, nuts, and raisins.

Some treasure-hunt clues:

1. If you get tired
   and lay down your head,
   clue number two
   will be there to be read.
   (It's on a couch or bed.)

2. An ice-cold clue
   sits waiting for you
   behind a closed door
   'mid chicken, steak, and more.
   (It's in the refrigerator.)

3. The treasure is hidden
   right under your nose
   in the place you get clean
   from your head to your toes.
   (It's in the bathtub.)

HANUKKAH PARTY

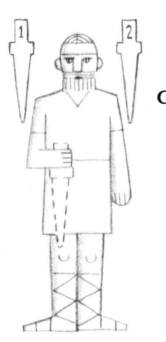

Gray, slushy midwinter is the perfect time for the holiday of candles, gifts, games, and good food. Ask each guest to bring an inexpensive (one dollar, tops), wrapped grab-bag gift. Put all the gifts in a pillow case or bag. Get as many Hanukkah menorahs (*hanukiyot*) as you can, so that a lot of people will have a chance to light candles. And get Hanukkah song sheets from Hebrew school, or copy them out of a songbook and use carbon paper for extra copies.

Games   *Dreidel*   This game is played with the small four-sided top described on page 92. From two to eight people can play, but it's most fun in groups of four to six. Everybody gets an equal number of pennies (or nuts) and puts one in the center for the pot. Each player gets a turn to spin the *dreidel*. If it lands with the נ *(nun)* up, the player gets nothing; with the ג *(gimel)* up, the player takes all the coins in the pot; with the ה *(heh)* up, the player takes half the coins from the pot; with the ש *(shin)* up, the unlucky player gives one penny to the pot. When the pot empties out after a gimel, each player puts a penny in and the game goes on.

Pin the sword on Judah   Draw and color a large Judah Maccabee on two large brown paper bags, opened and taped together. Make a paper sword for each player, write a name or number on it, and put a bit of tape at the top. Play it just like "Pin the Tail on the Donkey."

Lighting the Menorah   Set the menorahs on a table. Sing the blessings and light the candles. Make sure everybody has a chance to light a candle. Use the song sheets and sing more Hanukkah songs while you are gathered around the burning candles.

Grab-bag gifts   Bring out the bag and let everybody dig in.

Another way to give out gifts is to have a treasure hunt. Before the party prepare a hiding place for the bag of gifts and prepare two sets of three clues each. Divide the players into two groups, the Syrians and the Maccabees. Give each group its first clue. The first clue will lead to the second; the second will lead to the third; and the third will lead to the treasure! Members of the first team to reach the treasure can each get a small prize (such as a *dreidel* or chocolate coins in gold foil), and then everybody can grab for their gifts.

Food   *Latkes* (pancakes) or *sufganiyot* (Israeli doughnuts) are traditional Hanukkah treats. You'll find recipes for *latkes* in chapter 9 on page 132.

PURIM MISHLO'AH MANOT PARTY

Purim is the time to make believe you're somebody else. Ask everybody to wear a costume to your party. Or prepare a table full of craft supplies and paper bags and have each person make a mask. Paper bags should be large enough to fit over the head. Try them on and locate the eyes. Gently make a mark where the eyes are. Take the mask off and cut holes for the eyes. Then decorate.

You can make great mustaches out of construction paper by shaping the top to fit in your nostrils. See the diagram. See chapter 3 for other costume ideas.

When the masks are done, ask an adult or an older brother or sister to be the judge. Play marching music or a Purim record and have a parade around and around the room while the judge judges the masks and costumes. Silliest, prettiest, meanest, most colorful, scariest, hardest to make—have lots of categories so that everybody wins something. And have a funny paper medal or a small prize for each winner.

Games

Esther, Esther, Mordecai The players form a circle and one person, Haman, walks around the outside of the circle. He taps each person on the head as he walks, calling "Esther" to each one. When he calls someone "Mordecai" that person must chase him around the circle until Haman reaches Mordecai's place. If Mordecai catches Haman, then Haman is outside the circle again. If not, Mordecai becomes Haman.

Paper-bag Purim Play Choose two or more groups with at least four players in each. Give each group a paper bag containing five or six things (for example, a toothpaste tube, a potato, lipstick).

Each group will go off to a separate room or corner for about fifteen minutes and prepare a play about Purim using *all* the things in the paper bag as props. The groups will then perform for each other.

Food

Since this is a *mishlo'ah manot* party, invite each guest to bring a dish of sweets. But make sure you've prepared enough *hamantashen* and drinks for everybody. There's a recipe on page 134.

PASSOVER MAIMUNA PARTY

There are many kinds of Passover parties. The *seder* is a party for the family and guests—for grownups and kids together. The food is great, the *afikoman* hunt is fun, and the *Haggadah* tells a good story. Before the real thing you may have a tryout model *seder* at religious school.

At the end of Passover, just to make it last another day, try an old Moroccan custom and have a *maimuna*. It's a time when Moroccan Jews gather at picnics to sing, dance, meet old friends, and arrange marriages.

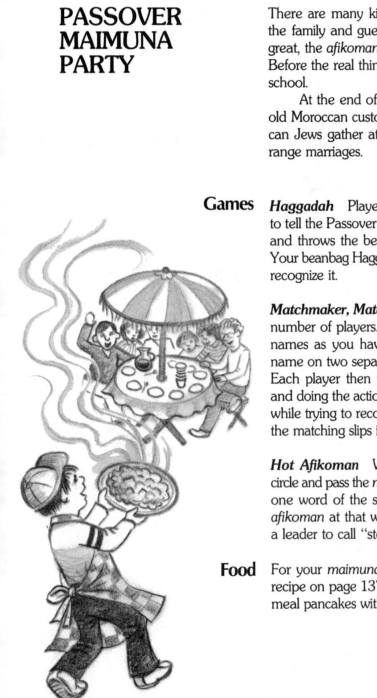

Games

Haggadah   Players sit in a circle. One holds a beanbag and starts to tell the Passover story. The storyteller stops at any point in the story and throws the beanbag to another player who continues the story. Your beanbag Haggadah will be so full of surprises even Moses wouldn't recognize it.

Matchmaker, Matchmaker   This game must be played with an even number of players. Count the players. Think of half as many animal names as you have players (6 animals for 12 players). Write each name on two separate slips of paper. Fold them and place in a bowl. Each player then picks a slip and walks around making the sound and doing the action of the animal (a horse might whinny and gallop), while trying to recognize his mate. (If this is serious matchmaking, put the matching slips in separate bowls—one for girls and one for boys.)

Hot Afikoman   Wrap a piece of *matzah* securely. Players sit in a circle and pass the *matzah*—the *afikoman*—while singing a song. Choose one word of the song to be the HOT one. Whoever is holding the *afikoman* at that word is out. Instead of a hot word you can choose a leader to call "stop" to catch the *afikoman* holder.

Food

For your *maimuna* party you can make Passover brownies (see the recipe on page 137), or *matzah brei* with honey and jam, or *matzah*-meal pancakes with sour cream. Have grape juice or punch to drink.

ISRAEL BIRTHDAY PARTY

Have a birthday party for the State of Israel. Decorate with streamers and balloons and a birthday cake in the center of the table. Iced cupcakes are good to use too. Put lots of birthday candles and tiny Israeli flags on the cake. You can make the flags or buy them in a Jewish book store.

Games

Aliyah   Before the state was established many Jews were stopped from entering Israel. They had to come secretly at night, jumping from ships off shore, or hiking across the borders, trying to escape the border guards. Play "Aliyah" outdoors. Mark off two opposite corners. One corner is Israel; the other corner is *galut* (the lands outside of Israel). One player is the border guard and stands in the middle. All the other players stand in the *galut* corner. Each has the name of a country. The border guard calls the name of a country and the person with that name tries to run to Israel without being tagged by the guard. If tagged, he or she becomes the new guard. If your group is large, have each player that is caught join the guard, and have the guard call out several countries at once. The winners are those who get safely to Israel.

Guard and Jews   This is a simpler Aliyah game, which is exactly like "Cat and Mouse." One player is a Jew, another is a guard, and the other players form a circle holding hands. The guard is outside the circle. The Jew is inside. The guard must try to catch the Jew. The people in the circle may help him by raising hands and letting him in, or they may keep hands down and protect the Jew. The Jew can only stay safely inside the circle for a few seconds, then he must run out to keep the chase going. He can run back in again if the people in the circle let him through.

Dancing

The *hora* is an Israeli dance in which the dancers hold hands or rest their arms on each other's shoulders as they move around and around in a circle. Whether you have four people or forty at your Israel birthday party, they can all dance the *hora*. See how in chapter 12.

Food

If you want more than birthday cake and a drink, try felafel and pita bread, a favorite snack in Israel. A recipe for felafel is on page 131.

Before you eat, light the birthday candles on the cake, make a great wish for yourself and for Israel, and blow. *Betayavon!* In Hebrew that means "hearty appetite."

LAG BA-OMER PICNIC

Hope for good weather and pack plenty of sandwiches and a canteen of water for your Lag Ba-Omer hike. Then head for a park or a forest with hiking trails.

Games

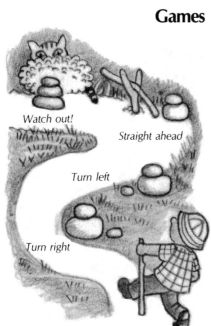

Watch out!

Straight ahead

Turn left

Turn right

Find bar Yoḥai's hideout Since this holiday recalls a time when Jews like Simeon bar Yoḥai hid in caves and forests to study Torah, this game will lead the players through the forest. Have a few people set up a trail for the group to follow. At the end of the trail hide a book of Bible stories to represent bar Yoḥai and his Torah. The trail has to be clear enough so that the trailblazers can find their way back—otherwise this may become a Hansel and Gretel game. Here are some trail signs you can use. Look for others in a scout handbook.

Silly races Archery and sports are traditional at Lag Ba-Omer. So are relay races and silly races like these:

- Wheelbarrow race: The first player holds the second player's legs up while the second player walks on his or her hands.
- Three-legged race: Two players stand side by side, and their inside legs are tied together at the ankle before they begin to run. (If you put your arms around each other's waists or shoulders, it helps to get you running in rhythm.)
- Sack race: The player steps into a large laundry bag or potato sack, holds it up to the waist and jumps forward.

Bar Kokhba's flag On La Ba-Omer many years ago Simeon bar Kokhba led a Jewish army against the Romans. In this game two teams, Romans and Jews, line up facing each other about thirty feet apart. Put a metal or plastic can or bottle midway between the sides. It represents the flag. Each team counts off so that the players on both sides have matching numbers. A non-player calls a number. The two matching players run out, and each tries to snatch the can and run back to his team without being caught by the matching player. In a rougher version of this game, the person who snatches the can must run to the opposing team and break through their line to get free.

Campfire

Bonfires are lit all over Israel at Lag Ba-Omer time. You could end your hike with a campfire and bake apples on a stick. In the park or backyard, a picnic barbecue would be fun and delicious.

Question: Who killed one-quarter of the people in the world with one blow?

Answer: Cain, the son of Adam and Eve, when he killed his brother Abel.

Question: When did all the people in the world hear one rooster crow?

Answer: When they were on Noah's ark.

Question: Why didn't the people play cards on Noah's ark?

Answer: Because Noah sat on the deck.

Question: Who was the first Jewish doctor?

Answer: Moses. He prescribed two tablets.

SHAVUOT SLEEP-OVER PARTY

A sleep-over party makes us think of pillow fights, late-night snacks, and ghost stories. On Shavuot many adult Jews have a kind of stay-awake party, but without pillow fights. They spend the whole night reading and studying together.

Your Shavuot sleep-over can be double fun. You can have the spookiness of a late night party, plus the dairy foods and special stories of the holiday. You'll need a bedroom with two or three beds pushed together and enough pillows and covers for everybody. Or you can ask your guests to bring sleeping bags and sleep on the carpet.

Things to do

- Read aloud the Book of Ruth from the Bible, or read a short version such as the one in *Pathways Through the Bible,* published by the Jewish Publication Society of America.

- Tell spooky stories in a circle. One person begins the story and stops at an exciting point. The next person continues the story and then the next, until everybody has a turn. Then somebody has to make up a terrific ending. Here are some opening lines:

  1. At midnight on the night before Shavuot the room was suddenly filled with a blinding light and I saw . . .

  2. As I was doing my homework, the prophet Elijah appeared in the doorway. "You may make three wishes," he said . . .

  3. Walking home from Hebrew school on a dark night, I heard a deep, humming noise and saw, floating over my head, a giant, silver . . .

- Tell riddles, jokes, anecdotes, and stories—they're all fun at sleep-over parties. You'll find books of jokes and riddles in your library.

- Think of important wishes to make at midnight. Legend tells that the heavens open for a split second at midnight and a wish made *that second* will come true.

Food

Snacks like cheese and crackers, nuts, fruits, and ice cream spooned into sugar cones will keep everybody well fed at night.

All of you can work together to make a scrumptious breakfast in the morning. Have homemade bagels ready (see the recipe on page 129) along with cream cheese, jelly, nuts, and raisins. Or give each person half a melon to fill with strawberries, cottage cheese, and sliced bananas. Or you could check out breakfast ideas in one of the children's cookbooks in the library. (Don't try sardines and ice cream on shredded wheat! We did, and nobody except the cat ate it.)

Happy Holiday!

1. Oneg Shabbat
2. Sukkot party
3. Ḥanukkah party
4. Purim *mishlo'aḥ manot* party

5. Passover Seder
6. Israel Birthday party
7. Lag Ba-Omer picnic
8. Shavuot sleep-over party

Holiday crafts

Paper, paint, clay, scraps from around the house—a little imagination and you can become an artist. Roll up your sleeves, for there are many exciting crafts to explore.

Mold a *Shabbat* candleholder from clay. Print a holiday greeting card. Create a model *sukkah*. See your favorite Bible story characters come to life as you recreate them in masks and puppets.

In this chapter you will discover many more crafts to try. By adding your own ideas to each project, they will become originals, handcrafted by you, the artist.

Easy-to-make holiday cards

yarn

mock stained glass

button people

YARN CARD

1. Fold a sheet of paper in half. Write a message or draw a picture inside the card.
2. Draw a simple holiday picture on the front of the card.
3. Trace with glue the lines of the design.
4. Press colored yarn on the glued lines.

MOCK STAINED-GLASS CARD

1. Fold a sheet of paper in half. Write a message or draw a picture inside the card.
2. On the cover of the card, pencil in designs to look like stained glass. Trace with a broad point black felt-tip pen the lines of the design. Fill in the designs with felt-tip pens in other colors.

BUTTON PEOPLE CARD

You will need:

construction paper, 6 inches by 6 inches, any color
pencil
white buttons, each with 2 holes
white glue
felt-tip pens, any color
fabric scraps
yarn scraps
envelope, 3⅝ inches by 6½ inches

1. Fold the paper in half.
2. On the front of the folded card, pencil in a design that includes "button people."
3. Place the buttons on the card, using the two holes as eyes, and glue down.
4. Draw eyebrows and a mouth with the pens. Add clothing by gluing on scraps of fabric. Add hair by gluing on yarn.
5. Trace over the penciled lines with the pens.
6. Write a holiday message inside the card. Insert in an envelope. With the pens, add a border of color to the envelope.

FOIL-BACKED WINDOW CARD

1. Fold in half a sheet of dark construction paper, 6 inches by 12 inches. Write a message or draw a picture inside the card.

2. Draw a design on construction paper of a lighter color, 2½ inches by 5½ inches, and cut it out. Cut household aluminum foil to the same size as the lighter construction paper.

3. Glue the foil behind the lighter color construction paper so the foil shows through the cut-outs. Mount on the cover of the folded construction paper.

foil-backed window

Clay Shabbat candleholders

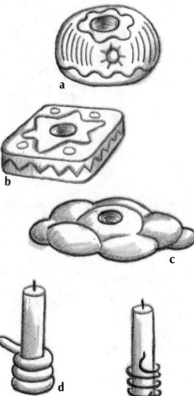

You will need:

clay that air hardens or "fires" hard in a home oven
tools to decorate clay (pointed stick, comb)
rolling pin

thin, pliable wire, about ⅛ inch diameter (from craft store)
2 Sabbath candles
Optional: acrylic or tempera paint, brush

1. For each candleholder, work with a lump of clay the size of a large apple.

2. Shape the clay by one of these methods:

a. *Roll and shape*—Roll clay into a ball, flatten the bottom so it stands securely, make a design with a pointed stick or a comb.

b. *Slab*—Roll the clay flat with a rolling pin and cut designs into the slab of clay.

c. *Braid*—Divide the lump of clay into three chunks, roll each chunk into a coil, braid the coils together in the shape of a ḥallah. Flatten the bottom so it stands securely.

d. *Coil*—Form a long coil by rolling the clay between your hands. Shape the coil around the bottom of a candle.

e. *Armature*—Twist a piece of thin wire around the bottom of a candle. Shape the clay around the twisted wire (the armature). This gives the finished candleholder added strength.

3. For methods (**a**), (**b**), and (**c**), insert a Sabbath candle about halfway down into the clay to make a hole. Wiggle the candle slightly to enlarge the hole. Remove the candle.

4. Let the candleholder dry according to the directions on the clay package.

5. Paint the candleholder if you wish.

Havdalah candles

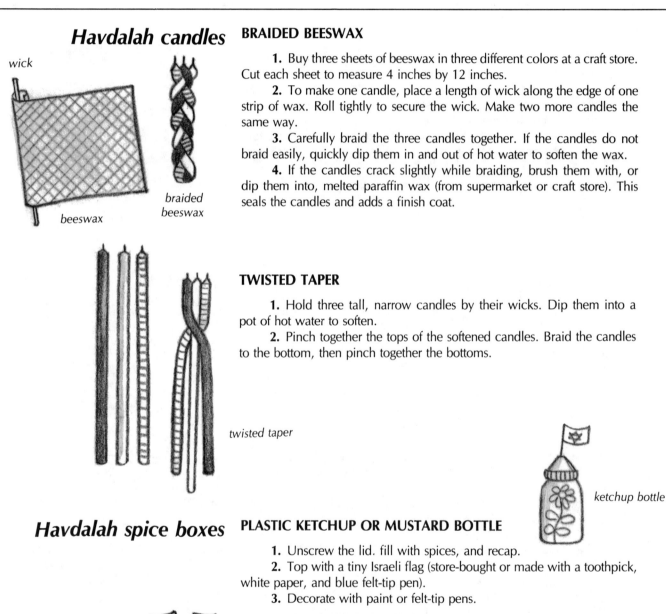

wick

beeswax

braided
beeswax

twisted taper

BRAIDED BEESWAX

1. Buy three sheets of beeswax in three different colors at a craft store. Cut each sheet to measure 4 inches by 12 inches.

2. To make one candle, place a length of wick along the edge of one strip of wax. Roll tightly to secure the wick. Make two more candles the same way.

3. Carefully braid the three candles together. If the candles do not braid easily, quickly dip them in and out of hot water to soften the wax.

4. If the candles crack slightly while braiding, brush them with, or dip them into, melted paraffin wax (from supermarket or craft store). This seals the candles and adds a finish coat.

TWISTED TAPER

1. Hold three tall, narrow candles by their wicks. Dip them into a pot of hot water to soften.

2. Pinch together the tops of the softened candles. Braid the candles to the bottom, then pinch together the bottoms.

ketchup bottle

Havdalah spice boxes

PLASTIC KETCHUP OR MUSTARD BOTTLE

1. Unscrew the lid. fill with spices, and recap.

2. Top with a tiny Israeli flag (store-bought or made with a toothpick, white paper, and blue felt-tip pen).

3. Decorate with paint or felt-tip pens.

SALT AND PEPPER SHAKERS

1. Place one flat-topped glass or plastic shaker on top of the other and secure with glue. Let dry.

2. Decorate with paint and let dry.

3. Stick one or more Israeli flags in the holes in the top shaker.

4. To fill with spices, snap off the cover of the top shaker.

salt and pepper shakers

EMPTY SPOOLS OF THREAD

1. Stack several empty spools, gluing one to the other.
2. Glue on a circle of wood or cardboard as a base.
3. Paint the entire structure and let dry.
4. Fill the center hole with spices.

spools

You will need:

1 shoe box	fruit (raisins, berries, figs, dates)
scissors	leaves
construction paper, any color	twigs
felt-tip pens, any color	1 large, shallow box
glue	sand
string	Optional: small cactus plants, cardboard, small dolls

Sukkah in a desert

1. Placing the shoe box on its side, cut out slits in the top (A). You may make slits in the walls, too.

2. Using the construction paper, felt-tip pens, and glue, decorate the inside of the *sukkah*.

3. String the fruit and hang from the roof.

4. Weave the leaves and twigs in and out of the roof. If you made slits in the walls, you may add twigs and leaves in the walls too.

5. Spread the sand evenly in the large, shallow box. Place the model *sukkah* in the sand.

6. You may add small cactus plants (real or artificial) or trees cut out of cardboard. Cardboard figures or little dolls may also be added (B).

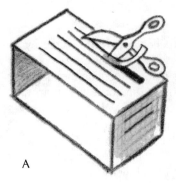

A

B

Simḥat Torah flags

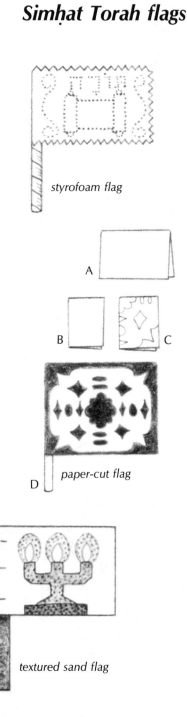

styrofoam flag

paper-cut flag

textured sand flag

STYROFOAM FLAG

1. Start with a styrofoam meat tray, about 7 inches by 9 inches. To make a scalloped border for the flag, cut around the edges of the tray with pinking shears.

2. Place the tray on a sheet of paper and trace around it. Remove the tray and draw a design within the penciled outline.

3. Tape the drawing to the tray. With a heavy-duty needle, poke holes through the outline of the design, piercing through the styrofoam. Remove the taped paper and check to be sure all the holes went through the tray.

4. Tape or glue one end of a crepe paper streamer to one end of a narrow wooden dowel, about 13 inches long (from craft or hobby store). Wind the crepe paper around the length of the dowel, gluing or taping down the end. Glue the dowel to the tray.

PAPER-CUT FLAG

1. To make the paper-cut, fold in half a sheet of white typing paper, 8½ inches by 11 inches (A). Then fold in half again (B). Draw a design that touches all edges of the folded paper (C).

2. With manicure scissors, carefully cut out the design, making sure not to cut apart the side fold of the paper.

3. To mount the cut-out, carefully open the folded, cut-out paper. Glue onto a sheet of colored construction paper, 8½ inches by 11 inches.

4. To make the flag, glue the mounted paper-cut to a narrow wooden dowel, about 15 inches long (craft or hobby store), as shown in (D).

TEXTURED SAND FLAG

1. Draw a design on a sheet of construction paper, 8½ inches by 11 inches. Glue the construction paper to a piece of cardboard, 8½ inches by 11 inches. Apply white glue to all the areas that will contain the first color of sand or glitter. Take a spoonful of colored sand or glitter (from craft store), and sprinkle it generously on the glued areas. Wait a few minutes for the glue to dry. Carefully tilt the flag to return excess sand or glitter to its container. Repeat for each additional color area of the flag.

2. Paint a flat wooden stick, about 15 inches long (hobby store or lumberyard). Let dry. Staple or tack the flag to the stick.

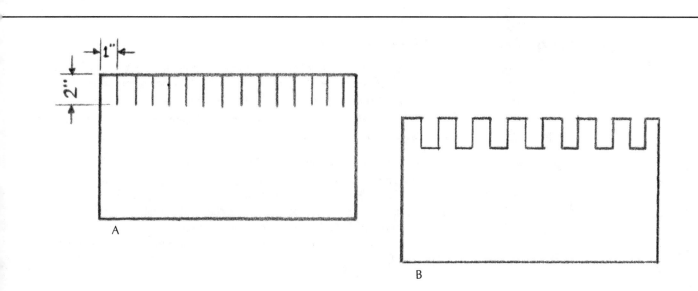

FELT-ON-FELT BANNER

1. Hold a ruler near the top of a piece of felt, 11 inches by 14 inches. Make 14 pencil marks, one inch apart. Draw a 2-inch line down from each mark (A).

2. Starting at the first drawn line, cut out every other strip (B). Fold over each remaining strip and glue down at the bottom only, forming eight loops (C). This is the back of the banner.

3. Turn over the felt. Cut scraps of felt in assorted colors into various shapes. Glue the shapes in a design on the banner.

4. Insert a narrow wooden dowel about 20 inches long (from craft or hobby store) through the loops (D). To use as a flag, hold one end of the dowel (not upright). After using, you may hang the banner as a wall decoration.

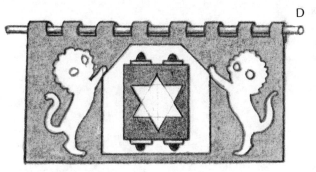

felt-on-felt banner

Ḥanukkah menorahs

PAPER CUP MENORAH

1. Start with ten small paper nut cups. Fill eight with sand.

2. To make the holder for the *shamash*, glue the bottom of one cup to the bottom of another cup. Fill the top one with sand. To use, place the cups in a row and insert a Ḥanukkah candle into the sand in each one.

FLOWER POT MENORAH

1. Start with eight small clay flower pots (the size used for tiny cacti) and one larger clay pot for the *shamash*. Turn them upside down.

2. Paint a design on each pot with acrylics. Let dry. Wiggle a candle into the drain hole in each pot. If the candle is too small for the hole, fill in with candle or floral adhesive (from craft store).

3. You may store the flower pot menorah from year to year by stacking the pots.

Easy-to-make dreidels

EGG CARTON DREIDEL

1. Cut a cup from the bottom of a styrofoam or cardboard egg carton. Cut deeply into the cup to make four pointed petals. Insert a sharpened pencil, pointed dowel, or long nail through the bottom of the cup.

2. With a ball-point pen, add one of the Hebrew letters on the opposite page on each of the four sides.

PING-PONG BALL DREIDEL

1. With small scissors (manicure) or a skewer, poke a hole through a ping-pong ball. Insert a dowel (from craft store) that has been sharpened to a point.

2. With felt-tip pens, print the Hebrew letters on the opposite page around the ball. Let dry.

egg carton

ping-pong ball

WHEEL WITH A COLLAR DREIDEL

1. Start with a wood or plastic wheel from a toy car, bead set, or building peg and block set. Glue a square paper or cardboard "collar" on the wheel.

2. Paint the Hebrew letters below around the wheel. Let dry. Insert a sharpened dowel through the hole in the wheel.

TOOTHPICK AND BUTTON DREIDEL

1. Start with a white button that has two holes. With a felt-tip pen, print the Hebrew letters below around the button. Push a round toothpick through each hole and glue or tape the bottoms together.

2. To spin the *dreidel,* squeeze the tops of the toothpicks together. The heavier the button, the faster and longer the spin.

CLAY DREIDEL

1. Mold the *dreidel* from clay that "fires" hard in a home oven. Let dry. Bake the clay according to package directions. Let cool.

2. Leave the clay its natural color or decorate with acrylic paints. Paint one of the Hebrew letters below on each of four sides. Let dry.

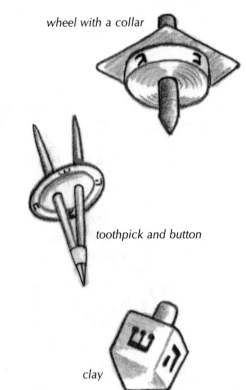

wheel with a collar

toothpick and button

clay

Purim masks

paper plate mask

construction paper mask

foil or styrofoam mask

transparent acetate mask

All these masks can be decorated with paint, paper cut-outs, yarn, fabric, buttons, glitter, or fake jewels (from variety store). If you are going to wear the mask, be sure to cut out eyes and mouth or nose so you can see and breathe. To use the masks, hold up in front of your face, or secure by stapling ribbons on each side of the mask to tie around your head or rubber bands to go around your ears. You may also hang the masks as wall decorations.

PAPER PLATE MASK

1. Paint a paper plate or start with one that is already patterned or colored.

2. Cut out eyes, nose, and neck.

3. Add yarn trim.

4. Glue, staple, or tack a stick or dowel (from craft store) to one side of the plate. This makes a handle for holding the mask over your face.

CONSTRUCTION PAPER MASK

1. This mask should be large enough to cover your entire head, including your hair.

2. To make the crown, hair, beard, and facial features, cut out pieces of colored construction paper and glue on with white glue.

FOIL OR STYROFOAM MASK

1. Gather some frozen-food pans, shallow foil tins, or styrofoam meat trays in a variety of sizes and shapes.

2. Combine several and staple together to form one mask.

3. Cut out features and trimmings and glue them on.

TRANSPARENT ACETATE MASK

1. Cut out a mask shape from a piece of transparent acetate (from craft or hobby store).

2. Dilute a small amount of glue that dries clear with an equal amount of water.

3. Glue shapes cut from colored tissue paper to the mask. Try overlapping colored tissue for an unusual effect.

4. Wipe off excess glue with a paper towel.

Purim puppets

OLD BALL

1. Make a hole in an old rubber ball or ping-pong ball.

2. Paint a face on the ball.

3. Add a crown, hair, mustache, or beard to decorate the head.

4. Drape a hankerchief around your forefinger and stick your finger in the hole of the head. Wiggle your finger to move the puppet.

old ball

SOCK

1. If you are right-handed, place a light-colored sock on your left hand, spreading your fingers to stretch the material.

2. With felt-tip pens, draw the character of your choice, making the waist at the base of your fingers.

3. Draw the rest of the body from the base of your fingers to the bottom of your hand. As you close your hand, the puppet bows at the waist.

PADDLE

1. Use a wooden paddle with a rubber band and ball attached. Glue on paper or yarn hair and paint Haman's face. Play a "paddle Haman" game (A).

2. You may remove the rubber band and ball and use the handle of the paddle to move the puppet (B).

TOOTHPASTE BOX

1. To make the mouth opening, cut the toothpaste box, as shown by the dotted line in (A).

2. Paint the box with acrylics and let dry. Glue on colored paper, yarn, buttons, or other trim (B).

3. Glue a tab to the back of the top half and tab to the back of the bottom half of the box to move the puppet and make it "talk" (C).

POPCORN BALL

1. Buy popcorn balls or make your own by mixing popcorn and white corn syrup.

2. Poke the hole in the popcorn ball and insert a popsicle stick for a handle.

3. Decorate the ball with a removable paper crown and dots of icing for facial features.

After the show, you can eat the puppet.

CARDBOARD TUBE

1. Give a small cardboard tube a base coat of acrylic or poster paint. Let dry.

2. To make the hair, stuff a wad of fluffed-out cotton in one hole.

3. Shape more cotton into a beard and eyebrows and glue on. Paint on eyes and costume decoration.

4. Let dry.

5. Cut out feet at one end of a long strip of cardboard.

6. Glue the bottom of the puppet to the cardboard strip, just above the feet. Use the other end of the strip to move the puppet.

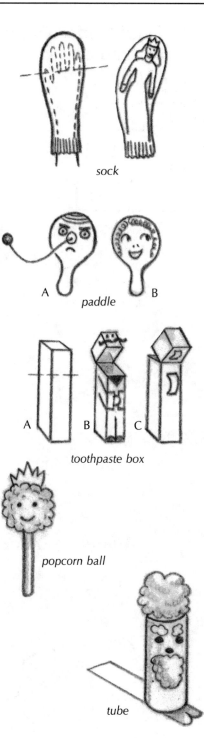

sock

A   *paddle*   B

toothpaste box

popcorn ball

tube

Liquid-embroidered matzah cover

A

B

C

You will need:

1 sheet of paper, about 14 inches square	1 sheet of dressmaker's carbon paper
pencil	tubes of liquid embroidery, any colors
4 light-colored pieces of cotton or linen material, each about 15 inches square	straight pins
	embroidery yarn, any color
	embroidery needle

1. Plan a design on paper that includes a simple object in each corner.

2. Pull one thread at a time along the edges of each of the four pieces of material. Unraveling the material about one-quarter inch all around makes a pretty fringed border.

3. Center a piece of dressmaker's carbon paper (it doesn't smear) face down on one of the pieces of fringed material. Place the paper with your design face up on the carbon paper and trace over it (A). Remove both sheets of paper. The design should appear on the material.

4. Using the liquid embroidery, paint the design, but not the corner designs. Let dry.

5. Pile up the four pieces of fringed material, with the painted one on top. Pin the pieces together in each corner (B).

6. Use a backstitch (C) to embroider the outline of the corner designs. Be sure to sew through all four layers. Remove the pins. The cover now has three sections.

7. You may embroider your name or initials and the date on the back of the matzah cover. Sew with thread or use liquid embroidery.

8. To use, place three whole pieces of *matzah* in the *matzah* cover, one in each of the three sections. After using, wash by hand.

Afikoman holder

A

B

You will need:

11 inch square of patterned adhesive-backed paper	staple gun or glue
	scissors
11 inch square of heavy-duty paper, any color	felt-tip pens, any colors

1. Peel the backing off the adhesive-backed paper and place it sticky side up (A).

2. Hold the heavy-duty paper over the sticky paper and, when centered, press it firmly down.

3. Fold one point of the square so the tip slightly overlaps the middle of the paper. Fold up the opposite point, as shown in (B).

4. Fold up another point and staple or glue together (C).

5. Fold the remaining point down. This flap opens to hold the *afikoman* (D).

6. With the handle of a pair of scissors, firmly press down along the folded parts of the holder.

7. With the felt-tip pens, decorate the front of the holder with the word "afikoman" in Hebrew and English (E).

E ‏אֶפִּיקוֹמָן‎   AFIKOMAN

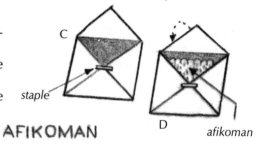

staple

D   afikoman

PLASTIC-COATED

You will need:

paper plate
felt-tip pens or acrylic paint

spray can of clear, liquid plastic
(from hardware or craft store)

1. Draw a design on a paper plate, using the illustration on this page as a guide to the order of the six items that belong on a *seder* plate. Color the design with felt-tip pens or acrylic paint.

2. With a back and forth motion, lightly spray the face of the plate with clear, liquid plastic spray. Several light coats should be applied, rather than one heavy coat, to prevent the colors from running. If the colors do run slightly, you just might like the effect. When the "face" of the plate is dry, turn it over and spray the back.

3. When thoroughly dry, the plate may be used. To clean, wipe with a damp sponge.

PAPER-COVERED

You will need:

paper plate
felt-tip pens or acrylic paint

clear, adhesive-backed paper
(from hardware or craft store)
scissors

1. Draw a design on a paper plate, using the illustration on this page as a guide to the order of the six items that belong on a *seder* plate. Paint the design with felt-tip pens or acrylic paint. Let dry.

2. Place the paper plate on the back of a piece of clear, adhesive-backed paper and draw around it. Cut around the penciled outline.

3. Peel the backing off the paper and hold the paper centered over the top of the paper plate, sticky side down. Press the paper on the plate, smoothing it from the center outward. Press firmly to the back of the plate.

4. Place the plate face down on another piece of clear, adhesive-backed paper. Draw around it, cut, and apply paper as in instruction 3.

5. After using, wipe with a damp sponge.

Paper seder plates

Cooking Jewish

Jewish cooks have always had a hard time. For instance, one morning in Egypt, about 3,500 years ago, the cooks had just finished setting their bread dough in the sun to rise when Moses came running and yelling, "Pack up! We're going into the desert!"

The cooks scraped up the flat loaves, loaded them onto the donkeys along with the babies and the dishes, and off they went. For the next forty years they did their cooking in the desert. It was no picnic.

Of course something good came out of all this (especially with butter and salt). The bread that stayed flat because it had no time to rise became our Passover *matzah*.

Since that morning in Egypt, Jewish cooks again and again have packed up their babies, dishes, and pots and moved on. In every new country they have found interesting dishes, such as Russian borsht with meat and sour cream, Turkish moussaka with eggplant, cheese, and chopped lamb, and American cheeseburgers. But even though their mouths were watering, the kosher Jewish cooks could not mix meat and dairy foods in the same meal. In each country they had to rewrite the recipes. They took the beef out of the borsht, the chopped lamb out of the moussaka, the cheese off of the cheeseburger . . . and, to everybody's surprise, the new dishes tasted just fine.

Today traditional Jewish recipes, like the ones in this chapter, come from all over the world. Each one is a little different, a little special, because Jewish cooks added a pinch of this, or took away a pinch of that, to make their food kosher and just right for a holiday or celebration.

WHAT'S KOSHER?

Kosher (*kasher* in Hebrew) means right, proper, or following the laws of the Jewish religion.

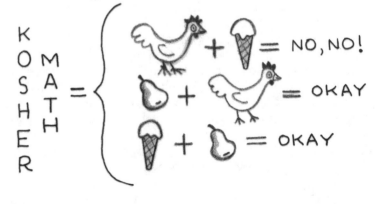

The Bible has rules that guide Jews in their daily lives. It also has rules about food. They tell us which foods people may eat and how the foods should be prepared. Over the years the rabbis have explained these rules in great detail.

Here is some basic information about kosher cooking and eating. You can learn more about it from your parents, rabbi, or Hebrew teachers.

1. There are three kinds of foods—dairy, meat, and pareve.

- *Dairy foods* are milk, butter, cheese, and other products made from milk.
- *Meat foods* are chicken and other poultry, lamb, beef, and products that contain meat, such as salami, frankfurters, or sausage.
- *Pareve foods* are fruits, vegetables, nuts, grains (including most bread and crackers), fish, vegetable oil, and vegetable margarine.

2. Dairy and meat foods may not be eaten or cooked together.
3. Pareve foods may be used with either meat or dairy foods.
4. Some foods, such as pork and shellfish, are not kosher.

LOOK BEFORE YOU COOK!

Here are some important rules for safe and successful cooking:

1. Make sure there's an adult around in case you need help. Many of these recipes are suitable only for older children.

2. Read the recipe. Check to see that you have all the ingredients (food) and utensils (tools and pots) that you need.

3. Wash your hands.

4. Put all the needed ingredients out on the table or counter.

5. Measure the ingredients carefully.

6. Do all cutting on a cutting board. Cut away from your body, not toward yourself.

7. Don't let pot handles stick out. Turn them in over the stove so you won't bump into them.

8. Keep *dry* pot holders handy (the heat goes right through wet ones) and use them to hold hot pot handles.

9. Turn off the stove and oven when you finish cooking.

10. Clean up.

Poor Jews in Eastern Europe ate dark peasant bread all week. For the Sabbath, they saved their money to buy white flour and made this braided bread. "The Sabbath is like a little taste of heaven," they said, "and in heaven, we will all be rich."

RECIPES

Heavenly ḥallah
makes 2 loaves

You will need:

¼ cup oil	measuring cup
extra oil for greasing the dough and the cookie sheet	measuring spoons
1 teaspoon salt	large mixing bowl
1 tablespoon sugar	mixing spoon
¾ cup hot water	2 small bowls
1 package dry yeast	fork
¼ cup lukewarm water	pastry board for kneading
2 eggs	clean dish towel
3½–4 cups flour	cookie sheet
extra flour for kneading dough	pastry brush
¼ cup sesame seeds or poppy seeds	

1. Pour the oil, salt, and sugar into the large mixing bowl. Add the hot water. Mix until the sugar melts.

2. Mix the yeast and the lukewarm water in one of the small bowls until the yeast melts.

3. Beat the eggs with the fork. Put aside 2 tablespoons of egg to brush on the ḥallah before baking. Pour the rest of the eggs into the large bowl. Add the yeast and mix.

4. Add the flour to the bowl, one cup at a time. Mix after every cupful. Continue mixing until the ingredients hold together in a ball of dough.

5. To keep the dough from sticking, spread a little flour on the board, your hands, and the ball of dough. Put the dough on the board and knead for about 5 minutes. Add flour if the dough starts sticking. Roll the dough into a ball again.

6. Put a few drops of oil on your hands. Pat the oil on the ball of dough. This will keep the surface from getting dry. Place the dough back in the bowl. Cover it with a towel and put it in a warm place to rise.

7. Let the dough rise for 1 hour or until it is twice as big as when you started. Put it on the floured board again. Knead it for 1 minute. Cut the dough into 6 equal pieces. Knead each one.

8. Roll each piece of dough between your hands until it is about 9 inches long. Braid 3 pieces of dough together for each loaf of ḥallah.

TO BRAID THE HALLAH:

LAY THREE ROLLED PIECES OF DOUGH SIDE BY SIDE

PINCH THE THREE ENDS TOGETHER

CROSS 1 OVER 2

CROSS 3 OVER 1

CROSS 2 OVER 3

REPEAT UNTIL YOU RUN OUT OF DOUGH, THEN PINCH THE THREE ENDS TOGETHER

Making ḥallah takes about 3½ hours from start to finish. But there's plenty of resting time in between while the yeast is working to raise the dough. That's a good time to do homework, clean your room, curl up with a good book, or maybe just rest.

127

Cooking Jewish

9. Grease the cookie sheet with a few drops of oil.

10. Put the 2 loaves on the cookie sheet. Cover them with the towel and let them rise for 45 minutes at room temperature.

11. Turn the oven on to 375 degrees. Dip the pastry brush in the leftover egg and lightly brush the top of each ḥallah. This will make the tops brown and shiny. Sprinkle on the seeds. Bake for 30 minutes or until the bread is toasty brown.

HALLAH CREATIONS

Here are three more ways to use yeast dough. After the dough rises for the first time (after step 6 of the ḥallah recipe), you can:

1. Break off plum-sized pieces and roll them into long, squiggly snakes. Put them on a greased cookie sheet and let them rise for 30 minutes. Sprinkle with cinnamon and sugar and bake till they are golden brown, about 30 minutes, at 350 degrees. They make great sandwich rolls for *Shabbat* lunch.

2. At Rosh Ha-Shanah you can roll the dough into thin coils and shape into ladders to carry your new year's wishes up to heaven. Let the ladders rise for 30 minutes, brush the surface with egg yolk, and bake for 30 minutes at 350 degrees.

3. At Purim you can roll the dough out with a rolling pin to ¼ inch or thinner. Cut circles with a 3-inch round cookie cutter, fill them with prune filling, and pinch shut (see page 134 for prune filling and pinching instructions). Let the yeast *hamentashen* rise for 30 minutes. Then bake them until golden brown, about 30 minutes, at 350 degrees.

TO KNEAD — PRESS DOWN ON THE DOUGH WITH THE HEELS OF YOUR HANDS AND PUSH IT AWAY FROM YOU. FOLD IT OVER AND GIVE IT A QUARTER TURN. PRESS, PUSH, FOLD OVER AND TURN AGAIN, AND AGAIN ... UNTIL THE DOUGH IS SMOOTH AND SPRINGY.

"When a poor man eats chicken, one of them is sick." A folk saying

Grandma's chicken soup
makes 5 cups of soup

You will need:

7 cups water
2½–3-pound chicken (pullet) cut into 8 pieces
1 large onion
1 teaspoon salt
2 stalks celery
2 carrots
1 small parsnip
10 sprigs fresh parsley or ¾ teaspoon dried parsley
10 sprigs fresh dill or ¾ teaspoon dried dill

measuring cup and spoons
large pot with lid
knife and cutting board
mixing spoon
vegetable brush
slotted spoon
10-inch square baking dish
string

WE SKIM THE SOUP TO LIFT OUT THE BITS OF FAT.

1. Measure the water into the pot. Bring to a boil. Add the chicken pieces. The water should cover the chicken. Add more water if necessary. Skim the top with the mixing spoon.

2. Peel the onion. Cut it vertically partway through. Add it to the soup. Add the salt. Skim again. Cover the pot and cook over medium heat for 30 minutes.

3. Scrub the celery, carrots, and parsnip with the brush. Cut the celery in half. Cut the carrots into thick slices. Add the celery, carrots, and whole parsnip to the soup. Bring to a boil. Then turn down the heat and simmer for another 30 minutes.

4. Using pot holders, remove the pot from the heat. Take out the pieces of chicken with the slotted spoon and place them in the baking dish. Take out the onion and throw it away.

5. Tie the fresh parsley and dill together with string and add to the soup. If your are using dried herbs, add them now. Simmer for 20 minutes more.

6. Take out the celery and the tied parsley and dill. Throw them away. Let the soup cool. Skim off the cooled fat. Reheat the soup before serving.

Bagels
makes 16–20

You will need:

⅛ cup oil
½ teaspoon salt
1 tablespoon sugar
½ cup hot water
1 package yeast (¼ ounce)
½ cup lukewarm water
1 egg
3–3½ cups flour
2 quarts water and 1 tablespoon
    salt for boiling the bagels
coarse salt, sesame seeds, or
    poppy seeds

measuring cup
measuring spoons
large mixing bowl
mixing spoon
2 small bowls
fork
floured pastry board or table
    surface
large saucepan
slotted spoon
greased cookie sheet

1. Put the oil, salt, and sugar in the large bowl. Add ½ cup of hot water. Mix until the salt and sugar melt.

2. Mix the yeast and ½ cup of lukewarm water in the small bowl until the yeast melts.

3. Beat the egg slightly. Add it to the large bowl. Add the yeast and mix.

4. Add the flour to the mixture one cup at a time. Mix after every cupful.

5. Place the dough on the floured board or table and knead until smooth. See the kneading instructions on page 127.

6. Pat some oil over the dough, put it back in the bowl, cover it, and let it rise in a warm place for one hour, or until it is twice as big as when you started.

7. Punch down the dough. Break off a piece slightly bigger than a plum. Roll it as thick as a cigar and about 7 inches long. To keep it from sticking to your hands, put about ½ cup of flour at the side of the table and dip the dough in it before rolling. Form a ring and pinch the ends together. Put the dough rings on the floured board or platter. Leave room between them for rising.

8. Let the bagels (dough rings) rise for 15 minutes at room temperature.

9. Heat the oven to 400 degrees. Bring the water and salt to a boil in the saucepan and turn the burner down to medium.

10. Gently drop the bagels into the water, 2 or 3 at a time, and cook them for about 2 minutes.

11. Remove the bagels with the slotted spoon, place on the cookie sheet, and sprinkle with salt or seeds.

12. Bake for 20 minutes.

WHAT'S A BAGEL?

A PETRIFIED DONUT

Pita is a flat bread that opens like an envelope. It is usually filled with felafel, which are deep-fried balls of mashed chick-peas. Tehina, a sauce made of sesame seeds, is poured on top. You can make felafel from a packaged mix or use the felafel recipe in this chapter. The pita, felafel mix, and tehina can be bought at a kosher butcher store, supermarket, or a store that sells foods from other countries.

Pita sandwiches
enough for 4 people

You will need:

½ onion
1 cucumber
1 green pepper
2 tomatoes
4 pita breads
16 felafel balls
    or 16 small pieces of hard cheese,
    or 16 small meatballs
tehina sauce

vegetable peeler
knife
cutting board
large mixing bowl
mixing spoon

The Israelis learned to make these spicy sandwiches from their Arab neighbors. They eat them on the run, just as we eat hot dogs.

1. Peel the onion and the cucumber. Cut the green pepper in half. Scoop out the seeds and white ribs and throw away. Slice the tomatoes. Cut all the vegetables into narrow strips. Then cut the strips into little pieces. Put them in the bowl and mix.

2. Slit the top edge of each pita, as shown in the illustration. Pull the sides apart to make an open "pocket." Fill each pocket with one quarter of the vegetables. Add 4 felafel, or 4 pieces of cheese, or 4 meatballs.

3. Pour tehina sauce over the filling in each pocket.

Felafel
makes 16 balls

You will need:

1 cup cooked or canned chick-peas (garbanzo beans), drained
1 clove garlic
½ teaspoon salt
⅛ teaspoon pepper
⅔ cup fine bread crumbs
2 eggs
2 tablespoons oil
oil for deep frying, enough to fill the pot about 3 inches

can opener
measuring cups and spoons
large mixing bowl
potato masher
knife
cutting board
mixing spoon
pot for deep frying
slotted spoon or frying basket
plate
paper towels

1. Mash the chick-peas in the large bowl. Cut the garlic into tiny pieces. Add the garlic, salt, pepper, and bread crumbs to the chick-peas. Mix. Add the eggs and oil. Mix thoroughly.

2. Heat the oil in the pot to 375 degrees, or until little bubbles rise to the surface.

3. Shape the mixture into balls, about 1 inch in diameter. Gently place the balls in the pot with the mixing spoon—don't drop them in because the hot oil may splash. Fry a few at a time until golden brown, about 5 minutes.

4. Remove the felafel with the slotted spoon. Drain on a plate covered with paper towels.

If you want to mix your own felafel, here is a recipe to use. Whether you buy a mix or make your own, be sure to ask an adult to help with the deep frying. Splattering oil can burn you.

You will need:

¾ cup tehina	can opener
⅓ cup lemon juice	measuring cups and spoon
⅛ teaspoon garlic powder	small mixing bowl
⅓ cup water	mixing spoon

1. Put the tehina, lemon juice, and garlic powder in the bowl. Mix until you have a smooth sauce.

2. Add the water, one teaspoon at a time, until the sauce is thin enough to pour.

3. Pour tehina over pita sandwiches or use as a dip for raw vegetables.

Tehina sauce
makes about 1 cup

Tehina is a paste made from sesame seeds. You can buy a can of tehina in stores that sell felafel or pita and turn it into tehina sauce.

IN ISRAEL ALL KINDS OF FOODS ARE ADDED TO A FELAFEL SANDWICH — FRIED CAULIFLOWER — EGGPLANT — PICKLED BEETS — ONIONS

Potato latkes

makes 16–20 pancakes

You will need:

3 medium potatoes
1 small onion
3 tablespoons flour
2 eggs
¼ teaspoon salt
dash of pepper
oil for frying

vegetable brush
small knife
grater
large bowl
measuring spoons
mixing spoon
large frying pan
tablespoon
spatula
plates and paper towels

1. Scrub the potatoes and cut out any dark spots.

2. Grate them into a large bowl, using the coarse side of the grater. Peel the onion and grate it into the bowl.

3. Add the flour, eggs, salt, and pepper. Mix well.

4. Heat the oil in the frying pan till it sizzles. Drop heaping tablespoons of the mixture into the oil. Flatten with the spoon and fry at medium heat till both sides are golden brown. Mix the batter in the bowl from time to time as you work.

5. Drain the *latkes* on plates, and cover them with paper towels. Serve with applesauce or sour cream.

If you're frying *latkes* for a lot of people, prepare them the day before. Wrap and refrigerate them. Twenty minutes before serving, preheat the oven to 350 degrees. Warm the *latkes* for 10 minutes on an ungreased pan.

WHY ARE LATKES MADE FOR HANUKKAH?

THEY'RE QUICK TO FRY, SO THE JEWS MADE THEM IN BETWEEN BATTLES WITH THE GREEKS

AND THEY ARE MADE WITH OIL LIKE THE OIL OF THE MENORAH

LET'S EAT!

LATKE VARIATIONS

CHEESE

Beat 2 eggs in a large bowl. Add 1 cup of drained cottage cheese, ½ cup of matzah meal, ¼ cup of water, 1 teaspoon of sugar, ¼ teaspoon of cinnamon, a dash of salt, and mix well. Drop the batter by heaping tablespoons into a heated, oiled frying pan and fry at medium heat till both sides are golden brown.

ZUCCHINI

Mix 2 cups of grated zucchini, one small grated onion, and 2 ounces of grated cheddar cheese. Add 2 eggs, ⅓ cup of wheat germ, 3 tablespoons of flour, and salt and pepper to taste. Mix well, and fry, as in the cheese *latke* recipe above.

You will need:

2 eggs
¾ cup honey
1 cup sugar
½ cup oil
2½ cups flour
1 teaspoon baking powder
1 teaspoon baking soda
1 teaspoon cinnamon
1 cup strong coffee, cooled
handful of sliced almonds

loaf pan, about 9 inches by 5 inches
waxed paper
large mixing bowl
egg beater or electric mixer
measuring cup and spoons
medium-size mixing bowl
mixing spoon
toothpick

Honey cake
serves 8–10 people

1. Turn the oven on to 325 degrees. Grease the pan. Cut the waxed paper to fit the bottom of the pan and put it in.

2. Break the eggs into the large bowl and beat until they are foamy. Slowly add the honey, sugar, and oil while continuing to mix.

3. Put the flour, baking powder, baking soda, and cinnamon in the medium-size bowl. Mix well with the spoon, counting 35 to 40 strokes. This will keep the batter from having holes or lumps.

4. Add half the coffee and half the flour mixture to the egg mixture. Mix well. Add the rest of the coffee and the flour mixture. Mix until smooth. Pour into the loaf pan. Sprinkle the almonds on top.

5. Bake for 1 hour or until a toothpick comes out dry when you poke it into the center of the cake.

Hamantashen
makes about 20 small pastries

For the filling, you will need:

1 pound uncooked prunes
1 small apple
2 teaspoons honey

knife
cutting board
medium-size saucepan
chopping bowl
chopping knife
medium-size mixing bowl
grater
measuring cup
mixing spoon

1. Put the prunes in the pan. Add enough water to cover. Bring to a boil and cook at medium heat for 20 minutes. Remove from heat. Let the prunes cool. Take out the pits. Chop or grind the prunes and put them in the bowl.

2. Wash and grate the apple and add it to the prunes. Add the honey and mix well. Set the filling aside.

To make the dough and shape the hamantashen, you will need:

¾ cup sugar
2 cups flour
2 teaspoons baking powder
¼ teaspoon salt
⅓ cup margarine
1 egg
2–3 tablespoons water
bowl of filling
extra flour for coating board and
    rolling pin

2 cookie sheets
large mixing bowl
fork
mixing spoon
pastry board
rolling pin
2 teaspoons

1. Grease the cookie sheets.

2. Put the sugar, flour, baking powder, and salt into the bowl. Mix well, counting 35 to 40 strokes, to blend thoroughly.

3. Cut the margarine into little pieces and add to the bowl. Mix with the fork or with your hands until you have an evenly crumbly mixture. Be patient—it'll take a few minutes. Add the egg and water. Mix until the dough sticks together in a ball.

4. Wash your hands if they are sticky. Sprinkle flour on the board, the rolling pin, and your hands. Leave a little extra flour on the back corner of the board.

5. Pinch off a piece of dough. Roll it between your hands into a 1½-inch round ball. Dip the ball in the extra flour. Roll it flat with the rolling pin to about ⅛-inch thickness. More experienced cooks may roll out *all* the dough and cut circles with a cookie cutter.

6. Take a teaspoon of filling. With the second teaspoon, scrape the filling off into the middle of the dough.

7. Fold up three edges of the dough and pinch them together to make a triangle. Put it on the cookie sheet. Repeat steps 5, 6, and 7 until you have used up all the dough.

8. Turn the oven on to 350 degrees. When it is warm, put in the cookie sheets and bake for 20 minutes.

Here are two other mixtures you can use to fill your hamantashen.
1. *Soak 1 cup of poppy seeds overnight. Drain them. Grind in a food grinder. Add 4 tablespoons of honey and mix.*
2. *Mix 3 ounces of cream cheese or farmer cheese, 2 teaspoons jam, and ¼ cup chopped nuts.*

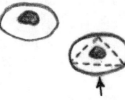

fold up on dotted lines

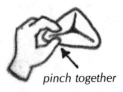

pinch together

Babanatza

A Sephardi raisin pudding for Passover
serves 4–5

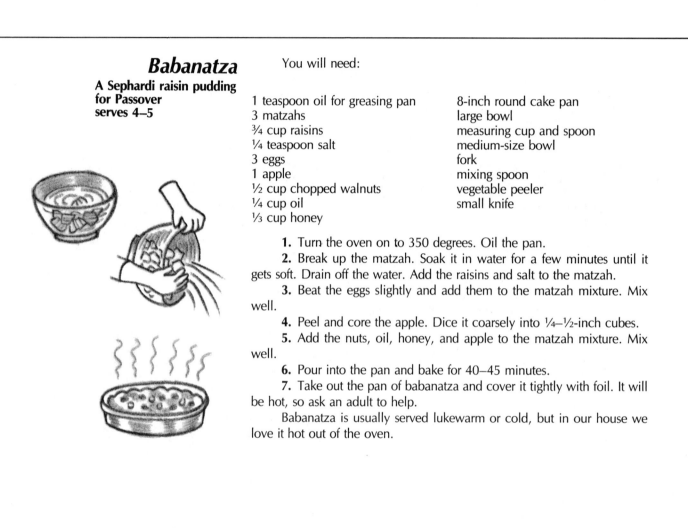

You will need:

1 teaspoon oil for greasing pan	8-inch round cake pan
3 matzahs	large bowl
¾ cup raisins	measuring cup and spoon
¼ teaspoon salt	medium-size bowl
3 eggs	fork
1 apple	mixing spoon
½ cup chopped walnuts	vegetable peeler
¼ cup oil	small knife
⅓ cup honey	

1. Turn the oven on to 350 degrees. Oil the pan.
2. Break up the matzah. Soak it in water for a few minutes until it gets soft. Drain off the water. Add the raisins and salt to the matzah.
3. Beat the eggs slightly and add them to the matzah mixture. Mix well.
4. Peel and core the apple. Dice it coarsely into ¼–½-inch cubes.
5. Add the nuts, oil, honey, and apple to the matzah mixture. Mix well.
6. Pour into the pan and bake for 40–45 minutes.
7. Take out the pan of babanatza and cover it tightly with foil. It will be hot, so ask an adult to help.

Babanatza is usually served lukewarm or cold, but in our house we love it hot out of the oven.

Haroset

Apple mixture for the *seder* dish, and for noshing.

You will need:

2 apples	grater
½ cup chopped walnuts	medium-sized bowl
1 teaspoon cinnamon	measuring cup and spoon
2 tablespoons of sweet red wine	mixing spoon

1. Grate the apples. Measure 1 cup of grated apple into the bowl.
2. Add the nuts and cinnamon and mix.
3. Add enough wine to hold the mixture together, about 2 tablespoons.

Passover Brownies

You will need:

¾ cup cocoa | baking pan, 9 by 9 by 2 inches
3 tablespoons oil | small bowl
4 eggs | measuring cup and spoons
1¾ cups sugar | fork
⅓ cup oil | egg beater
¼ teaspoon salt | large bowl
½ cup potato starch | mixing spoon
½ cup chopped nuts

1. Heat the oven to 350 degrees. Grease the baking pan.

2. Mix the cocoa and 3 tablespoons of oil in the small bowl.

3. Beat the eggs in the large bowl till thick and foamy. Add the sugar slowly and keep beating.

4. Add ⅓ cup of oil to the large bowl and mix. Add the salt, potato starch, and nuts. Mix well.

5. Add the cocoa-oil mixture to the batter and mix.

6. Pour the batter into the baking pan. Bake about 30 minutes or until a toothpick poked into the center comes out dry.

7. Cut the brownies into squares while they're hot.

Passover Pizza ? ! !
Pizza started out 2,000 years ago as a Roman-Jewish dish when Roman soldiers put olive oil and cheese on Passover matzah.

People's Almanac

Grandma's remedies

TEA from Russia and Greece
For a fever or an upset stomach.
Brew lots of mint or fennel herb tea, or regular tea with lemon, and drink, drink, drink.

HONEY AND MILK from Russia
For a sore throat.
Mix ½ cup of hot milk and ½ cup hot water. Dissolve 2 tablespoons of honey in the mixture. Drink up!

SALT IN A SOCK from Greece
For a chest cold. **Don't eat this!**
Heat the salt in a pan. Pour it into a sock and tie the sock shut. Place it on your chest or back.

Another cure for chest colds.
Make a thick paste of flax seed and hot olive oil. Smear it on flannel and apply the flannel to the back and chest.

PAIN KILLER from Morocco
For toothaches.
Soak a piece of cotton in *arak* (a Middle Eastern liquor). Sprinkle pepper and salt on the cotton and place it on the tooth.

EGGPLANT JUICE from Turkey
For a bad cough.
Bake an eggplant till it's soft. Squeeze out the juice and drink it up.

GUGGLE MUGGLE from Poland
For a cold, or if your grandma decides you look pale and run-down.
Put 1 raw egg, ½ teaspoon of vanilla, 1 cup of warm milk, and 1 tablespoon of sugar in a mixing bowl. Beat with an egg beater till it's well mixed and bubbly. Drink up!

GARLIC
To keep you from catching anything from anybody because you smell so strong that no one will come near you.
Peel several cloves of garlic. Tie them into a handkerchief or gauze bag and hang them around your neck with a red ribbon.

"A meal at which words of Torah are not discussed is a wasted meal." Talmud

TWO 'EVERYTHING' FOODS

You can start a civil war between a European (Ashkenazi) Jew and an Eastern (Sephardi) Jew if you ask which food is perfect for almost everything.

"Shmaltz!" says the Ashkenazi.

"Skhoog!" says the Sephardi.

Don't let them fight it out. Try both recipes and decide for yourself.

Skhoog

You will need:
6 or 8 hot peppers (the long, thin peppers)
4 cloves of garlic
olive oil
a dash of tumeric
a dash of cumin powder.

1. Put on rubber gloves (the peppers can burn) and grate the peppers and garlic into a bowl.

2. Add enough olive oil to make a paste. Add the spices.

3. Refrigerate the mixture overnight.

Use a TINY BIT (at least until you get used to it) on bread, salad, or with main courses.

A spoonful of *skhoog* strikes like a bolt of lightening. It clears the head, makes the body tingle, and you can't wait to get more food into your mouth to wash it down.

Shmaltz

You will need:
about ¼ pound of fresh chicken fat or fat skimmed off the top of cooled chicken soup
a diced onion
salt

1. Cut the chicken fat into small pieces and fry at low heat until it melts.

2. Add the onion and keep frying until the onion turns golden brown. Add salt to taste.

3. Pour the mixture into a jar and let it cool until it becomes solid. Some cooks strain the mixture to remove the onions and bits of meat before pouring it into the jar.

Use *shmaltz* on bread, vegetables, and other nondairy foods the same way as you would use butter with dairy foods.

• Keep *skhoog* and *shmaltz* in the refrigerator.

Holy books

In small Jewish towns in Eastern Europe people waited impatiently for spring to come. When the snow melted and the muddy road dried, the bookseller trudged into town pulling his heavy cart. Boys and girls, market women, rabbis, shoemakers—everybody came running to buy, or at least to look over, the new books. The bookseller was such a welcome guest that a famous Jewish writer took the name Mendele Mokher Seforim, which means "Mendele the bookseller."

A pious Jew was asked what he expected to find in heaven. "Ah," he smiled, "in heaven there must be a great, big library where people can read and study forever and ever." People who find such "heavenly" pleasure in reading surely deserve the name "People of the Book." Reading their holy books gives Jews more than pleasure. It is also a guide to their daily lives.

It may seem strange that books written centuries ago are still guiding us today. The laws of the United States are also based on an old book, the Constitution, which was written about 200 years ago. Each year Congress passes new laws. Many of them are reviewed by the Supreme Court. If the court decides that a law is against the Constitution, the law is thrown out.

This chapter tells how Jewish laws grew out of the opinions and interpretations of many leaders, built up over more than 2,000 years and based on the "constitution" of the Jewish people—the Torah of Moses.

TORAH

Sometimes the word Torah is used to mean only the Five Books of Moses. Sometimes it's used to mean all three sections of the Bible.

Another name for the three sections is "Tanach." In Hebrew תַּנַ״ךְ *, Tanach, comes from the first letter of the name of each section.*

תּוֹרָה *Torah (Five Books of Moses)*
נְבִיאִים *Nevi'im (Prophets)*
כְּתוּבִים *Ketuvim (Writings)*

Jewish holy books tell about the rules that God gave to Moses and the Jewish people. These words were first written in the Torah, or Five Books of Moses. All the other holy books start out with the words of the Torah and then add ideas, stories, and explanations. The Torah is like the foundation of a building; the other books are the walls and upper floors. The Five Books of Moses, Prophets, and Writings are the three sections of the Hebrew Bible.

The actual Torah that is read in the synagogue is handwritten on scrolls of parchment. The Five Books of Moses are printed in a book called the *Ḥumash,* which is used for Torah study and for following along with the reading of the Torah in the synagogue.

The Torah tells stories of how the world began and developed, such as the stories of Adam and Eve, Noah and the great flood, and the tower of Babel. It also tells about the beginnings of the Jewish people—from Abraham the first Jew, to the slavery in Egypt, to the

The illustration shows blocks of a wall labeled, from bottom to top: HUMASH, PROPHETS AND WRITINGS, MISHNAH, GEMARA, and at the top COMMENTATORS, RESPONSA, SIDDUR, HAGGADAH. Along the right side vertically: TALMUD, TORAH. A sign reads: JEWISH LAW UNDER CONSTRUCTION — COMPLETION DATE: WHEN MESSIAH COMES

going out (Exodus) from Egypt under the leadership of Moses. It tells how Moses received the Ten Commandments and taught the laws of God to his people. Then he led them to the border of the Land of Israel but died before he could enter the Promised Land. The Jews went into their land to begin a new life.

The other two sections of the Bible, Prophets and Writings, describe how the Jewish people built a kingdom and a temple in Israel. There are happy parts, like the many beautiful poems of praise to God, and sad parts, like the prophets' angry scoldings when the peo-

The Bible is a worldwide best-seller. It has been translated into more than 1,000 languages, including the Mohawk and Chippewa languages. Hebrew biblical words like babel, hallelujah, cherub, amen, and jubilee are now part of the English language.

ple broke the laws of the Torah. The Book of Jeremiah describes a terrible war in which the Temple was destroyed and the Jewish people were forced to leave their land. But later, the Books of Ezra and Nehemiah tell how the people came home, rebuilt the Temple, and joyfully promised to live by the rules of the Torah.

Each week a section of the Prophets is read after the Torah reading in the synagogue. It is called the *haftarah*.

TALMUD

A young Talmud student came to his teacher and asked to be ordained as a rabbi. The teacher tested him with a question. He asked, "What would you do if a man cut his hand on Shabbat and began to bleed heavily?"

The student thought, then he said, "Wait a minute, I'll look it up in the Talmud."

"Never mind," said his teacher. "Go home and study some more. By the time you looked it up the poor man would have bled to death."

The Talmud has two parts: Mishnah and Gemara. It took 400 years to write the first part, the Mishnah. This is why.

For a long time the Torah guided the Jewish people, but then new rulers took power. They brought new customs and new ideas about God and the world. There was a war, and the Second Temple was destroyed. People became confused and frightened. It seemed that they couldn't find answers to their questions in the Torah anymore.

"The Torah is the word of God," said the rabbis. "All the wisdom and truth that we need is in there. We have to search it until we find the answers."

Teachers and rabbis such as Hillel and Shammai listened to the people's problems. Then they studied the laws of the Torah and discussed them together, seeking advice and answers for the problems. After 400 years, Judah Ha-Nasi gathered all the discussions and answers into a great book called the Mishnah.

Life got even more complicated when the Jews were forced to leave the Land of Israel and scatter to faraway countries. They found new languages and strange new ideas about medicine, astronomy, and philosophy. The rabbis and their students kept working. They studied Torah, Mishnah, and also everything around them—from the care of donkeys and oxen to the latest developments in medicine and astronomy. Then they added other rules for the new times.

The rabbis also told stories to explain the Torah. Tales of devils and princesses, talking animals, treasures of gold and diamonds were embroidered around the Torah stories. The laws, science, legends, and stories are mixed together in the Gemara, the second part of the Talmud. It is a collection of 300 years of work that was finally written down in 500 C.E.

According to tradition the Mishnah and Gemara, like the Torah, are the words of God.

"When I pray, I pray quickly, because I am talking to God. When I read the Torah I read slowly, because God is talking to me."—a folk saying

COMMENTARIES

Anybody who opened the Talmud to look for an answer to a question might drown in that great sea of words. The rabbis quickly became lifeguards. They wrote "commentaries" that explained the Torah and the Talmud. Some of them rearranged the Talmud text to make it more clear. Rashi, Alfasi, and Maimonides were famous commentators.

Here is a page of the Talmud. The section inside the dotted line is the Talmud text. All the rest is commentary.

RESPONSA

When a Jew couldn't solve a problem he brought it to his rabbi. If the rabbi couldn't find an answer, he sent a letter to the wisest rabbi he knew and asked for his advice. The letter might be carried across many countries until it finally reached the wise one. He would ponder, study, pray . . . and finally send an answer. Such letters became known as "responsa."

Here is a question sent to Maimonides, a famous North African rabbi, in 1160 C.E.: "The Muslim rulers of our land want to kill all non-Muslims. Shall we die as Jews, or shall we give up Judaism and become Muslims?"

Maimonides answered the anxious writer: "Pretend to become a Muslim. Then wait with hope and patience until you can openly become a Jew again."

Rabbis are still writing responsa. Today there are questions like these: "If there is only one kidney machine and several very sick people, who should use the machine?"

"Should women take part in synagogue services equally with men?"

Responsa research is easier than it used to be. Fifteen hundred years of responsa have been programmed into a computer at Bar-Ilan University in Israel. If a scholar or rabbi punches the right keys the computer will shower him or her with opinions. Now there's a new problem—which opinion to accept.

Questions of the Future

SIDDUR

When Jews read aloud from the *siddur*, the daily prayer book, they're using the same words that Moses spoke in the desert, as well as many more. Some prayers in the *siddur*, such as *Shema Yisra'el*, are 4,000 years old. The long silent prayer, the *Amidah* or *Shemoneh Esreh*, is almost new by comparison—it was written in its present form only some 1,900 years ago.

The *siddur* was put into the order we use today in 860 C.E. But every few hundred years some prayers are added and others left out. For example, in 1948 a prayer for the welfare of the new State of Israel was added.

COMMENTATORS
RESPONSA
SIDDUR
HAGGADAH

HIDDEN TREASURE IN THE GENIZAH

The Jews of Cairo, Egypt, had a problem: What should they do with their old religious books? They couldn't throw them out—that would be like throwing out a grandfather or an old friend. So they piled them up in the dusty synagogue attic. Year after year the pile of books grew, for 1,300 years.

About 100 years ago Solomon Schechter, a British scholar, climbed up to explore the attic. He came down covered with dust and bursting with excitement. The attic was full of ancient manuscripts (handwritten books) of the Bible, Talmud, and responsa. Some of them were older than any Jewish books he had ever seen.

Schechter collected manuscripts in the dusty Cairo *Genizah* (the Hebrew word for "storage place") for a whole year. Then he took them back to England and spent more years sorting and studying them. Now the *Genizah* manuscripts are being used again.

Only a long-distance swimmer could make it through the "sea of the Talmud." More than 2,000 rabbis are quoted in the Talmud, and one set of Talmud, in English translation, has 35 thick volumes.

A TALMUD STORY

Nine hundred and seventy-four generations before God created heaven and earth, He created the Torah. He wrote the words in black fire on white fire.

When God began to think about creating the world, He asked the Torah for her opinion. The Torah answered: "It would be good to have a world to do your bidding. But the people of the world may disobey the laws you entrusted to me."

God reassured her. "Don't worry," He said, "people may disobey the laws, but when they see their mistakes they will try to do better, and I will forgive them."

HAGGADAH

The *Haggadah* is an old, old book that always stays young. It tells the story of Passover, and we read it at the *seder* meal. The four cups of wine, the story of the four sons, and the order of the *Haggadah* haven't changed for about 1,800 years. But new songs and stories are always being added.

Because Passover is a holiday of freedom, some families add readings from the Prophets and sing "Let My People Go." Other families change the custom of having the *seder* leader hide the *afikoman*—they have the kids hide it and the adults hunt for it.

Most old Jewish books had no pictures, but the *Haggadah* was always filled with art. One *Haggadah* from the Middle Ages is called the "Bird *Haggadah*" because all the people in the illustrations have birds' heads.

Before printing was invented, every book had to be copied slowly by hand. It took years to copy a Talmud, and each precious copy was read over and over by teachers and students. But church leaders in the Middle Ages fought Judaism by burning copies of the Talmud. In 1242 C.E. in Paris, twenty-four cartloads of Talmuds were burned. In 1288 ten rabbis were burned along with their libraries of manuscripts. The Jews cried for the loss of their beloved books as well as for the loss of their rabbis.

DEAD SEA SCROLLS

"May your left ear drop off and fall into your right pocket, you good-for-nothing goat!" The Bedouin boy was very angry. He had been climbing around the cliffs near the Dead Sea for hours, hunting for his lost goat. He stopped to rest on a ledge and found himself staring into a dark cave opening. Could the goat be in there? The boy tossed in a rock. No goat came running out. Instead he heard the sound of pottery breaking.

Pottery? In an empty cave in the desert? The boy scrambled down and hurried to tell his family. The next day he and other Bedouins crawled into the cave. They found eight tall clay jars. Inside each was a rolled scroll with strange writing. Such scrolls must be worth money, they thought. The Bedouins carried two of the scrolls to a dealer in Bethlehem.

The year was 1947, a dangerous time. War would soon break out between Arabs and Jews. But when Professor Eliezer Sukenik, a Jewish archaeologist, saw a tiny piece of one of the scrolls, he knew he had to see more, even at the risk of his life. One night he came to Arab Bethlehem, to the dealer's house. He carefully unrolled a scroll and read the beautiful Hebrew writing. Suddenly Sukenik realized he was looking at a treasure that had not been read for 2,000 years.

Professor Sukenik bought the scrolls. Later more were bought. They contain the writings of Isaiah and Psalms and more. Desperate Jews had hidden these precious writings from their enemies 2,000 years before. They became a birthday present for the State of Israel, which was established soon after.

But to this day nobody knows what happened to the goat.

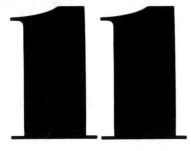

A list of good books

Here's a short list of some of the many good books about Jewish life written for young readers. It was prepared with the help of Marcia Posner, who also prepared a more complete list of Jewish books for young readers, which is available from the

Jewish Book Council
15 East 26th Street
New York, New York 10010.

To receive a current list of books, just write to the Jewish Book Council, or call (212) 532-4949.

BIBLE STORIES

Aratan, Harry. *Two by Two: Favorite Bible Stories.* Rockville, MD: Kar-Ben, 1991, 32 pp. (ages 3–6)

Briefly told Bible stories, accompanied by witty poster art in bright primary colors outlined in black.

Bach, Alice, and Exum, J. Cheryl. *Moses' Ark: Stories from the Bible.* Illustrated by Leo and Diane Dillon. New York: Delacorte Press, 1989, 184 pp. (ages 9–14)

Thirteen Bible stories, sensitively told. Dramatic black and white illustrations.

Brenner, Barbara. *Noah and the Flood.* Illustrated by Annie Mitra. (Bank Street Ready-to-Read, Level 3). New York: Bantam Books/Little Rooster, 1992. 48 pp. (ages 4–8)

Contains a rollicking dialogue by God and chorus. Naif-style illustrations in watercolors edged in white.

Brent, Isabelle. *Noah's Ark.* Illuminated by the author. Boston: Little, Brown, 1992, unpaged. (ages 7–up)

Exquisitely illustrated edition based on Revised English Bible, which does not conflict with the Jewish version of the Noah story.

Chaikin, Miriam. *Children's Bible Stories from Genesis to Daniel.* Illustrated by Yvonne Gilbert. New York: Dial Books, 1993, 94 pp. (ages 6–10)

A master storyteller retells stories from the Bible in simple but lyrical text. Magnificently illustrated in colored pencil.

Gellman, Marc. *Does God Have a Big Toe? Stories About Stories in the Bible.* Illustrated by Oscar de Mejo. New York: Harper & Row, 1989, 88 pp. (ages 9–12)

Original midrashim on Bible tales; sometimes irreverent, but always wise and witty.

Hoffman, Yair. *The World of the Bible for Young Readers.* New York: Viking/Kestrel, 1989, 96 pp. (ages 10–14)

Oversized volume, packed with information about the Hebrews and their neighbors from 2000 B.C.E. to the third century C.E.

Segal, Lore. *From Adam to Moses.* Illustrated by Leonard Baskin. New York: Knopf/Random House, 1987, 144 pp. *The Story of King Saul and King David.* Illustrated. New York: Schocken/Pantheon Books, 1991, 123 pp. Oversized format. (ages 10–16)

Sections of the Bible pertaining to the title characters are translated into beautiful contemporary prose. Illustrated with reproductions.

Williams, Marcia. *Joseph and his Magnificent Coat of Many Colors.* Cambridge, MA: Candlewick Press, 1992, unpaged. (ages 4–8)

Joseph's adventures as a cartoon strip, with dialogue in balloons.

JEWISH HOLIDAYS (younger readers)

Chaikin, Miriam. *Esther.* Illustrated by Vera Rosenberry. Philadelphia: The Jewish Publication Society, 1987, 32 pp. (ages 5–8)

A retelling of the Esther story with exquisite illustrations.

Chaikin, Miriam. *Hanukkah.* Illustrated by Ellen Weiss. New York: Holiday House, 1990, 32 pp. (ages 3–7)

A fine first book that describes the history of the holiday.

Drucker, Malka. *Grandma's Latkes.* Illustrated by Eve Chwast. San Diego: Gulliver/Harcourt Brace Jovanovich, 1992, 32 pp. (ages 3–7)

Grandma tells Molly the story of Hanukkah while they prepare latkes. Unusual woodcuts painted in muted watercolors.

Goldin, Barbara Diamond. *Cakes and Miracles: A Purim Tale.* Illustrated by Erika Weihs. New York: Viking, 1991, 32 pp. (ages 4–8)

An artistic blind boy "sees" in his mind and helps his mother by fashioning fanciful cakes for her to sell at Purim.

Goldin, Barbara Diamond. *Just Enough Is Plenty.* Illustrated by Seymour Chwast. New York; Viking, 1989, 32 pp. (ages 4–8)

A mysterious peddler, invited to join a poor tailor's Hanukkah table, entertains the family with stories and songs.

Goldin, Barbara Diamond. *The Magician's Visit,* from a tale by I. L. Peretz. Illustrated by Robert Andrew Parker. New York: Viking, 1992, 32 pp. (ages 4–8)

A mysterious magician provides a Seder feast for a poor couple. Mystical watercolor illustrations and masterful writing.

Greenberg, Melanie Hope. *Celebrations: Our Jewish Holidays.* Illustrated. Philadelphia: The Jewish Publication Society, 1991, unpaged. (ages 4–7)

Small-scale book describing Jewish holidays, with simple text and tiny illustrations in bright, flat areas of color.

Jaffe, Nina. *In the Month of Kislev: A Story for Hanukkah.* Illustrated by Louise August. New York: Viking, 1992, 32 pp. (ages 6–10)

A poor man tricks a miserly merchant into giving charity during Hanukkah.

Kimmel, Eric A. *The Chanukah Guest.* Illustrated by Giora Carmi. New York: Holiday House, 1988, unpaged. (ages 4–8)

Bubba Brayna mistakes a bear for the rabbi, with hilarious results.

Kimmel, Eric A. *Hershel and the Hanukkah Goblins.* Illustrated by Trina Schart Hyman. New York: Holiday House, 1989, unpaged. (ages 4–8)

Using his wits, Hershel vanquishes the goblins that would extinguish the Hanukkah lights.

Kimmelman, Leslie. *Hanukkah Lights, Hanukkah Nights.* Illustrated by John Himmelman. New York: HarperCollins, 1992, 32 pp. (ages 3–5)

With each night, another candle and custom appears, with the menorah glowing brighter each day.

Manushkin, Fran. *Latkes and Applesauce: A Hanukkah Story.* Illustrated by Robin Spowart. New York: Scholastic, 1990, unpaged. (ages 6–10)

A starving cat and dog, sheltered from a storm during Hanukkah, return the favor.

Modesitt, Jeanne. *Songs of Chanukah.* Illustrated by Robin Spowart. Musical arrangements by Uri Ophir. Boston: Little, Brown, 1992, 32 pp. (ages 6–10)

Songs in English and Hebrew, arranged for two-handed piano, touch on every facet of the holiday.

Nerlove, Miriam. *Hanukkah. Passover.* Both books illustrated by the author. Niles, IL: Albert Whitman, 1989, unpaged. (ages 4–6)

Simple text and illustrations explain the holidays.

Rosen, Michael J. *Elijah's Angel: A Story for Chanukah and Christmas.* Illustrated by Aminah Brenda Lynn Robinson. Harcourt Brace Jovanovich, 1992, 32 pp. (ages 6–10)

A tale of friendship and respect between an African-American barber/woodcarver and a little Jewish boy.

Schotter, Roni. *Hanukkah.* Illustrated by Marilyn Hafner. Boston: Little, Brown/Joy Books, 1990, 32 pp. (ages 6–10)

Image-rich, poetic text describes the meanings and traditions of the holiday as five children celebrate with their family.

Silverman, Maida. *Festival of Esther: The Story of Purim.* Illustrated by Carolyn S. Ewing. New York: Simon & Schuster/Little Simon, 1989, unpaged. (ages 6–10)

Elaborate illustrations in the classical style embellish this simply told story.

Zalben, Jane Breslin. *Beni's First Chanukah* (1988). *Happy Passover, Rosie* (1990). *Leo and Blossom's Sukkah* (1990), and *Goldie's Purim* (1991). Illustrated by the author. New York: Holt, 32 pp. ea. (ages 3–6)

Charming mini-books about a family of bears preparing for Jewish holidays.

JEWISH HOLIDAYS (older readers)

Chaikin, Miriam. *Ask Another Question* (1986). *The Story and Meaning of Passover* (1981). *Light Another Candle: The Story and Meaning of Hanukkah* (1983). *Make Noise, Make Merry: The Story and Meaning of Purim* (1984). *Shake a Palm Branch: The Story and Meaning of Sukkot* (1986). *Sound the Shofar: The Story and Meaning of Rosh Hashanah and Yom Kippur* (1986). New York: Clarion Books, 96 pp. each. (ages 8–12)

The finest books about the holidays for this age range, incorporating meaning, lore, how the holidays originated, and how they are observed by Jews around the world. Written clearly and based on solid research.

Kimmel, Eric A. *Days of Awe: Stories for Rosh Hashanah and Yom Kippur.* Illustrated by Erika Weihs. New York: Viking, 1991, 48 pp. (ages 8–12)

Explanation of the holidays, followed by three tales related to the holiday themes.

Levine, Arthur. *All the Lights in the Night.* Illustrated by James E. Ransome. New York: Tambourine/Morrow, 1991, 32 pp. (ages 8–10)

A small oil lamp with miraculous powers comforts two brothers fleeing to Palestine from Czarist Russia.

Schram, Peninnah and Steven M. Rosman. *Eight Tales for Eight Nights: Stories for Chanukah.* Illustrated by Tsirl Waletzky. Northvale, NJ: Jason Aronson, 1990, 160 pp. (ages 8–12)

Tales highlighting the customs and meaning of Hanukkah around the world and throughout Jewish history.

Sussman, Susan. *Hanukkah: Eight Lights Around the World.* Illustrated by Judith Friedman. Niles, IL: Albert Whitman, 1988, 40 pp. (ages 7–12)

Themes of Hanukkah—freedom, charity, security, and heroism—are integrated in brief stories for each night of Hanukkah.

FICTION (younger readers)

Adler, David A. *The Number on My Grandfather's Arm.* Illustrated with photographs by Rose Eichenbaum. New York: UAHC Press, 1987, 28 pp. (ages 5–9)

In this photo-essay, the narrator gently discloses the story of the Holocaust to his granddaughter when she asks about the numbers on his arm.

Blanc, Esther Silverstein. *Berchick.* Illustrated by Tennessee Dixon. Volcano, CA: Volcano Press, 1989, 32 pp. (ages 7–10)

A Jewish family in the West at the turn of the century adopts an orphaned colt.

Edwards, Michelle. *Chicken Man.* Illustrated. New York: Lothrop, 1991, 32 pp. (ages 5–8)

Because Rody loves his job, others in the kibbutz jealously believe it must be better than theirs—until they try it!

Gilman, Phoebe. *Something from Nothing.* Ontario: North Winds Press/Scholastic, 1992, 32 pp. (ages 4–8)

In this richly illustrated humorous tale set in Eastern Europe, the mice under the floor add to their home with each transformation of Joseph's "little blanket."

Greene, Jacqueline Dembar. *What His Father Did.* Illustrated by John O'Brien. Boston: Houghton Mifflin, 1992, 32 pp. (ages 4–8)

Herschel makes an innkeeper give him dinner by threatening to "do what his father did when not provided dinner."

Hautzig, Esther. *Riches.* Illustrated by Donna Diamond. New York: HarperCollins, 1992, 43 pp. (ages 7–10)

The rabbi's advice about what Samuel should do when he retires is surprising, but it enables him to discover what is truly of value.

Lanton, Sandy. *Daddy's Chair.* Illustrated by Shelly O. Haas. Rockville, MD: Kar-Ben, 1991, unpaged. (ages 5–8)

A child's reaction to his father's death suggests future healing.

Oppenheim, Shulamith Levey. *The Lily Cupboard.* Illustrated by Ronald Himler. New York: Charlotte Zolotow Books/HarperCollins, 1992, 32 pp. (ages 5–9)

Hidden by a Dutch farm family during the Nazi occupation, a little Jewish girl finds comfort in her pet rabbit.

Polacco, Patricia. *The Keeping Quilt.* Illustrated by the author. New York: Simon & Schuster, 1988, 32 pp. (ages 4–8)

A pieced quilt made of fabric from four generations plays an important role in a family's life-cycle events.

Polacco, Patricia. *Mrs. Katz and Tush.* Illustrated by the author. New York: Bantam Books, 1992, 32 pp. (ages 4–8)

A warm Passover story about an elderly Jewish woman, an African-American child, and a cat.

Ross, Lillian Hammer. *Buba Leah and Her Paper Children.* Illustrated by Mary Morgan. Philadelphia: Jewish Publication Society, 1991, 32 pp. (ages 7–10)

Chava discovers the meaning of the "paper children" about whom her great-aunt speaks, when she emigrates to America.

Schwartz, Howard and Rush, Barbara (retellers). *The Sabbath Lion: A Jewish Folktale from Algeria.* Illustrated by Stephen Fieser. New York: HarperCollins, 1992, unpaged. (ages 6–10)

Because of Yosef's piety, the Sabbath Queen sends a great lion to guard and guide him on his journey through the desert on his way to Egypt.

FICTION (older readers)

Banks, Lynne Reid. *One More River.* New York: Morrow, 1992 (Rev. Ed.) 256 pp. (ages 10–up)

Leslie, a spoiled teenager, reluctantly moves with her parents from Canada to an Israeli kibbutz.

Barrie, Barbara. *Lone Star.* New York: Delacorte Press, 1990, 182 pp. (ages 10–14)

When her dysfunctional family moves to largely Christian Corpus Christi, Texas, a young Jewish girl struggles to adjust by over-assimilating.

Baylis-White, Mary. *Sheltering Rebecca.* New York: Dutton/Lodestar, 1991, 91 pp. (ages 8–12)

Friendship between an English girl from a working-class family and a German-Jewish refugee.

Bergman, Tamar. *Along the Tracks.* Translated from the Hebrew by Michael Swirsky. New York: Houghton, 1991, 256 pp. (ages 10–14)

Yankele, separated from his mother and siblings at the age of six, spends years filled with harrowing escapes and adventures searching for them.

Greene, Jacqueline Denbar. *Out of Many Waters.* Walker, 1988, 208 pp. (ages 10–14)

Kidnapped during the Portuguese Inquisition and forced to work for cruel monks in Brazil, two sisters plan their escape.

Herman, Charlotte. *A Summer on Thirteenth Street.* New York: Dutton, 1991, 128 pp. (ages 10–14)

Recaptures the magic of hot summers in the city during the 1940s, when an 11-year-old tomboy feels the first stirrings of love, and, later, the cruelty of death.

Hesse, Karen. *Letters from Rifka.* New York: Holt, 1992, 148 pp. (ages 10–14)

Rifka describes her family's narrow escapes and other adventures. Lively flashes of humorous Yiddish proverbs.

Ish-Kishor, Sulamith. *Our Eddie.* New York: Knopf, 1992 (Reissue), 183 pp. (ages 10–14)

Teenager Eddie is a good boy and a loving son, but he can never please his stern father, a Hebrew school principal.

Kaye, Marilyn. *The Atonement of Mindy Wise.* New York: Harcourt Brace Jovanovich, 1991, 160 pp. (ages 11–14)

During Yom Kippur services, Mindy reflects on the wrong choices she made because of her eagerness for approval from the "in" crowd at school.

Laird, Christa. *Shadow of the Wall.* New York: Greenwillow Books, 1990, 144 pp. (ages 11–16)

Set against the background of Dr. Janusz Korczak's school and orphanage in the Warsaw ghetto.

Lehrman, Robert. *The Store That Mama Built.* New York: Macmillan, 1992, 126 pp. (ages 11–up)

Mama takes charge when Papa dies before he can open a grocery store in a poor black neighborhood.

Levitin, Sonia. *The Return.* New York: Atheneum, 1987, 183 pp. (ages 11–up)

A dramatic novel about an Ethiopian Jewish family's perilous flight to Israel.

Lowry, Lois. *Number the Stars.* Boston: Houghton Mifflin, 1989, 160 pp. (ages 8–12)

A story about friendship, heroic Danish Christians, and frightened children who draw on hidden reserves of courage.

Mayerson, Evelyn Wilde. *The Cat Who Escaped from Steerage: A Bubbemeiser.* New York: Charles Scribner's Sons, 1990, 64 pp. (ages 9–12)

Two irrepressible children and their cat cross the Atlantic.

Morpurgo, Michael. *Waiting for Anya.* New York: Viking, 1991, 172 pp. (ages 8–14)

In an occupied French town during World War II, a village boy, an elderly Christian widow, and her Jewish son-in-law smuggle Jewish children into Spain.

Nixon, Joan Lowry. *Land of Hope.* New York: Bantam Books, 1992, 172 pp. (ages 10–14)

Rebeccah, a 15-year-old, arriving in America in 1902, has to delay her education to work in a sweatshop.

Orlev, Uri. *The Man from the Other Side.* Translated from the Hebrew by Hillel Halkin. Boston: Houghton, 1991, 186 pp. (ages 10–16)

A Polish boy and his stepfather smuggle Jews out of the ghetto.

Pitt, Nancy. *Beyond the High White Wall.* New York: Charles Scribner's Sons, 1986, 135 pp. (ages 10–14)

While trying to bring a murderous Russian peasant to justice in Czarist Russia, a 13-year-old wealthy Jewish girl brings disaster to her family.

Provost, Gary and Gail Levine. *David and Max.* Philadelphia: The Jewish Publication Society, 1988, 180 pp. (ages 8–12)

David helps his grandfather track down a fellow Holocaust survivor.

Sacks, Margaret. *Beyond Safe Boundaries.* New York: Dutton/Lodestar, 1989, 160 pp. (ages 12–up)

A coming-of-age novel that provides an insightful look into Jewish life in South Africa in the 1950s and 1960s.

Segal, Jerry. *The Place Where Nobody Stopped.* Illustrated by Dav Pilkey. New York: Orchard Books/Franklin Watts, 1991, 160 pp. (ages 10–14)

Part historical fiction, part farce, and part folklore about a lonely Russian baker who agrees to hide a Jewish man.

Semel, Nava. *Becoming Gershona.* Translated by Seymour Simckes. New York: Viking, 1990, 153 pp. (ages 10–14)

A pre-teenager in Tel-Aviv discovers her emerging sensuality when a new boy moves into the neighborhood.

Sherman, Eileen Bluestone. *Independence Avenue.* Philadelphia: The Jewish Publication Society, 1990, 164 pp. (ages 10–14)

Adventures of a 14-year-old Russian Jewish boy who immigrated to America in 1907, arriving in Texas rather than Ellis Island.

Vos, Ida. *Hide and Seek.* Translated from the Dutch. Boston: Houghton, 1991, 144 pp. (ages 10–14)

First-person narrative recaptures the tenseness and fear felt when hiding during the Nazi occupation of Holland.

Yolen, Jane. *The Devil's Arithmetic.* New York: Viking/Kestrel, 1988, 160 pp. (ages 10–14)

Hannah, tired of hearing about the Holocaust and her grandfather's ranting against the Nazis, is transported back into the Holocaust. A dramatic fantasy.

Weissenberg, Fran. *The Streets Are Paved with Gold.* Tucson, AZ: Harbinger, 1990, 145 pp. (ages 10–14)

Eighth-grader Deborah worries about how to reconcile life with her traditional Jewish family and her friendships outside the Jewish community. Realistic, lively dialogue.

Zalben, Jane Breslin. *The Fortuneteller in 5B.* New York: Holt, 1991, 144 pp. (ages 9–12)

At first, Allie is suspicious and frightened of the elderly fortune-teller who moves into her apartment house, but later their common experiences and grief help her put the pain from her father's death in perspective.

STORY COLLECTIONS

Geras, Adele. *My Grandmother's Stories.* Illustrated by Jael Jordan. New York: Knopf, 1990, 96 pp. (ages 8–12)

Set in Tel-Aviv, these are stories within stories, some traditional and others from the author's grandmother's Russian girlhood.

Gold, Sharlya, and Mishael Maswari Caspi. *The Answered Prayer and Other Yemenite Folktales.* Illustrated by Marjory Wunsch. Philadelphia: The Jewish Publication Society, 1990, 80 pp. (ages 8–12)

A collection of tales about tricksters and pashas.

Goldin, Barbara Diamond. *A Child's Book of Midrash: 52 Jewish Stories from the Sages.* Northvale, NJ: Jason Aronson, 1990, 110 pp. (ages 9–14)

Stories from rabbinic literature that illuminate Jewish ethical and moral values, gracefully adapted for children.

Kimmel, Eric A. *The Spotted Pony: A Collection of Hanukkah Stories.* Illustrated by Leonard Everett Fisher. New York: Holiday House, 1992, 70 pp. (ages 7–11)

A story for each night of Hanukkah, with a brief shammes story preceding each. Rich in plot, character, and tradition.

Patterson, Jose. *Angels, Prophets, Rabbis and Kings from the Stories of the Jewish People.* Illustrated by Claire Bushe. New York: Peter Bedrick Books/Blackie, 1991, 144 pp. (ages 7–10)

A treasury of Jewish tales grouped into 13 sections, prefaced by an interpretation and source of each tale.

Schwartz, Howard, and Barbara Rush. *The Diamond Tree: Jewish Tales from Around the World.* Illustrated by Uri Shulevitz. New York: HarperCollins, 1991, 120 pp. (ages 7–10)

Fifteen brief tales are gracefully retold, with introductions explaining unfamiliar ideas and characters.

NON-FICTION

Brenner, Barbara. *If You Were There in 1492.* New York: Bradbury Press, 1991, 112 pp. (ages 8–12)

Highlights pivotal events of 1492.

Chaikin, Miriam. *A Nightmare in History: the Holocaust 1933–1945.* New York: Clarion Books, 1992, 150 pp. (ages 10–14)

Excellent, detailed history containing eyewitness accounts, statistics, maps, photos, chronology, and commentary.

Chaikin, Miriam. *Menorahs, Mezuzas and Other Jewish Symbols.* Illustrated by Erika Weihs. New York: Clarion Books, 1990, 102 pp. (ages 8–12)

Explains the meaning of symbols in Jewish life.

Edwards, Michelle. *Alef-Bet: A Hebrew Alphabet Book.* New York: UAHC Press, 1992, 32 pp. (ages 4–8)

Features an engaging family and charming illustrations.

Freedman, Rabbi E. B., Jan Greenberg, and Karen Katz. *What Does Being Jewish Mean? Read-Aloud Responses to Questions Jewish Children Ask About History, Culture, and Religion.* New York: Prentice-Hall Press, 1991, 136 pp. (ages 8–13; parents)

Answers to children's most-asked questions about Judaism, arranged in categories.

Gellman, Marc, and Thomas Hartman. *Where Does God Live? A Book for Parents and Kids with Questions About God.* New York: Triumph/Gleneida, 1991, 144 pp. (ages 8–up; parents with children ages 6–up)

A rabbi and Roman Catholic priest offer answers to children's most frequently asked questions about God.

Kolatch, Alfred J. *The Jewish Child's First Book of Why.* Illustrated by Harry Araten. Queens Village, NY: Jonathan David, 1992, 32 pp. (ages 6–10)

Children's version of the acclaimed Jewish Book of Why.

Resnick, Abraham. *The Holocaust* (Overview Series). San Diego, CA: Lucent, 1991, 128 pp. (ages 9–14)

A solid history of the Holocaust and the establishment of Israel.

Rogasky, Barbara. *Smoke and Ashes: The Story of the Holocaust.* New York: Holiday House, 1988, 187 pp. (ages 11–16)

Excellent, detailed history with large format and many photos, eyewitness accounts, chronology, commentary.

Rosenblum, Richard. *Journey to the Golden Land.* Illustrated. Philadelphia: The Jewish Publication Society, 1992, unpaged. (ages 6–10)

After leaving Czarist Russia, Benjamin and his family undergo a difficult ocean crossing and arrive at Ellis Island to start a new life in America.

Sasso, Sandy Eisenberg. *God's Paintbrush.* Illustrated by Annette Comptom. Woodstock, VT: Jewish Lights, 1992. 32 pp. (ages 5–9)

Children are encouraged to imagine God through nature, thoughts, and deeds.

Zakon, Miriam. *The Kids' Kosher Cookbook.* Illustrated and designed by Lori Feld and Diane Liff. Spring Valley, New York: Targum/Feldheim, 1991, 72 pp. (ages 7–10)

Cheerfully designed and illustrated.

BIOGRAPHIES AND MEMOIRS

Behrman, Carol H. *Fiddler to the World: The Inspiring Life of Itzhak Perlman.* Crozet, VA: Betterway, 1992, 128 pp. (ages 10–14)

The essence of Itzhak Perlman—his talent, sweetness, sense of humor, and menschlekeit—comes through in this illustrated biography.

Berkow, Ira. *Hank Greenberg: Hall-of-Fame Slugger.* Illustrated by Mick Ellison (Young Biography Series). Philadelphia: The Jewish Publication Society, 1991, 108 pp. (ages 10–14)

An exceptional biography of the first Jewish athlete to be elected to the Baseball Hall of Fame.

Drucker, Malka. *Eliezer Ben-Yehuda: The Father of Modern Hebrew.* Illustrated with photos. New York: Dutton/Lodestar, 1987, 128 pp. (ages 10–14)

How Ben-Yehuda overcame all obstacles to fulfill his vision of a one-language, cohesive country instead of a "Tower of Babel."

Drucker, Olga Levy. *Kindertransport.* New York: Holt, 1992, 146 pp. (ages 10–14)

When her parents recognized what the Third Reich meant for Jews in Germany, the author was sent to England, where she spent ten difficult years.

Finkelstein, Norman H. *Captain of Innocence: France and the Dreyfus Affair.* Illustrated. New York: Putnam, 1991. 160 pp. (ages 12–up)

A gripping account of a time of madness in 19th century France.

Finkelstein, Norman H. *Theodore Herzl.* New York: Franklin Watts, 1987, 128 pp. (ages 10–14)

A compelling portrait of Herzl, who—shocked by the Dreyfus trial—formulated his dream of a homeland for the Jews.

Hautzig, Esther. *The Endless Steppe: Growing Up in Siberia.* New York: HarperCollins, 1992, 256 pp. (ages 10–14)

The author recounts the difficult years of exile in Siberia that saved her parents and herself from the death camps.

Henry, Sondra, and Emily Taitz. *Everyone Wears His Name: A Biography of Levi Strauss.* Minneapolis, MN: Dillon, 1990, 128 pp. (ages 10–14)

The best of three available biographies. Explains Levi Strauss's involvement in the Jewish community.

Krantz, Hazel. *Daughter of My People: Henrietta Szold and Hadassah.* New York: Dutton/Lodestar, 1987, 117 pp. (ages 10–14)

A brilliant student, and later an editor at The Jewish Publication Society. An insightful, exciting biography.

Linnéa, Sharon. *Raoul Wallenberg: The Man Who Stopped Death.* Illustrated with photographs. Philadelphia: The Jewish Publication Society, 1993, 168 pp. (ages 12–up).

A dramatic biography of the Swedish diplomat who saved more than 100,000 Jews from the Nazis, then disappeared in the final days of World War II.

Perl, Lila. *Molly Picon: A Gift of Laughter.* Illustrated by Donna Ruff. Philadelphia: The Jewish Publication Society, 1990, 66 pp. (ages 9–12)

A sensitive portrayal of the star from early childhood through her career and marriage.

Roth-Hano, Renee. *Touch Wood: A Girlhood in Occupied France.* New York: Four Winds Press, 1988, 256 pp. (ages 11–15)

A diary of the years the author and her two sisters spent in a French convent hiding from the Nazis.

Strom, Yale. *A Tree Still Stands: Jewish Youth in Eastern Europe Today.* Illustrated with photographs by the author. Introduction by Sonia Levitin. New York: Philomel Books, 1990, 111 pp. (ages 12–15)

Interviews with children with at least one parent or grandparent who survived the Holocaust.

What did people do on long winter evenings before they had television, radio, or movies? They sat around the fireplace and told stories. Grandparents remembered stories they had heard long before and told them to their grandchildren. Peddlers and travelers wandering from town to town stopped in for a hot meal and told stories about faraway places. Teachers and rabbis taught lessons by telling them as stories.

In the days before newspapers and jet planes, travelers' tales were the best way to find out about the world. When a traveler came to a small town before the Sabbath, he went straight to the synagogue. Somebody was sure to invite him home for a Sabbath meal, and over the chicken soup and gefilte fish he would answer questions about the great outside world with a few facts and a lot of imagination. But not many travelers could have told stories as fantastic as two that are retold in this chapter, "The Ten Lost Tribes" and "The Guest."

Life was dangerous for small communities of Jews surrounded by unfriendly neighbors. They were often attacked by mobs of anti-Semites. People felt helpless and prayed that the Messiah would come quickly to save them. If not the Messiah, then at least a superhero who could smash their enemies. "The Golem of Prague," another story retold in this chapter, tells of a supercreature who answered their prayers.

When there was no superman to save them, the Jews could only laugh at their troubles and dangers. Folk tales about a wacky town called Chelm made people laugh until they cried. There are several Chelm stories in this chapter. The Yiddish writer Sholom Aleichem also wrote stories that made people laugh and cry at the same time. *Fiddler on the Roof,* an American musical, is based on his stories.

Prayer, study, and trying to earn a living kept people busy. A religious group called Hasidim felt this was a dull, cold way to live. "We need more joy in God and in His world, not more study," they said. They worshiped God with singing, dancing, and devotion to their rabbis. Isaac Leib Peretz wrote many stores about Hasidim. One of them, "Maybe Even Higher," is retold here. There are also two stories about Israel during its early days as an independent state and two stories about Jewish American children.

People don't tell stories around the fireplace very much these days. But the storytellers are still hard at work. You'll find their new and old stories about Jewish life at your bookstore and library. Check the list in chapter 11 for some good titles.

WHEN Solomon became king of Israel, God said to him, "Choose whatever you want and I will give it to you."

"I don't want wealth or glory," said Solomon. "I only want wisdom."

God granted his request. Soon after, Solomon needed to use all his wisdom to decide a difficult case.

Two women came before him carrying a baby between them.

Solomon and the Baby
a story from the Bible

"We live in the same house," said one of the women, "and each of us had a baby. A few nights ago that woman's baby died." She pointed to her neighbor. "She tiptoed to my bed, took my baby away, and put her dead child next to me."

"No, no, I did not," cried the other. "It was *your* baby that died. This child is mine!"

"He's mine! Give him to me," shouted the first woman.

"No, he's my baby," the other cried.

The baby started to wail.

King Solomon raised his scepter. "Unsheath your sword," he commanded his guard. "Take the baby from these women. Since we can't tell who is the true mother, you will cut the baby in two and give each woman half."

The guard lifted his sword over the crying baby. One of the women stepped back and waited. But the other fell to the ground before the king. "No, don't kill the child," she sobbed. "Better that she should have him than that he should die."

"Put down the sword," the king ordered his guard. "The woman who could not let the baby be killed is the true mother. Give the child to her."

Jonah's Journey

a story from the Bible and Midrash

GOD told the prophet Jonah to go to Nineveh and tell the people there to turn from their evil ways and follow God's laws.

Jonah did not want to go to Nineveh. He tried to escape from God by sailing away in a ship. A terrible storm broke out at sea. The ship was thrown up and smashed down by the waves until it was about to sink.

"The gods have sent the storm—they must be angry at one of us," cried the passengers. They drew lots to see who was guilty. The lot fell on Jonah, and they tossed him overboard. Immediately the storm ended.

A large fish that was swimming beside the ship gulped down the frightened prophet. To his surprise, Jonah found the inside of the fish very comfortable. He could look out through its eyes and see the other fish and plants and even wrecked ships lying on the sea bottom. The belly of the fish was warm and well lit by layers of sparkling diamonds that it had swallowed.

For three days the fish took Jonah on a sightseeing trip through the oceans of the world. Jonah was so busy looking around that he forgot God was angry at him and that he was being punished. Suddenly a giant fish, larger than Jonah's, came racing after them. She was a mother fish, carrying a load of 365,000 young ones. God had sent her to take Jonah away from his friendly host.

Against his will, Jonah had to move to the belly of the bigger fish. His new quarters were very fishy smelling and very crowded with the 365,000 babies. He soon remembered God and began to cry and pray, "All right God, I give up, I'll go to Nineveh. Just get me out of this fish!"

God ordered the fish to spew Jonah out onto the shore. The prophet dried himself off, and without wasting a minute, made his way to the city of Nineveh.

"Listen to the word of the Lord," he cried out at the city gates. "You will all die because of your evil deeds."

The king of Nineveh heard Jonah's warning. He ordered his people to fast and repent for three days. When God saw that the people of Nineveh were trying to change their evil ways, He pitied them and pardoned them for their sins.

Then Jonah begged God also to pardon him for disobeying His word and running away. And God pardoned Jonah too.

The Best Caretakers

a biblical legend

ACCORDING to tradition, the prophet Elijah never died. He still roams the world and tries to help people. One day he saw a poor farmer working in the field. "Farmer," said Elijah, "God will grant you seven good years. Do you want them now or in the last years of your life?"

The farmer was frightened. He didn't know if Elijah was a wizard or a real messenger from God. He rushed home and told his wife what had happened.

"We are poor, and we have nothing to lose. Ask for the seven years now," she said. The farmer returned to the field and answered Elijah as his wife had suggested.

"Return home," said the prophet. "Good fortune has come to you."

As he turned toward home the farmer's children came running to meet him. "Papa, papa," they cried, "we were digging in the yard and found a giant box filled with gold and silver."

That night, as the family sat counting the treasure, the farmer's wife said, "The stranger promised that we will have seven years of prosperity. Let's share our good luck with the poor and needy."

And so they did. For the next seven years the farmer and his wife helped everyone who was in need.

After seven years Elijah came to the farmer again. "I am here to take back what I gave you," he said.

"Let me go and tell my wife what is to happen before I return it to you," said the farmer. He hurried home and told his wife that the messenger had come back to take the treasure.

"Tell this to the messenger," she advised: "If you can find anyone who will take better care of this gift than we have, we will gladly give it back to you."

When the man repeated his wife's words to Elijah, the prophet smiled. "Truly, you have cared for the treasure well," he said. "You may keep it."

The Ten Lost Tribes

told by

Eldad the Danite in 883 C.E.

Jews were scattered from one end of the world to the other after they left the Land of Israel. Merchants, rabbis, messengers, and beggars traveled from community to community carrying news, letters, and stories. But some Jews disappeared from sight. They were called the Ten Lost Tribes of Israel. Where could they be, people wondered. They listened eagerly as travelers told tales of the golden, hidden kingdom of the Ten Lost Tribes.

The Guest

by Sholom Aleichem

translated from Yiddish by Chaya M. Burstein

We had such a guest for Passover, such a guest as nobody had before. His eyes sparkled above rosy cheeks and a round, gray beard. He wore a fur hat and a robe striped blue, yellow, and red. And he didn't speak Yiddish, only a strange Hebrew that was full of ah-ah-ah's.

I am puffed up with pride as I follow my father and his guest home from the synagogue. All my friends watch me with envy.

My father offers the guest the chair with the cushion, and my mother and Rikel the maid stare at him as though he is something more than human. When it is time to say *kiddush* over the wine, my father and the guest hold a Hebrew conversation.

I am proud to find that I understand nearly every word.

My father: *Nu?* (That means, "Won't you make the *kiddush?*")

The guest: *Nu, nu.* ("Please, *you* make it.")

My father: *Nu-ah?* ("Why not you?")

The guest: *Ah-nu?* ("Why not *you?*")

My father: *Ee-ah.* ("You first.")

The guest: *Ah-ee* ("*You* first.")

My father: *Eh-ah-ee* ("I beg you to make it.")

The guest: *Ee-ah-eh* ("I beg *you* to make it.")

My father: *Ee-eh-ah-nu?* ("Why shouldn't *you* make it?")

The guest: *Eh-ah-eh-nu-nu.* ("Well, if you really want me to, I'll do it.")

We finish the first part of the *seder*. While my mother and Rikel the maid serve the fish, my father asks the guest questions. What is your name? Where do you come from? As the guest answers, my father translates for us. My mother is overcome with everything she hears, and so is Rikel the maid.

No wonder! It's not everyday that a person comes from a land 2,000 miles away, beyond seven seas, a huge desert, and a mountain whose top reaches the clouds and is covered with ice. The land itself is like a Garden of Eden, filled with spices, herbs, and every kind of fruit. The houses have silver roofs and golden furniture. (The guest looks at our silver spoons, forks, and knives.) Pearls and diamonds clutter the streets. Nobody even bothers to pick them up. (He looks at my mother's necklace and holiday earrings.)

The guest tells us more and more thrilling things about his land. The country belongs to the Jews, he says. They have a king who rides in a golden carriage pulled by six fiery horses. There is a huge temple with an altar and golden vessels and Levites who sing during the services, just as we used to have in the days of Solomon.

As I listen I feel a great desire to visit that wonderful land. I'll speak to our guest secretly and beg him to take me back with him. He'll surely do it. He is such a kind, friendly man. He looks at everyone, even Rikel the maid, in such a friendly way.

That night I dream about the guest. I dream that I climb the mountains and reach his land. Diamonds and pearls are everyplace. I stuff and stuff and stuff them in my pockets, and still there is room for more. Then I dream of the beautiful temple. I hear the Levites singing and want to go inside, but I can't—something is pulling me back. I toss and turn.

I wake and see my mother and father standing there, pale and half-dressed. Something terrible has happened. Our guest has disappeared. And a lot of things have disappeared with him —the silverware, my mother's jewelry . . . and Rikel the maid.

Tears filled my eyes. Not because of the silverware or the jewelry. And not because of Rikel the maid — good riddance! But because of the rich, happy land, because of the temple and the Levites, because of all the beautiful things that have been taken from me.

I turn my face to the wall and cry.

In the beginning God made the world and all living things. Then he filled two sacks with souls, one with brainy souls and one with foolish souls, and sent an angel out to spread them around. The angel flapped along tossing out souls like grass seed until he reached the town of Chelm. There, one of the sacks caught on the pointy tip of a mountain and ripped open. All the souls poured out on the same spot, on the little town of Chelm. Historians did not record which sack ripped open—the sack of brainy souls or the sack of foolish souls. You'll have to read these stories and decide for yourself.

The Wise People of Chelm

folk tales from Eastern Europe

THE tailors of Chelm were very busy before Passover. All the mothers brought all their children to be measured for new holiday clothing. Leah the fishseller was waiting impatiently with her flock while Hannah's daughter was being measured.

"Leave plenty of material so she shouldn't outgrow the new dress by Shavuot," said Hannah.

"Certainly, certainly," the tailor nodded, "but where should I leave it, at the bottom or at the top? From which end does your daughter grow?"

Hannah looked at the little girl carefully. "I think she grows from the bottom," she said. "When you made this skirt it was so long it dragged on the ground, and now it's at her knees."

"Nonsense," Leah interrupted, "it's the other way around. Children grow from the top. Just look here at my four children. Their feet are evenly on the ground, but on top they're each a different size."

CHELM was a poor town. There was no money to fix the leaky synagogue roof or to buy a stove for the bathhouse or to make a proper wedding for orphan girls. The elders tugged their beards and looked up to heaven for a suggestion.

"Aha!" cried the wisest elder, "heaven just gave me a fantastic idea." He pointed to the thin sliver of the moon in the sky. "Each month religious Jews must bless the new moon, right?"

"Right."

"In two weeks, when the moon is fat and round, we will capture it. We'll lock it up safely and wait. When the new month begins the moon won't appear because it will be down here in Chelm. Jews from everywhere will have to come to us to be able to bless the new moon. We'll charge each Jew a penny or two, and then we'll have plenty of money."

"Brilliant! But how can we capture the moon?" the other elders asked.

"We'll nail together all the ladders in Chelm and climb up to the moon and pull it down," said the wisest elder.

"No, no. Somebody might fall and get hurt, heaven forbid," said the rabbi. "Let's make the moon come to us. We'll scrub out our biggest herring barrel, fill it with water and put it in the market-place. As the moon passes over, it will dip into the barrel. At that moment we'll cover the barrel tightly and capture the moon."

The plan worked perfectly. The moment the moon was reflected in the water of the barrel they slammed on the cover. Then the Chelmites waited.

But when the month ended the out-of-town Jews didn't come running. In fact, the people of Chelm heard that Jews were blessing the new moon just as if it were still up in the sky.

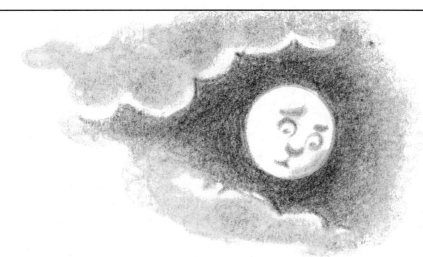

"Pull out the barrel," ordered the rabbi. "We must get to the bottom of this."

Everybody gathered around. The rabbi lifted the cover slowly, slowly . . . and found that the moon was gone!

"A thief stole the moon!" cried the Chelmites.

"We learned our lesson," the elders said. "The next time we capture the moon we'll watch it day and night so that nobody will be able to steal it."

THE most outstanding Chelmite of all was the rabbi. He could answer the deepest, most difficult questions with perfect logic. And the people of Chelm loved to ask deep questions.

On a dark, moonless night the town's only bathhouse caught fire. The townspeople rushed out to pass buckets of water from the well to put out the fire.

"Rabbi, Rabbi, how will we bathe for the Sabbath?" they cried as they worked. "How could the Good Lord let such a terrible fire happen?"

The rabbi's wisdom didn't fail him. "Don't be ungrateful to God," he panted. "He created the fire for our benefit. If it weren't for the light of the fire, how could we see to pass the water buckets on such a dark night?"

Luckily for the United States, a few Chelmites crossed the ocean and settled here. Even in America they did not change. Once a Chelmite, always a Chelmite.

AN American great-grandson of Chelm decided to become an astronaut.

"Why?" asked his worried mother.

"Because I want to land on the sun," said the astronaut.

"*Oy vay,* you'll burn your feet. The sun is hot!" cried the mother.

"Don't worry, Ma," he said impatiently. "I'm no dummy—I'll land at night."

The Golem of Prague

a legend of the Middle Ages

THE mob raced through the streets of the Prague Ghetto, smashing everything in its way and yelling, "Kill the murderers of our children! Death to the Jews!"

In the shuttered synagogue Rabbi Loew bowed his head and prayed, "Please God, show me how to save my people. How can I prove to the Christians that we don't use the blood of their children to make *matzah?*"

Golden letters suddenly danced in the darkness before his eyes.

Rabbi Loew whispered the words: "Create . . . a Golem . . . of . . . clay . . . to destroy . . . the enemies of Israel!"

Before dawn the rabbi and two helpers crept through the empty streets to the river bank. On the shore they shaped the huge figure of a man out of clay. Seven times they walked around it reciting mysterious prayers. As the sky brightened, the three men recited these final words: "And God breathed into his nostrils the breath of life."

The great figure trembled and stood up.

Quickly the helpers dressed the creature while Rabbi Loew spoke to him. "Golem," he said, "you have been created to protect the Jews. I will tell you what you must do, and you must obey me!"

From that morning on the Golem roamed through the ghetto. He drove off thieves and attackers, and he searched every wagon that came into the ghetto. On the very next Passover the Golem found the body of a little boy under the straw of a farmer's wagon. The body was to be left near a Jewish home so that the Jews could be accused of murder. But the Golem lifted the kicking, screaming farmer, tied him up, and dragged him and his wagon to the City Hall.

Each year the Golem grew stronger. The enemies of the Jews were terrified. The attacks and blood libels ended. The ghetto was safe again. But the giant Golem still roamed the streets hunting for enemies. People ran when they saw him coming, and he lumbered after them crushing fences and carts and trees.

"Stop him!" the people cried to Rabbi Loew.

Sadly the rabbi went out to face the Golem. The creature towered over him and raised its fists.

"You must obey me," commanded Rabbi Loew, "because my prayers gave you life! Tonight you must go up to the attic of the synagogue to sleep."

The Golem stared silently into the rabbi's eyes, then dropped his fists and turned away.

At midnight the rabbi and his helpers climbed up to the attic. Seven times they walked around the Golem's huge body and recited mysterious prayers. On the last word the Golem reared up, then fell back—a heap of clay.

The men wrapped prayer shawls around the figure and covered it with old prayer books. A week later Rabbi Loew proclaimed, "Nobody may ever again go up to the synagogue attic."

Nobody ever has. Some say the Golem is still up there waiting to be called to help when new troubles arise for the Jewish people.

A Rabbi, a Genius

a folk tale

JACOB the tailor lived in a house so small that his five children shared one bed in the bedroom and he and his wife, Sarah, slept in the kitchen. Their clothing hung on lines strung across the room. When Sarah cooked supper the long underwear kept dipping into the soup. When she swept she tripped over boots and children.

Before Passover Jacob brought the special dishes and pots down from the eaves, and the house became more crowded than ever. Sarah threw down her broom and yelled, "Jacob, do something! This house is too small for Passover."

The tailor ran to the rabbi. "My wife says our house is too small for Passover," he cried. "What should I do?"

"Bring your two goats into the house," said the rabbi.

The goats clattered in, climbed on the beds, and ate the long underwear.

"Help!" Jacob yelled, running back to the rabbi. "Now the house is even smaller. What should I do?"

"Bring in your rooster and eight chickens and four geese," ordered the rabbi.

"*Koo-koo-ree-koo!*" crowed the rooster from atop the clothes-

line. *"Meh-eh-eh,"* answered the goats. And the chickens and geese clucked and gabbled and nipped the children and laid eggs in the boots.

"Oy vay!" Jacob put his fingers in his ears and ran to the rabbi again. "The house is smaller than ever. NOW what should I do?"

"Now," said the rabbi, "take out the goats, the rooster and chickens, and the geese."

"Shoo, shoo, scat, out!" Jacob and Sarah and the children chased all their guests out into the yard. Then they shut the door and turned around and looked.

"Our rabbi, long may he live, is a miracle worker, a genius!" cried Sarah. "Now the house is big enough for us, and even big enough to invite company for the *seder.*"

Maybe Even Higher

from a story by I. L. Peretz

EVERY year at *Seliḥot* time, just before Rosh Ha-Shanah, the Rabbi of Nemirov would disappear. The townspeople did not worry. They said, "Instead of praying in the synagogue our rabbi goes right up to heaven to talk to God."

One autumn a stranger arrived in town. "To heaven?" he sneered when he heard the story. "What nonsense! Even Moses couldn't get into heaven while he was alive." He decided to follow the rabbi and see where he really went.

On the evening of *Seliḥot* the stranger stole into the rabbi's house and hid under his bed. After a while the rabbi climbed into bed. He tossed and turned and sighed. The stranger began to worry. Maybe the townspeople were right. The rabbi might be praying and preparing to go up to heaven and argue for his people. He got goose bumps and began to shiver, but he wouldn't budge.

In the middle of the night the other townspeople got up and went to the synagogue for the special *Seliḥot* prayer. But the rabbi and the stranger just tossed and turned, one *on* the bed and one *under* the bed. Finally, at dawn, the rabbi got out of bed and put on work clothes and heavy boots. He tucked an axe into his belt and went out. The stranger tiptoed after him.

They went into the dark woods at the edge of town. The rabbi pulled out his axe and chopped down a tree. Then he cut it into small pieces, tied them together, and carried them back to town. The puzzled stranger followed.

At a tumbledown little house the rabbi stopped and knocked on the door.

"Who's there?" a weak voice asked.

"The woodcutter," he answered, "I have wood to warm your house."

"I'm poor and sick. I have no money to pay you," the voice answered.

The rabbi pushed open the door and carried in the wood. "You'll pay some other time," he said. The stranger peeked in after him and saw a small, dark room. A woman lay on a bed in the corner. "I'll never be able to pay you," she groaned.

"Foolish woman," said the rabbi, "I trust you. I believe that you will pay me back. And you must trust your God. He is great and powerful and He will help you."

"But I'm too sick to light the fire," the woman sighed.

"I'll light it," said the rabbi.

As he put the wood into the stove he said the first part of his prayers. As he started the fire he said the second part. And when the stove was hot he recited the third part and shut the door.

After that morning the stranger became a follower of the Rabbi of Nemirov. When the townspeople told how their rabbi went up to heaven before Rosh Ha-Shanah, the stranger would nod and say, "Maybe even higher."

IT happened at the beginning of May 1948 when the British were preparing to leave the country. To the east of our kibbutz there still remained a camp with British soldiers. To the west there were little Arab villages whose orange groves were beside our own.

In our grove, life continued as usual. There, among the trees, three of us worked together, doing the most necessary summer tasks. Eli and Moshe were moving the pipes which watered the grove, and I was pruning the dry branches.

On the morning of the day I am going to describe, we ate our breakfast as usual. We made a salad, fried eggs, and brewed very strong coffee. Then at the end of the meal, before each went on his way, Moshe suddenly told me with half a smile:

"Don't forget to take your gun and the hand grenades."

"I won't forget," I answered.

"And if you happen to come across the enemy, don't ask *him* to pull the trigger . . ."

I tried hard to smile, but did not succeed very well. I did not like the conversation, and I did not like to wear the grenade-belt, nor the gun. The noise of the last hand grenade practice still echoed in my ears. But I faithfully obeyed Moshe's order.

The part of the grove where I was to work that day was far off from the kibbutz, close to the road leading to the British camp. Somehow I had never paid much attention to it, but now, suddenly, I saw that the farther north I went, the farther south my friends went. There were many, many trees between us, and the days were days of fear and worry. In almost every corner of the country Jews and Arabs were fighting, even as our "referees" were getting ready to leave us. There was a feeling of war everywhere, and danger seemed to hide behind every bush.

I reached the trees I still had left to prune. The time passed slowly and I began to feel bored. I knew that Moshe and Eli were placing the water pipes at the other end of the grove, moving farther and farther from me. Sometime later I glanced at my watch: eleven o'clock. In another hour we were to meet in the well-shed and have our lunch together.

I was working, working and singing in a whisper. Then all of a sudden I saw them: three men coming in the direction of our grove! They were moving slowly, looking about carefully as they went. I was in the fourth row from the road, and the men were already at the first row. What should I do? I held my breath. The three were getting

When Pruning Shears Shoot

by Sara Eshel

translated from the Hebrew

closer. Then they disappeared. The trees were hiding them. The trees were also hiding me! I didn't move. *I'll wait,* I thought. *This isn't happening. Perhaps I am dreaming? Should I run to the shed . . . and what if they come after me? They are three and I am alone.* I was well-covered by the grapefruit tree, which I was pruning. Nothing moved. I could not see the men—it was as if the earth had swallowed them.

Perhaps it was only a vision. I opened the pruning shears again and quickly started cutting, cutting with speed, and each falling branch made a terrible noise. Suddenly, one of the men got up and looked straight at me with wide eyes, his gaze falling on my sharp pruning shears gleaming in the sun. . . . A mighty yell escaped him and all three ran away as fast as they could.

When I didn't arrive on time for lunch, Moshe and Eli came to look for me and we met halfway. When I told them what had happened, they asked me to show them exactly where I had seen the three men. I led them to the end of the grove. There, above the water-canal, which was full to the brim, we saw some military clothes scattered about. "Ah," said Eli, "They were probably hot soldiers who came to have a quiet bath."

"Did you open fire?" asked Moshe.

"No," I answered calmly, "I opened my pruning shears."

Felicia to Felicia
by Terri Beverly Bernstein

IT was often hard for Felicia Weissman to be Jewish. So hard that usually she pretended she wasn't. On holidays she went to services because Mom and Dad went. Other times she tried to forget. It was painful. It wasn't important to her, and besides, none of her friends were Jewish. As for cousins and other relatives, she had none.

Felicia's parents had come to America after World War II. They had been in Auschwitz, and somehow they survived. When Felicia was very young she realized that all her aunts, uncles, cousins, and grandparents were dead because of the Nazis and because they were Jews. On holidays and birthdays, family came to visit all her friends. No one came to see Felicia because no one was alive to come. There was only Tante Gretel in England, Dad's aunt. So being Jewish meant pain and death, but most of all loneliness, to Felicia.

Felicia had never met Tante Gretel and never expected to. But one night at dinner Dad announced that she was coming in July.

"Landing at Philadelphia Airport," he said.

The next weeks were spent in endless discussion of where she'd be most comfortable and what she'd like to eat.

"She's not that old and hard to please, is she?" cried Felicia.

"No," Mom agreed. "But she is over seventy. She isn't well, and she is used to Austrian food and friends, I think. We want to make her comfortable here."

Felicia shivered. She thought of ghettos and accents and poverty and persecution back in Austria. She did not look forward to meeting Tante Gretel.

When Tante Gretel got off the plane, Dad pointed her out.

"There. In the blue coat."

She was an old lady, but not that old, and not hardly the wrinkled crone Felicia expected. Her short hair was brown, sprinkled with gray. She was only a bit stooped and nicely dressed. When she hugged Felicia she was not frail and sagging, and although she had an Austrian accent, she spoke English as well as Dad did. In fact, it sounded nice. On her arm Felicia saw the familiar series of black numbers burnt into her skin. Tante Gretel, too, had survived the concentration camps. And around her neck she wore a little Star of David.

"So this is Felicia!" She smiled, but there was a sadness in her clear brown eyes. "How much you look like your grandmother, my dear sister."

Felicia turned away. She was not sure why, but she felt hurt and perhaps even a little embarrassed.

Tante Gretel settled in with no fuss, not at all like an old European lady of seventy. As Felicia passed her aunt's room on the way to bed, Tante Gretel called her in.

"Felicia, dear! Come in a minute."

She stepped in. Tante Gretel wore a light blue bathrobe and was unpacking her suitcase.

"I wanted to get to know my great-niece! Sit down, darling"

Felicia sat, stiff and awkward.

"I have something for you."

Tante Gretel pressed a piece of cardboard into Felicia's hand. When she looked at it, Felicia saw herself in the picture. The hair was different, fixed in old-style waves, and the young woman wore a silk dress with button sleeves. The picture was all in gloomy old brown tones—but it was Felicia's own face.

"Your grandmother," Tante Gretel said softly. "My sister Felicia. You were named for her, you know. That's the only picture that survived. I must show it to your father. But it's for you to keep. She would have wanted you to have it."

Felicia stared at the picture.

"I wish she could have seen you, darling. Known you."

"I—I wish I had known her."

Tante Gretel sighed. She fingered the numbers burnt into her arm.

"Life is hard . . . it hurts, sometimes. But it carries on—that's what children are for, no? To carry on for us and keep up our old ways—to keep our people alive as we add to what was done in the past. It's an endless chain. Felicia to Felicia, no?" She hugged Felicia. "You carry on for your grandmother and for yourself and for all of us . . . But enough of me! I babble like an old woman. Tell me about you, about school!"

School and friends suddenly didn't seem that important. Not important like the picture in her hand. Not important like the Sabbath candles she helped her mother light for the first time that Friday night. She lit them to carry on for her grandmother, and that was important.

Keren Kayemet (Jewish National Fund) was founded in 1901 to purchase and develop land for Israel.

Nahalat Goldstein

adapted from a Hebrew play by Yehuda Haezrahi

NATAN and Zvi of Kibbutz Ramat Dan were riding a tractor toward the south field when they first saw the old man and his wife. The man was pointing a rifle at the two kibbutzniks.

"What do you want with us?" Natan asked.

"I want my land. That's all."

"Now listen, Mr. and Mrs. . . . ."

"Goldstein. Meir and Rivke Goldstein, if you please," the old man's wife said politely.

"Mr. and Mrs. Goldstein, *boker tov,* good morning. There must be some mistake. This land is to be Ramat Dan's wheat field."

"Oh no it's not. No one puts wheat on my land. Only trees will be planted here. This is *Nahalat Goldstein—The Goldstein Estate.*"

It was then that the couple stepped aside so that the kibbutzniks could see the sign in blue paint on a white board:

NAHALAT GOLDSTEIN

"Look, Mr. Goldstein. There must be some mistake."

"There's no mistake. I am Meir Goldstein and here is a certificate from the Keren Kayemet. You see, it says here that a piece of land, 20 dunam, on the left shore of the wadi near Ramat Dan, is to be known as *Nahalat Goldstein.*"

Natan and Zvi looked at the certificate.

"But this can't be," Natan said. "This land belongs to Ramat Dan."

"Mr. Goldstein," Zvi said, "we'll plant for you the best wheat. Then we'll sit and talk."

"I say what's planted here, and I want trees. See, I have the certificates—20 dunams of land, 200 trees on a dunam, so that's . . ."

"That's 4,000 trees," Mrs. Goldstein said cheerfully.

"But you can't own this land, Mr. Goldstein. None of us do . . . and all of us do. This land belongs to all Israel. That's the way the Keren Kayemet works."

"Young man, don't tell me how Keren Kayemet works. I have been giving to the Keren Kayemet all my life so that it could buy land to plant trees. And last month I sold my tailor shop and took the money to Jerusalem to the Keren Kayemet secretary. I gave him my money on the condition that it would pay for this land for *Nahalat Goldstein.*"

"But how did you convince the secretary to do that?"

The old man stared off into the sky. "I'd rather not say."

Mrs. Goldstein's eyes filled with tears. "We paid for the land, this land, before we bought it," she whispered.

Zvi suddenly remembered something. "Mr. Goldstein, where did you get the gun?"

"The gun? It was Duvidl's, of course."

"Mr. Goldstein, of course, your son. Yes, he was Davidka. Mr. and Mrs. Goldstein, your Davidka was very brave . . . like you."

"You knew him? He died right here, you know." Mrs. Goldstein was weeping softly.

"He held this outpost, defending the south side of the kibbutz. He was shot before we could send help. The trees, are they for him?"

"Yes, he died for this land."

"Mr. Goldstein, did you know that Davidka, your Duvidl, had decided to join the kibbutz? He told us the night before the fighting."

"We didn't know."

"Mr. Goldstein, Davidka died for all the land. He loved it. He shared our dream for the wheat fields and for the new tree groves on the ridge in the north."

Mr. and Mrs. Goldstein looked toward the kibbutz, the ridge, and the fields beyond.

"He would have wanted the wheat here, don't you think?" the old man asked his wife.

"Yes, I think so."

"And he would have wanted this sign here," Natan said, "to mark *Naḥalat Goldstein*. We'll leave it."

"The sun is so hot," Zvi said. "Come with us to Ramat Dan for lunch."

Mr. Goldstein gave his gun to Natan and the four of them walked together toward the kibbutz.

The Tallit

by Lois Ruby

"WHO'S Aunt Rhoda?"

"Oh, Judith, you remember. She's Aunt Ellen's husband's sister from Cleveland."

"And *she's* coming to the bar mitzvah?"

"Everyone's coming."

Of course. You would think my brother Jeff was being crowned King of Israel, Kansas City branch, and I, the mere ten-year-old sister, was only a servant in the castle.

"Get me the guest list, will you, Judith," my mother would say. "We're crossing off Uncle Sidney because he's having gall-bladder surgery. Of all times."

If you ask me, which no one would, Uncle Sidney picked a good time. He doesn't have to be here watching King Jeffrey parade through our house as if he were inspecting his army, tossing words of Hebrew over his shoulder. Outside of his Torah portion, I'm sure he knows *only* about six words. I learned a hundred times more than that just in my first year of Hebrew. What's he been *doing* for five years in Hebrew school?

The presents pour in. Jeff rips the wrapping off and tears into each box, only to find *Roget's Thesaurus,* four more *kiddush* cups, six copies of *Pirke Avot,* and some Israeli Bonds. No baseballs, no foreign stamps, no gift certificates from the bowling alley, and no chocolates. Mother scurries around to make a list of who sent what, with a little square Jeff is to fill in when he mails each thank-you note.

Jeff is supposed to be humbled by the experience of becoming a bar mitzvah, isn't he? Oh, but history never knew my brother Jeff! He has let the honor go to his head. But he is to be punished for such shameless pride: He has to write thank you notes at the rate of ten a day for the next month. I love that part.

Mother is baking and freezing, and the freezer is cataloged like a library: 12.5 dozen pieces of strudel; 6.5 dozen brownies; 4 dozen miniature cherry blintzes, etc. On another shelf there are foil pans of noodle kugel and ḥalot with sweet poppy seeds on top. Before this month she never baked a ḥallah in her life.

My father goes around smiling and saying, "Look how he's grown up, our boy," as if no one ever got to be thirteen before in the entire history of the Jewish people. I've got news for my father: Jeff will have to stand on a Coca Cola case to be seen over the podium on the *bimah.* That's the only thing that keeps me going. That, and the thank you notes.

On Saturday morning everyone is racing around and getting dressed. The aunts are putting the final touches on their little darlings, my cousins, and I've finished dressing in the closet. I knock on Jeffrey's door. A weak, unkingly voice says, "Come in." He's standing in the center of the room in his new blue suit and shiny shoes. There's a satin *kippah* on his head, almost hidden among his brown curls. But what strikes me most is the *tallit* draped over his shoulders. It was our great-grandfather's. He brought it with him when he left Russia seventy years ago. The satin is yellowed with age, and the embroidery of blue and gold threads is worn and flattened by the years. When Jeff was born, it was folded away in our cedar chest, waiting for just this morning.

The *tallit* hangs nearly to Jeff's ankles, telling us how very tall our great-grandfather must have been. Jeff strokes the cloth gently with the palm of his hand. "Beautiful, isn't it?" he asks.

I smile and nod, knowing suddenly that nothing else today will compare with this moment: not the presents or honor or speeches, not even the privilege of being called to the Torah. I know that *this* is the moment Jeff will become a true bar mitzvah, this moment when he has felt the tug of generations in the soft folds of our great-grandfather's *tallit*.

And I am the only one who has shared it with him.

Music, songs, and dances

FROM THE BEGINNING THERE WAS MUSIC

When you sit by a campfire toasting marshmallows and singing Hebrew songs, you're making Jewish music. When you chant prayers in the synagogue, you're making Jewish music too. And when the band at a wedding plays fast and loud and everybody, from your grandma to your littlest cousin, dances a stamping, kicking *hora,* you're doing a Jewish dance to Jewish music. It's an old habit. Singing and dancing and making music have been part of Jewish life from the very beginning.

In the days of the Bible the Jews would go up to the Holy Temple in Jerusalem at holiday time. They would bring grapes and wheat and other fruits of their harvest as gifts to God. Then they would thank Him for the harvest by singing and dancing in the Temple courtyard. We don't know what the music sounded like because there were no records or tape recordings. There wasn't even a way of writing music. People learned the words and tunes by listening and memorizing.

All kinds of instruments were played in the Temple. There were drums and golden trumpets, recorders, whistles, rattles, and stringed instruments like our modern harps and guitars. The singers in the Temple choir and the musicians were all supposed to come from one Hebrew tribe, the tribe of Levi. But that didn't keep everybody else from joining in. On the Sukkot holiday the people sang *U-she'avtem Mayim* to thank God for bringing water for their crops. Then they danced all night, balancing jugs of water and blazing torches while the Levite musicians played. Even the solemn holiday of Yom Kippur was a time for dancing and singing in the days of the Temple.

The Temple was destroyed in 70 C.E. after a bloody war, and the Jews were driven from Israel. In faraway lands they built synagogues and prayed again, but there were no happy torch dances and blaring golden trumpets. The rabbis decided not to allow musical instruments in the synagogue so that the Jews would never forget their sadness at the loss of their Temple in Jerusalem.

But at home, on happy occasions, there still was music. What would a wedding be like without singing and dancing? What would the Purim holiday be like without a group of merrymaking musicians, *Purimshpiler,* prancing and clowning to make people laugh and throw pennies? Music was so important that in Eastern Europe bands of folk musicians called *klezmer* traveled from town to town to play at celebrations. Well-known *klezmer* were hired for non-Jewish parties too because their music made everybody want to dance.

For a group of Jews called Hasidim, dancing and singing was as important as praying. Their leader, the Ba'al Shem Tov (which means "master of a good name"), said that song was the ladder to the throne of God. Some of the first Hasidim were poor people who couldn't afford to go to school for long. They didn't have much Jewish education, but could they sing and dance! And the more they sang and danced, the closer they felt to God. Mostly it was the men who danced, sometimes the women, but *never* together. (Even among Jews who were not Hasidim, men and women seldom danced together. And when they did, even if they were married to each other, they held opposite ends of a scarf.) If there is a Hasidic synagogue near you, visit it on Simḥat Torah and feel the joy of singing and dancing your prayers to God.

Today there are as many kinds of Jewish music as there are kinds of Jews. Jewish composers like Leonard Bernstein write for symphony orchestras. Modern bands of *klezmer* tickle people's toes with old and new songs. There are Israeli rock groups and folk singers. There is even Hasi-Disco, dance-band music written to words from the Bible and prayer book.

Jewish songs are being written even in Russia, where Jews are

not allowed to study Hebrew. They tell of the Russian Jews' hope to live as free people. The songs must be sung in secret and smuggled out of the country.

Many popular songs and dances come from Israel. Each year there is a Hasidic Song Festival in Israel, and every few years there is a Folk Dance Festival. Composers and choreographers from all over the world bring their best ideas to be performed and judged. Soon afterwards the rest of us get to learn and enjoy the new music and dances at Jewish camps, schools, and synagogues.

It's a long, long time since the Levite orchestra played in the Temple courtyard and the people danced with blazing torches. We make different music today: Russian Jewish kids sing softly in a Moscow apartment, Israeli kids shout a marching song as they hike across the hills, and Jews chant their prayers and sway in synagogues around the world. Jewish music and dance today help us pray and enjoy and share with other Jews just as it did way back in the time of the Temple.

Look through the next two sections of songs and dances. Try them. Enjoy them. But please—no torches!

WHERE TO BUY JEWISH MUSIC

Hasidic Song Festival tapes and records can be bought or ordered at Jewish bookstores or stores that sell religious articles.

Klezmer music can be ordered from Arhoolie Records, El Cerrito, California, or can be found in catalogs under the names of individual musicians, such as Giora Feidman.

Israeli folk dance records and tapes can be found at Jewish bookstores or ordered from the American Zionist Youth Foundation at 515 Park Avenue, New York, New York 10022.

There's good new Jewish music being made all the time. To see how much, write to these suppliers and ask for their catalog and order blank:

Hebraica Record Distributors
50 Andover Road
Roslyn Heights, New York 11577

Tara Publications
29 Derby Avenue
Cedarhurst, New York 11516

Worldtone Records
230 Seventh Avenue
New York, New York 10011

Songs and poems are both called shirim in Hebrew. One of the oldest song-poems in the Bible may have been written by thirsty Israelites during the long trek from Egypt to Israel more than 3,000 years ago.

Song of the Well
Spring up, O well—sing to it.
The well that the princes dug,
That the nobles dug
With the scepter (of Moses) and with
*   their staffs.*

Num. 21

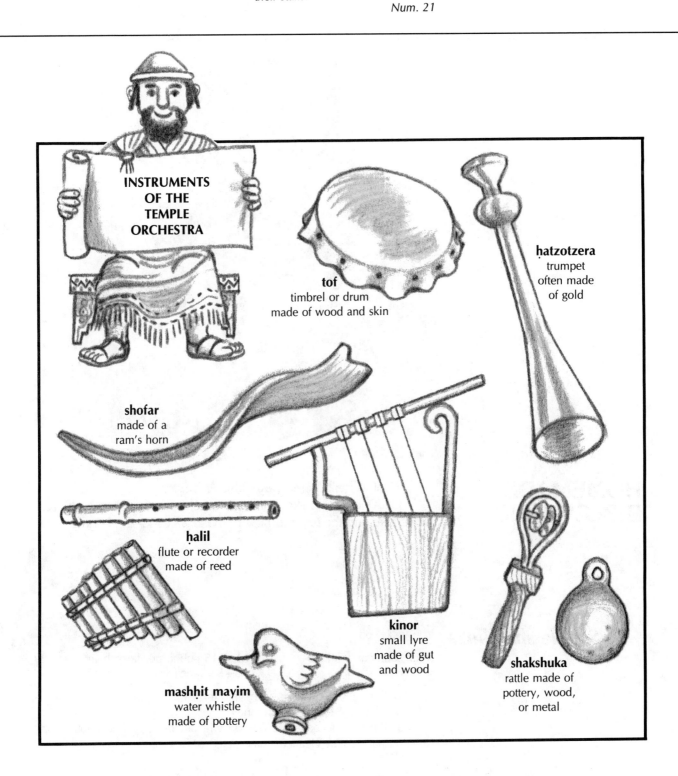

INSTRUMENTS OF THE TEMPLE ORCHESTRA

tof
timbrel or drum
made of wood and skin

ḥatzotzera
trumpet
often made
of gold

shofar
made of a
ram's horn

ḥalil
flute or recorder
made of reed

kinor
small lyre
made of gut
and wood

shakshuka
rattle made of
pottery, wood,
or metal

mashḥit mayim
water whistle
made of pottery

HOMEMADE BIBLE MUSIC

Want to make some very old-time music?

Here's how to make simple instruments that look like the biblical *shakshuka* and the *tof*, and how to make a not-so-simple *ḥalil*.

Simple shakshuka

You will need:

small soda can with tab-type opening

10 or 15 pebbles or large beans
masking tape

1. Drop the pebbles or beans into the can.

2. Close the opening with tape.

3. Paint or decorate the outside with adhesive-backed paper, construction paper, pipe cleaners, glitter, etc.

Be sure to ask an adult to help, or to be nearby, when you use a hammer, file, knife, drill, or other tools.

Slingshot shakshuka

Be careful with the hanger. Hangers have pointy ends.

You will need:

wire clothes hanger, the kind that has a cardboard tube as a bottom

about 10 inches of string
tape
4–6 large, metal washers

1. Take the cardboard tube off the hanger. Squeeze the sides of the hanger together until they're about 4 inches apart.

2. Tie one end of the string around a hanger end. Tape it in place.

3. Thread the washers onto the free end of the string. Pull the string taut and tie it around the opposite hanger end. Tape it in place.

4. Fancy up your *shakshuka* by squeezing the hanger hook together and dressing it in a brightly colored mitten or sock. Hold it on with a rubber band or ribbon.

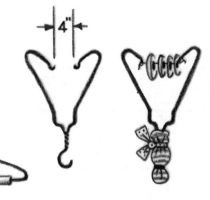

Tof

You will need:

2- or 3-pound coffee can with a plastic cover
can opener
nail punch or large nail

hammer
6 small bells (from a craft or hobby store)
6 freezer ties

1. Remove bottom of can with the can opener.

2. Working on a board or workbench, hammer 6 holes, evenly spaced, around the bottom of the can.

3. Thread the freezer ties through the holes and through the bell loops. Twist the ends together and tape them to the inside of the can.

4. The plastic lid is the *tof*'s face. Decorate the sides by gluing on brightly colored paper, cloth, or ribbons, or by painting. The *tof* can also be used without bells.

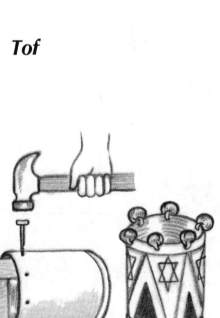

Ḥalil

shepherd's pipe, a simple recorder

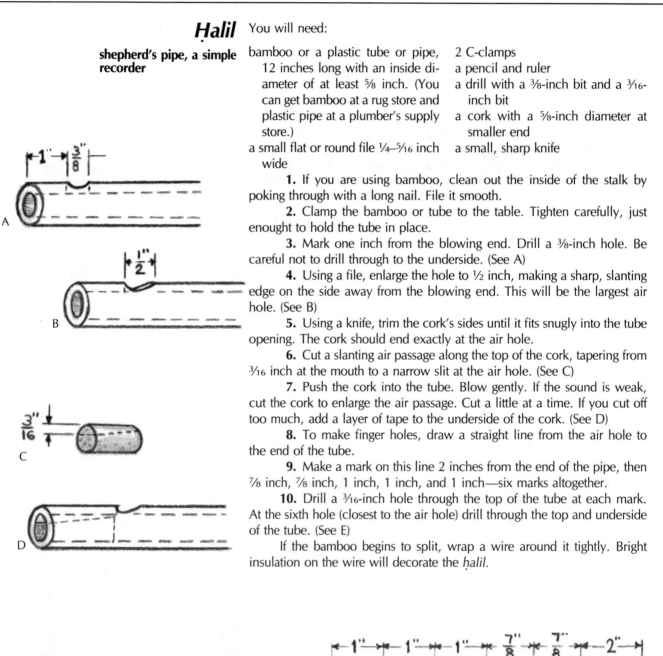

You will need:

bamboo or a plastic tube or pipe, 12 inches long with an inside diameter of at least ⅝ inch. (You can get bamboo at a rug store and plastic pipe at a plumber's supply store.)

a small flat or round file ¼–5⁄16 inch wide

2 C-clamps

a pencil and ruler

a drill with a ⅜-inch bit and a 3⁄16-inch bit

a cork with a ⅝-inch diameter at smaller end

a small, sharp knife

1. If you are using bamboo, clean out the inside of the stalk by poking through with a long nail. File it smooth.

2. Clamp the bamboo or tube to the table. Tighten carefully, just enought to hold the tube in place.

3. Mark one inch from the blowing end. Drill a ⅜-inch hole. Be careful not to drill through to the underside. (See A)

4. Using a file, enlarge the hole to ½ inch, making a sharp, slanting edge on the side away from the blowing end. This will be the largest air hole. (See B)

5. Using a knife, trim the cork's sides until it fits snugly into the tube opening. The cork should end exactly at the air hole.

6. Cut a slanting air passage along the top of the cork, tapering from 3⁄16 inch at the mouth to a narrow slit at the air hole. (See C)

7. Push the cork into the tube. Blow gently. If the sound is weak, cut the cork to enlarge the air passage. Cut a little at a time. If you cut off too much, add a layer of tape to the underside of the cork. (See D)

8. To make finger holes, draw a straight line from the air hole to the end of the tube.

9. Make a mark on this line 2 inches from the end of the pipe, then ⅞ inch, ⅞ inch, 1 inch, 1 inch, and 1 inch—six marks altogether.

10. Drill a 3⁄16-inch hole through the top of the tube at each mark. At the sixth hole (closest to the air hole) drill through the top and underside of the tube. (See E)

If the bamboo begins to split, wrap a wire around it tightly. Bright insulation on the wire will decorate the *ḥalil*.

A shepherd had a lot of time to sit around practicing, so he learned to get a good tune out of his *ḥalil*. And even if he was a little off-key, the sheep and goats didn't complain. You'll need practice too. Here's how to start.

Learning to blow the ḥalil:

Place your fingers over the first three holes. Now blow gently, the way you blow to make a sound with a soda-pop bottle. If you blow harder you can make a high, loud sound. If you blow more gently the tone will get lower. You'll be able to make a sound like the wind, or a pigeon, or a train whistle.

To play a scale:

Cover all the *ḥalil* holes with your fingers. The thumb of your right hand covers the hole on the underside of the *ḥalil*. Blow gently into the *ḥalil*. Lift your fingers from each hole, one at a time, starting at the bottom of the *ḥalil*.

SONGS

ARTZA ALINU

אַרְצָה עָלִינוּ

The early settlers in Palestine (before Israel became a state) didn't know how to plow or plant or pick fruit. They had been students and city people before they came to build their homeland. But they sang as they worked and waited for the harvest.

אַרְצָה עָלִינוּ	We've come to the land.
אַרְצָה עָלִינוּ	We've come to the land.
אַרְצָה עָלִינוּ, עָלִינוּ (all three lines, 2 times)	
כְּבָר חָרַשְׁנוּ	We've already plowed,
וְגַם זָרַעְנוּ (both lines, 2 times)	And we've also planted,
אֲבָל עוֹד לֹא קָצַרְנוּ (4 times)	But we haven't yet harvested.

(whole line, 2 times) הָבָה נָגִילָה (3 times) וְנִשְׂמְחָה	Let's be happy.
(whole line, 2 times) הָבָה נְרַנְנָה (3 times) וְנִשְׂמְחָה	Let's sing and be happy.
עוּרוּ, עוּרוּ אַחִים	Get up, get up brothers and sisters.
(4 times) עוּרוּ אַחִים בְּלֵב שָׂמֵחַ	Get up brothers and sisters with happy hearts.
עוּרוּ אַחִים, עוּרוּ אַחִים, בְּלֵב שָׂמֵחַ	Get up brothers and sisters with happy hearts.

HAVAH NAGILAH
הָבָה נָגִילָה

HA-TIKVAH
הַתִּקְוָה

The national anthem of the State of Israel was written in the 1890s when a Jewish homeland was only a hope and a dream.

כָּל עוֹד בַּלֵּבָב פְּנִימָה	As long as in our hearts
נֶפֶשׁ יְהוּדִי הוֹמִיָּה	There is a Jewish spirit,
וּלְפַאֲתֵי מִזְרָח קָדִימָה	And toward the east
עַיִן לְצִיּוֹן צוֹפִיָּה	Our eyes turn . . . to Zion,
עוֹד לֹא אָבְדָה תִקְוָתֵנוּ	Our hope is not lost,
הַתִּקְוָה בַּת שְׁנוֹת אַלְפַּיִם	The hope of 2,000 years,
לִהְיוֹת עַם חָפְשִׁי בְּאַרְצֵנוּ	To be a free nation in our own land,
בְּאֶרֶץ צִיּוֹן וִירוּשָׁלַיִם	In the land of Zion, in Jerusalem.

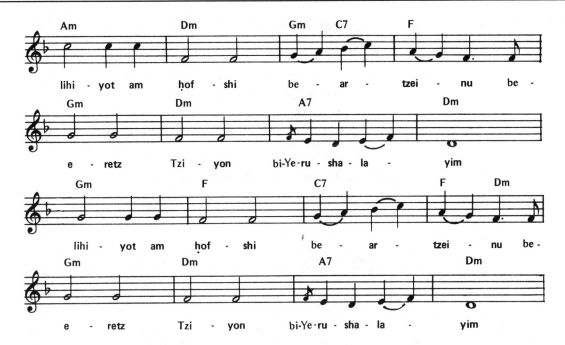

lihi - yot am ḥof - shi be - ar - tzei - nu be -

e - retz Tzi - yon bi-Ye - ru - sha - la - yim

lihi - yot am ḥof - shi be - ar - tzei - nu be -

e - retz Tzi - yon bi-Ye - ru - sha - la - yim

This melody without words is fun just to hum, and even more fun to hum while dancing.

DEBKA
דֶּבְּקָה

AZ DER REBBE ZINGT

אַז דער רבי זינגט

The Hasidim copied every move their rebbe made, says this Yiddish folk song.

און אַז דער רבי זינגט (2 times)	And when the rebbe sings,
זינגען אַלע חסידים (2 times)	All the Hasidim sing.
און אַז דער רבי זינגט (2 times)	And when the rebbe sings,
זינגען אַלע חסידים (2 times)	All the Hasidim sing.

To sing "When the rebbe dances . . .," substitute the word *tanst* for *zingt* and *tantsen* for *zingen*. To sing "When the rebbe sleeps . . .," substitute *shloft* for *zingt* and *shlofen* for *zingen*.

A sweet song for the sweetest holiday of all—the weekly day of rest.

SHABBAT SHALOM
שַׁבָּת שָׁלוֹם

בִּם בָּם	Bim, bam,
בִּם בָּם בִּם בָּם	Bim, bam,
בִּם בָּם בִּם בָּם בִּם בָּם	Bim, bam.
שַׁבָּת שָׁלוֹם (2 times)	Have a peaceful Sabbath.
שַׁבָּת, שַׁבָּת, שַׁבָּת, שַׁבָּת שָׁלוֹם	
שַׁבָּת שָׁלוֹם (2 times)	
שַׁבָּת, שַׁבָּת, שַׁבָּת, שַׁבָּת שָׁלוֹם	
בִּם בָּם	
בִּם בָּם בִּם בָּם	
בִּם בָּם בִּם בָּם בִּם בָּם	

HINEI MAH TOV
הִנֵּה מַה טוֹב

Hinei Mah Tov can be sung as a round. The second group starts when the first group gets to the second verse.

הִנֵּה מַה טוֹב וּמַה נָּעִים	How good it is and how pleasant
(both lines, 2 times) שֶׁבֶת אַחִים גַּם יַחַד	When brothers and sisters live together.
הִנֵּה מַה טוֹב	How good it is
(both lines, 2 times) שֶׁבֶת אַחִים גַּם יַחַד	When brothers and sisters live together.

MAYIM, MAYIM
מַיִם, מַיִם

In ancient Israel farmers sang this song when they prayed for rain. Today we sing it as we dance the *Mayim* dance. You'll find the steps for the dance on page 198.

שְׁאַבְתֶּם מַיִם בְּשָׂשׂוֹן	Draw up water with joy
(both lines, 2 times) מִמַּעַיְנֵי הַיְשׁוּעָה	from the wells of salvation.
מַיִם, מַיִם, מַיִם, מַיִם	Water, water, water, water,
(both lines, 2 times) הֵי מַיִם בְּשָׂשׂוֹן	Hey, water with joy.
הֵי, הֵי, הֵי, הֵי	Hey, hey, hey, hey
מַיִם, מַיִם, מַיִם, מַיִם	Water, water, water, water,
(both lines, 2 times) מַיִם, מַיִם, בְּשָׂשׂוֹן	Water, water with joy.

Am · · · · · C · · E7

Ushe -av -tem ma-yim be - sa - son___ mi ma'ayenei ha- ye-shu-ah ushe -

Am · · · · · F · C · Am

av- tem ma-yim be - sa - son mi ma'aye nei ha - ye- -shu- ah

F · Am · F · Em · Am

ma- yim ma- yim ma-yim ma-yim hei ma-yim be- sa - son

F · Am · F · C · Em · E7

ma-yim ma- yim ma-yim ma-yim hei ma- yim be- sa - son

G7

hei hei hei hei ma-yim ma- yim

G7 · C · G7

ma-yim ma- yim ma-yim ma-yim be- sa - son

G7 · C · E7 · Am

mayim mayim ma- yim ma-yim ma- yim ma-yim be- sa - son

SOME GOOD BOOKS ON JEWISH MUSIC AND DANCE

A history of the Jewish dance and an instruction manual. Dances include those of Eastern Europe, modern Israel, Yemenite Jews, and others.

Berk, Fred. *Ha-Rikud: The Jewish Dance.* New York: Union of American Hebrew Congregations, 1972. 102 pp. in paperback.

This is the original hardcover compendium of Jewish music for children, including Hebrew, Yiddish, Israeli, liturgical, and folk songs.

Coopersmith, Harry. *The Songs We Sing.* New York: United Synagogue Commission on Jewish Education, 1950. 450 pp.

A hardcover collection of additional songs, bringing The Songs We Sing *up to date.*

Coopersmith, Harry. *More of the Songs We Sing.* New York: United Synagogue Commission on Jewish Education, 1971. 266 pp.

A hardcover collection of songs and music for children from three to eight. Contains more than 250 songs for holidays, day-to-day experiences, and prayers. Lyrics are in Hebrew, English, and transliterations.

Eisenstein, Judith, and Prensky, Frieda. *Songs of Childhood.* New York: United Synagogue Commission on Jewish Education, 1955. 321 pp.

An overview of the music of Israel: music predating the modern State of Israel, Hasidic and liturgical music, and contemporary popular Israeli songs, for piano and voice.

Pasternak, Velvel, and Neumann, Richard, editors, compilers, and arrangers. *Great Songs of Israel,* and *Israel in Song.* New York: Tara Publications of the Board of Jewish Education of Greater New York, 1976 and 1974. 107 pp. each, in paperback.

The early settlers, the *ḥalutzim*, brought the *hora* to Palestine from Eastern Europe. The children of those first *ḥalutzim*, who are great-grandparents now, boast that they used to dance the *hora* half the night and then go out and work in the fields all the next day. Try it and see if you believe them.

The *hora* has six basic steps that are repeated over and over. The instructions show a dancer with a white leg and a shaded leg. The dancer's *weight* is on the *shaded* leg. *Artza Alinu* is a good *hora* song (words page 188). Dancers form a circle and put their hands on each other's shoulders or hold hands.

TWO JEWISH DANCES

1. Hora

1	2	3
STEP RIGHT WITH RIGHT FOOT	PLACE LEFT FOOT BEHIND RIGHT FOOT	STEP RIGHT WITH RIGHT FOOT
AR-	TZA	A-

4	5	6
HOP ON RIGHT FOOT	STEP LEFT WITH LEFT FOOT	HOP ON LEFT FOOT
LI-	NU	AR-

2. Mayim This dance is much younger than the *hora*, but the words of the song are very, very old. Two thousand years ago, Jews sang it when they came to the Temple for the Sukkot holiday. Maybe they had a *mayim* dance too. Maybe it was a little like this one. Who knows?

Part One Do the *mayim* steps 1–4, eight times.

1	2	3	4
STEP RIGHT WITH RIGHT FOOT	PLACE LEFT FOOT IN FRONT OF RIGHT	STEP RIGHT WITH RIGHT FOOT	PLACE LEFT FOOT BEHIND RIGHT
USHE'AV-	TEM	MA-	YIM . . .

Part Two Do steps 1–8 twice.

1	2	3	4
RUN 4 STEPS FORWARD (TOWARD CENTER), STARTING WITH RIGHT FOOT. RAISE ARMS.			
MAYIM	MAYIM	MAYIM	MAYIM

5	6	7	8
LOWER ARMS AND RUN 4 STEPS BACKWARD, STARTING WITH RIGHT FOOT			
HEY	MAYIM	BE-	SASON

The song *Mayim* (page 194) is the music for this dance. The instructions show a dancer with a white leg and a shaded leg. The dancer's *weight* is on the *shaded* leg. Dancers form a circle, face the center, and hold hands.

Part Three   Do steps 5–8 twice.   Do steps 9–12 twice.

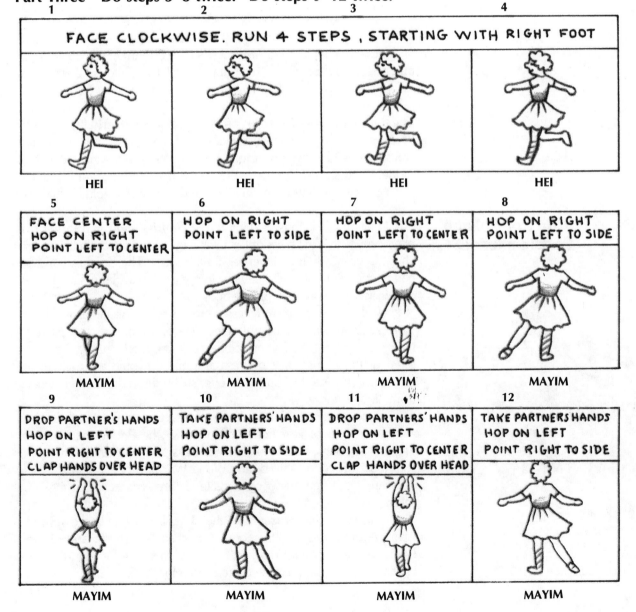

14  Traveling Jewish

ACROSS THE UNITED STATES

Since 1654 American Jews have scattered from Homosassa, Florida, to Walla Walla, Washington. Some dug for gold, some prospected for oil, some opened grocery stores, and some raised chickens. First they set up synagogues and schools. Later they bought land for cemeteries. And much later many Jews collected their candlesticks, menorahs, Torahs, and other treasures into museums for the rest of us to see.

All across this country you'll find Jewish places to explore and Jewish things to see. We can only tell you about a few of them. You'll find more in a book called *American Jewish Landmarks,* a travel guide and history by Bernard Postal and Lionel Koppman, published by Fleet Press in New York, 1977.

1 California

The ***Judah Magnes Museum*** on Russell Street in **Berkeley** is a cozy house set in the middle of a shady, lush garden. Inside you'll find crafts, books, displays on history, ceremonial objects, and exhibits of modern Jewish art. You can take a tour from the museum to some of the six nearby Jewish cemeteries that date back to Gold Rush days.

2 District of Columbia (Washington, D.C.)

The "Nation of Nations" exhibit at the ***Smithsonian Institution*** displays one of the first pairs of Levi jeans ever made. So what's Jewish about Levis? Only their inventor, Levi Strauss. The Smithsonian also has a collection of really Jewish things such as Ḥanukkah lamps, circumcision knives, and prayer books.

At the ***Library of Congress*** there's a huge collection of Torahs, Talmuds, and other Hebrew books. One of them, the great Bible of Mainz, is five hundred years old. And if they ever had a Passover *seder* at the Library of Congress, the guests would get their pages mixed up because the library has over six hundred different *Haggadot* from all over the world.

Check out the ***National Wax Museum*** on E Street, S.W. It shows a model of four heroic chaplains of the Protestant, Catholic, and Jewish faiths who gave their life belts to sailors and went down with their torpedoed ship during World War II. Models of Albert Einstein and other famous people make history come alive at this museum.

The ***Klutznick Museum*** at the B'nai B'rith building on Rhode Island Avenue has exhibits about American Jewish life and history. Look for the pen that President Harry Truman used to sign the declaration recognizing the new State of Israel in 1948.

This brass Ḥanukkah lamp was made in the nineteenth century in Eastern Europe. It is part of a Judaica (Jewish objects) collection in Ohio.

3 Florida

The *Gamble Mansion* in **Ellenton** was Judah Benjamin's hideout after the Civil War. He had been the Confederate secretary of state, and the federal government put a reward of $50,000 on his head. Soldiers marched up one day and nearly caught Judah. He hid in the bushes behind the house and then escaped to England. The house and bushes and a ruined sugar mill are interesting to explore, but watch out for poison ivy!

At **Homosassa Springs** you'll find *David Yulee's mansion* and sugar plantation. In 1845 he became the first Jew to serve in the U.S. Senate.

4 Illinois On East Wacker Drive in **Chicago,** look for the statue of President George Washington with Robert Morris, treasurer of the American Revolutionary government, and Haym Salomon, the Jewish financier who helped raise the money to fight the Revolutionary War.

Also in Chicago, the ***Spertus Museum*** has a fine collection of Judaica and shows the work of modern Jewish artists.

5 Maryland In 1845 the Jews of **Baltimore** built a synagogue on Lloyd Street. The third oldest synagogue in the country, it was a bustling place with a *matzah* bakery in the basement and a *mikvah* on the ground floor. It is still bustling today—not with prayer but with tourists.

6 Massachusetts A book of Hebrew grammar was the first Hebrew book printed in North America. ***Harvard University*** in **Cambridge** published it in 1735. The university library kept collecting Hebrew books, and today it has one of the largest Semitic collections in the world. One of its most valuable books is a handwritten copy of Maimonides' commentary on the Torah. In Harvard's Semitic Museum you can look at coins, statues, rocks, plants and other finds from Israel and nearby countries.

7 New York In **New York City** take the ferry from Battery Park to Liberty Island to visit the ***Statue of Liberty.*** Climb the winding staircase up, up, up into Ms. Liberty's head, then look across the harbor at the skyscrapers on Manhattan Island. Back on the ground, go to the Immigration Museum in Fort Wood by the base of the statue. Maybe you'll find a picture of one of your relatives, taken when he or she was a new immigrant. Look for the inscription of Emma Lazarus's famous poem on the statue's base. It welcomes all new immigrants to the United States. When you step off the ferry at Battery Park, remember that the first Jewish immigrants stepped ashore at this very same spot in 1654.

Roam around the ***Lower East Side*** of Manhattan, near Delancey and Essex streets. Eat a knish or a bagel, buy a pickle out of a barrel, and look up at the old tenement buildings and synagogues. Most Jewish immigrants in the early 1900s lived in these houses for at least a while. Jews come to the Lower East Side today to buy Hebrew books and records, *mezuzot,* prayer shawls, and other ceremonial objects. They find good pumpernickel bread and lots of bargains too.

Inside **Shearith Israel Synagogue** on Central Park West in Manhattan, you'll find a reconstruction of the first synagogue ever built in this country, the Mill Street Synagogue. In 1728 the Jews paid 100 English pounds, one loaf of sugar, and one pound of tea to buy land on Mill Street for a synagogue. When the small building was finished, the street became known as Jews' Alley.

A dignified old mansion on Fifth Avenue in Manhattan is the **Jewish Museum of the Jewish Theological Seminary.** It's filled with archaeological finds, modern crafts and paintings, and ceremonial objects. There is also a children's room with special exhibits, and a crafts room where kids can paint and draw and make holiday crafts. The center staircase has a great banister for sliding down, if only they would let you.

Hebrew Union College on Clifton Avenue in **Cincinnati** is the oldest rabbinical school in the country. Ancient books from all over the world are in the college library, including fifty-nine Chinese-Hebrew manuscripts from the long-gone Chinese Jewish community of Kaifeng. There is also a treasure of Hebrew books from Germany. They were buried and saved from the Nazis. After World War II they were dug up and brought to their new home in Cincinnati.

8   Ohio

The **Fenster Gallery** of Jewish art at Congregation B'nai Emuna in **Tulsa** has one of the biggest public collections of Jewish art in the country. A prized possession is a 1,900-year-old Ḥanukkah menorah from Israel.

If you pass the town of **Velma**, Oklahoma, wave to the Sholom Aleichem Oil Field. It's named after a friendly Jewish newspaperman who greeted the oilmen with *"shalom aleikhem"* instead of "hello."

9   Oklahoma

You'll walk back into the 1700s when you stroll down Independence Mall in **Philadelphia.** *Mikveh Israel,* the second oldest Jewish congregation in the country, stands there, as well as the **Museum of American Jewish History.** The nearby Jewish cemetery on Spruce Street is a national historic landmark. Haym Salomon and thirty-three soldiers of the American Revolution are buried there.

10   Pennsylvania

The oldest board for rolling *matzah* dough in the United States is inside the oldest existing synagogue in the United States. It's the **Touro Synagogue** in **Newport,** a national historic site built in 1763. No nails

11   Rhode Island

were used in building this synagogue, only wooden pegs. Be sure to peek under the reader's desk. You'll see the door of a secret passageway that used to lead to the street. The Jews of Newport remembered how their ancestors had been persecuted in Spain. In case of trouble, they wanted to be sure that they could escape quickly.

12 Tennessee The world's tiniest Torah, housed in a silver case, is in the *Harris Swift Museum of Religion and Ceremonial Arts* in **Chattanooga.** The museum also has many other beautiful ceremonial objects.

While you're in town, climb up to the *Adolph Ochs Observatory and Museum* in Lookout Mountain Park. If it's a clear day you'll see miles of the Great Smoky Mountains and the Blue Ridge Mountains. Adolph Ochs was a Jewish philanthropist and newspaper editor in Chattanooga. Later he became owner of a newspaper, the *New York Times.*

13 Texas There's a quiet Garden of Memories in *Lewis Park* in **Dallas.** It's a memorial to the 6 million Jews who were killed by the Nazis during World War II. Six lamps burn day and night on top of a stone wall. The story of the Holocaust is inscribed on the wall. A sculpture called *The Last March* stands in the garden and reminds us of the tragic final hours of our lost brothers and sisters.

14 Virginia When you visit *Monticello,* the beautiful home of Thomas Jefferson in **Charlottesville,** remember that it was saved from ruin by Commodore Uriah Levy. After Jefferson's death Monticello was neglected and began to fall apart. Levy had respected and admired Thomas Jefferson, the writer of the Declaration of Independence, so he bought and repaired the house, brought back the furnishings that had been taken from it, and added more land to the estate. Today the Thomas Jefferson Memorial Foundation takes care of the estate, which is visited by people from many countries.

Whenever you and your parents are planning a trip, get a few travel books from the library that describe the country you plan to visit. Look for Jewish landmarks in the index under "synagogue" or "Jewish." Also check "museums" or "special interests" in the index or table of contents.

Shalom! Have a good trip!

Here's a list of a few interesting places to visit in Israel. You'll find hundreds more in a good guidebook. To find the location of each listed place, look at the map of Israel and find the place number.

PLACES TO GO IN ISRAEL

Bring binoculars and peek through the papyrus reeds at ducks, geese, migrating storks (in the spring), and huge water buffalo. Hula was a wild mosquito-filled swamp until the Israelis drained it. Now most of the area is rich farmland. Only in the nature reserve can you see a bit of long-ago Hula—without the mosquitoes.

1 Hula Nature Reserve

Go sailing, fishing, and swimming in this blue lake. Then soak your aching bones in the hot springs on the shore just like the Roman emperors and talmudic sages did. Maybe Maimonides, who is buried nearby, bathed there too. You'll find mosaic floors and columns of ancient synagogues near the lake.

2 Yam Kinneret

Many Jews came to this mountaintop city after they were expelled from Spain in 1492. Safed became an important center of learning. Four-hundred-year-old synagogues sit on narrow winding streets, and modern artists paint in the ancient olive groves and stone houses on the hillsides. Safed is up so high that you can look east and see the Kinneret and look west and see the Mediterranean.

3 Safed

Fill your canteen, load your back pack and your camera, and climb the hiking trails to the highest peak in northern Israel. Be careful not to step on wildflowers, and watch for wild boar, polecats, salamanders, and dormice. The tomb of Rabbi Simeon bar Yoḥai is on Mt. Meron.

4 Mt. Meron Nature Reserve

This modern port city is built on the slopes of Mt. Carmel. Oil tankers, navy ships, and tourist boats crowd each other in the harbor, and sailors from all over the world stroll down Haifa's main streets eating felafel sandwiches. On Mt. Carmel, high above, young men and women study engineering and science at the Haifa Technion.

5 Haifa

The Land of Israel has been fought over for centuries. Seven hundred years ago the Crusaders conquered the land and built a great stone castle here. The thick stone walls, moats, and tumbled boulders of Montfort are great to explore. Don't look for Crusaders—they are long gone.

6 Montfort

7 Caesarea King Herod built a port here 2,000 years ago. Climb into the ancient amphitheater and watch the rolling waves while you listen to a concert (bring a pillow—Herod forgot to pad the stone seats). There's also a white sand beach for swimming, acres of Roman statues and ruins, and a modern golf course.

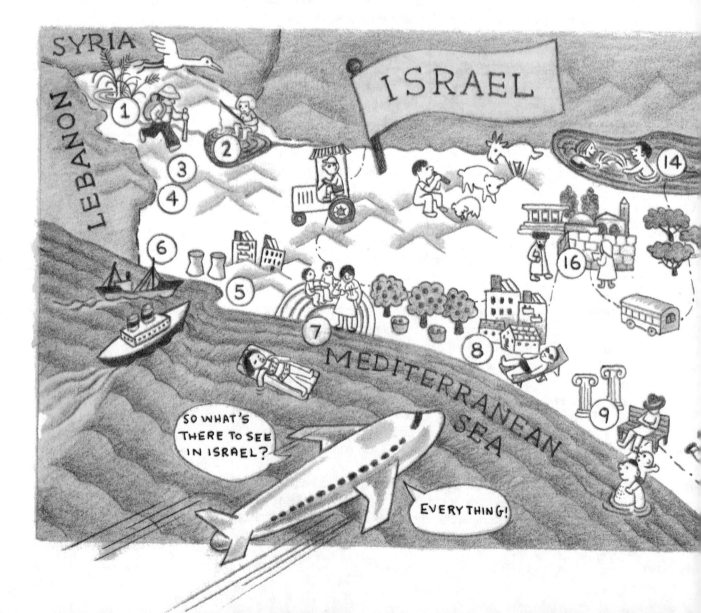

It's time to rest. Sit at an outdoor café, sip some Israeli iced coffee (a little coffee and a lot of ice cream), and watch the world go by. Early Zionists began to build Tel Aviv on sand dunes near the sea in 1909. Today it's Israel's biggest city, with skyscrapers, museums, theaters, and a bustling pushcart market. Don't miss the Museum of the Jewish Diaspora at Tel Aviv University. It uses dolls, dioramas, films, and more to tell the story of 2,500 years of Jewish life.

8   Tel Aviv

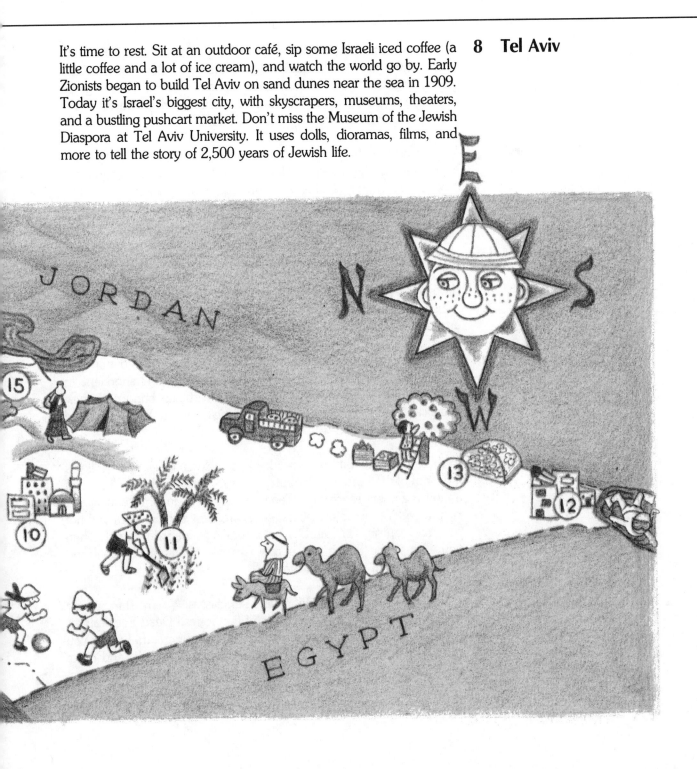

9 Ashkelon   Samson met a pretty Philistine girl called Delilah in this town many years ago. It was all downhill for him after that. But you shouldn't have any trouble here. The beach and pools are cool, and the green parks are filled with interesting Roman and Greek ruins. Just north of Ashkelon is the busy modern port of Ashdod.

10 Beersheva   In biblical times the patriarch Abraham dug a well here. Today Beersheva is a growing city in the Negev desert. Flocks of sheep and goats tended by Bedouin children share the roads with modern trucks and buses. You can get your picture taken on a Bedouin's camel at the sunny camel market or explore the campus of Ben-Gurion University.

11 Avdat   In the middle of the desert a spring of water bubbles out of the rocks. Over a thousand years ago Nabatean people learned to use each drop of this precious water for their farms. Wander through the spooky ruins of the town of Avdat on the hill. Then come back to the spring and see how Israelis are learning to use Nabatean farming methods.

12 Eilat   Even in January, the water off Eilat's beach is as warm as bath water. Brightly colored tropical fish whisk past swimmers and snorklers. In biblical times King Solomon built a port nearby to bring perfumes, peacocks, and ivory into Israel from Africa and Arabia. Today the harbor of Eilat is filled with yachts and oil tankers.

13 Ketura and Yahel   At these desert kibbutzim avocados and melons, roses and gladiolus grow out of the sand! In a kibbutz (there are many kibbutzim in Israel) all the members share the village property and income equally. At Ketura and Yahel the members also share a lot of hard work and hot sun. You can say "Hi" and "What's cooking?" in plain English when you stop at the dining hall because many members of Yahel and Ketura are from the United States.

14 Dead Sea   Put on your hat, suntan lotion, and sunglasses. You're standing on the lowest spot on earth—and one of the hottest! Dead Sea water is warm as chicken soup and thick (with salt) as sour cream. Even if you can't swim, you won't sink. Israel is mining salt, potash, and other minerals out of this rich sea.

15 Masada

The lonely rock of Masada looms high beside the Dead Sea. Judah Maccabee, the hero of the Ḥanukkah story, built the first fort here. Many years later the Jews held out against their Roman enemies for three years on Masada. Their water cisterns and the walls of their synagogues, homes, and storehouses can still be seen. If you feel very strong, climb to the top of Masada by the "snake path," as Israeli soldiers do. Start walking at dawn to beat the hot sun. Otherwise you can ride the cable car most of the way.

16 Jerusalem

The City of David, capital of ancient Israel and of modern Israel, is high in the hills of Judea. To Jews the most holy site in the city is the Western Wall, the last remaining wall of the Holy Temple. All day and night men, women, and children stand and pray by its great stones. The Old City of Jerusalem is holy to three religions and has many synagogues, churches, and mosques. As you walk along crowded, narrow streets, you'll bump sides with donkeys, black goats, and hurrying people. The Knesset (parliament building) and the Israel Museum (where the Dead Sea Scrolls are kept) are beautiful modern buildings. When you get tired of serious history, take the bus to the Biblical Zoo and feed the monkeys. It'll still be history—all the animals at the zoo are mentioned in the Bible—but you and the monkeys are sure to find something to laugh about.

WARNING TO ALL CAMERA-TOTING TOURISTS
DON'T TAKE HARD-TO-SEE PICTURES

Like this

or this

or this

- Hold the camera firmly (no shaking) when you click the shutter.
- Stand with the sun or other light source behind you and shining on your subject.
- Find your subject in the view-finder of the camera and center it.

15

An asterisk (*) next to a word means there's more information in another chapter. Look it up in the index.

Mini-encyclopedia

A

Abraham (about nineteenth century B.C.E.) The first Jew and the "father of the Jewish people."

Adam and Eve The first people on earth. The Book of Genesis tells how they lived in the Garden of Eden until they disobeyed God's rule and were driven out.

Aggadah Stories and sayings based on the Bible. Many are included in the Talmud.

Agnon, Shmuel Yosef (1888–1970) Israeli writer of novels and stories about life among the Jews of the Eastern European *shtetl* and among early Jewish pioneers in Palestine. He won the Nobel Prize for literature.

Ahad Ha-Am (1856–1927) An early Russian Zionist and writer. He thought it was more important that Palestine should be a cultural center for the Jews than an independent Jewish state.

*Ahasuerus (about 475 B.C.E.) Persian king. See *Purim.*

*Akiva ben Joseph (about 50–135 C.E.) Scholar, teacher, and editor of the Mishnah in the time when the Romans ruled Judea. Rabbi Akiva helped Bar Kokhba to revolt against the Romans and was executed by them.

*Aliyah Hebrew for "going up." Going to settle in Israel is known as going on *aliyah.* The honor of being called *up* to the Torah in synagogue is an *aliyah.*

*Anielewicz, Mordecai (1919–43) Young Zionist leader of the Warsaw Ghetto Revolt during World War II. He died fighting the Nazis.

Antiochus IV (ruled 175–64 B.C.E.) King of Syria who tried to stop Jewish worship in Judea. The fight to drive out Antiochus is described in the Ḥanukkah story.

*Anti-Semitism A feeling of hatred for Jews. After they left the Land of Israel, Jews lived all over the world. Since their customs and religion often seemed strange to their neighbors, it was easy for religious enemies or business rivals to stir up fear and anger. They spread terrible lies about Jews. One was the "blood libel," in which Jews were accused of using the blood of Christian children to make *matzah.* Another was the *Protocols of the Elders of Zion,* a forgery that tried to show a worldwide Jewish conspiracy to control all other people. Over the centuries, Jews were attacked and expelled from their homes again and again because of anti-Semitism. The Nazi Holocaust, which killed 6 million Jews during World War II, is often described as the most terrible anti-Semitic event in history. See *Holocaust.*

Apocrypha. Greek for "hidden." The religious books known as Apocrypha were written by Jews during the time of the Second Temple, but they were not included in the written text of the Bible.

*Arabs People of the Middle East. Some live in Israel; most live in lands bordering on Israel and nearby. They are mostly Muslim and speak Arabic. According to Jewish and Arab tradition, the Arabs are descended from Ishmael, the son of Abraham and Hagar.

Aramaic Language once used by many people in the Middle East. Much of the Talmud and *siddur* is written in Aramaic, as well as the song Ḥad Gadya ("One Little Goat") from the Passover *seder.*

*Archaeology The study of objects and structures left by ancient people. In Israel everybody is an amateur archaeologist because ancient statues, coins, or pots seem to turn up wherever a field is plowed or a foundation is dug. Archaeological finds in Caesarea, Jerusalem, Avdat, and other cities have taught us a lot about the early customs of the Jews.

Aron Kodesh Hebrew for "holy ark." The Ten Commandments were carried in the *aron kodesh* for forty years while the Jews wandered in the desert. Later the *aron* was placed in the Holy Temple in Jerusalem. Today the Torah is kept in an *aron kodesh* in the synagogue.

A little bit about a lot of Jewish matters

*Ashkenazim Hebrew for "Germans." The term is used to describe Jews from a Yiddish-speaking culture, often from Germany, France, Russia, and Poland.

Atonement, Day of See *Yom Kippur*.

B

*Ba'al Shem Tov (about 1700–60) Hebrew for "master of a good name." Israel Ba'al Shem Tov, the founder of Hasidism, was a deeply religious man who used to pray in the forest and worked at simple, hard jobs. He taught that loving God and enjoying prayer were more important than great learning. Poor Jews with little education followed him happily. Soon educated Jews became Hasidim too.

*Balfour Declaration A document issued by the British government in 1917 supporting the establishment of a Jewish homeland in Palestine.

*Bar Kokhba (about 100–35 C.E.) Leader of a revolt against the Roman rulers of Judea. At first the Judeans (Jews) beat back the enemy. They celebrated their independence joyously and minted new coins. But the Romans returned and destroyed Bar Kokhba and his army at Betar on the ninth of Av, 135 C.E.

*Bar Mitzvah Hebrew for "son of the commandment." A boy becomes a *bar mitzvah* at age thirteen and he is called up to the reading of the Torah. In some synagogues a girl becomes a *bat mitzvah*, a "daughter of the commandment," in the same way.

Begin, Menahem (1913–) Zionist who was the leader of the Irgun, an underground army that fought the British in Palestine. When the State of Israel was established in 1948, Begin became leader of the Ḥerut party and later prime minister of the country.

*Ben-Gurion, David (1886–1973) First prime minister of the State of Israel. He worked as a *ḥalutz* (pioneer), fought in the Jewish Legion during World War I, and then led the struggle to drive the

British out of Palestine. In 1948 he issued the proclamation that established the State of Israel in spite of warnings that the new state would be quickly destroyed.

*Benjamin, Judah (1811–84) U.S. senator from Louisiana who became secretary of state for the Confederacy during the Civil War.

*Ben-Yehuda, Eliezer (1858–1922) The "father of modern Hebrew." Ben-Yehuda spent his life modernizing the Hebrew language and educating the Jews of Palestine to use it. He wrote a fifteen-volume dictionary of old and new Hebrew words.

Bet Ha-Mikdash See *Temple*.

*Bialik, Hayyim Nahman (1873–1934) Famous Hebrew poet who wrote about love, nature, religion, and even about pogroms (attacks on Jews). "The City of Slaughter," a poem about the tragic pogrom in Kishinev in 1903, roused young Jews to fight and defend themselves. In Israel, Bialik prizes are given each year for the best writing.

*Bible Comprises the most holy books of the Jewish people. The Bible tells the early history of the Jewish people and sets forth many laws and moral principles by which Jews must live. The first five books of the Bible are the Torah.

Bikkurim Hebrew for "first fruits." The first grains and fruits harvested in late spring, and the first-born chicks, kids, and calves were called *bikkurim*. They were brought to the Temple in Jerusalem as offerings for the Shavuot holiday.

*Bilu A movement of young Zionists who left Russia in the 1880s to go to Palestine as *ḥalutzim* (pioneers).

Blood Libel See *Anti-Semitism*.

Brandeis, Louis D. (1856–1941) Justice of the U.S. Supreme Court and Zionist leader. Brandeis was called the "people's lawyer" because he often defended working people against employers. Brandeis University in Waltham, Massachusetts, is named after him.

*Brit Milah Hebrew for "covenant of circumcision." In a *brit milah* ceremony the foreskin of baby boys is removed as a sign of the covenant between God and Abraham.

C

*Calendar, Hebrew The cycle of the Jewish year, in which each month begins with the appearance of the new moon. Every few years an extra month (Adar Bet) is added to keep the months in the same season.

212

Mini-encyclopedia

An asterisk (*) next to a word means there's more information in another chapter. Look it up in the index.

*Camp David Accords Agreement between Israel and Egypt signed at Camp David, Maryland, in 1979. It is a first hopeful step toward peace between Israel and her neighbors.

Canaan Early name for Israel, which had been settled by Canaanite tribes before the time of Abraham.

Charity In Hebrew called *tzedakah*, which means "righteousness." Giving to help needy people is a very important principle of Judaism. It is part of Purim, Passover, and other holiday celebrations. Some people set aside money for *tzedakah* each week before the Sabbath.

*Christianity A religion founded in the first century C.E. by a small group of Jews who believed that their leader Jesus was the Messiah. As other peoples adopted Christianity, they dropped most Jewish customs and added to the Hebrew Bible a new book of religious writings, known as the New Testament.

Circumcision See *Brit Milah.*

*Confirmation A group ceremony held in some synagogues, often at Shavuot, in which boys and girls graduating from religious school celebrate their ties to Judaism.

*Conservative Judaism Branch of Judaism that changed some religious practices, such as seating men and women together and shortening the prayer service, while keeping the traditional symbols and spirit of the observances.

*Crusaders Armies of European Christians who tried to recapture Palestine and Jerusalem from the Muslims in the eleventh, twelfth, and thirteenth centuries. Many Jewish communities were destroyed by the marching Crusaders.

D

David (reigned about 1010–970 B.C.E.) The second king of Israel. David was a strong leader who unified the Hebrew tribes and captured Jerusalem. He also was a singer and musician, and he composed many psalms, songs to God, that we still sing today.

Dayan, Moshe (1915–81) Israeli political leader who served as an army general and as minister of defense. Dayan was known for his black eye patch and his independent ideas.

*Dead Sea Scrolls Biblical manuscripts of the first century C.E., discovered by an Arab shepherd boy near the Dead Sea in Israel. See *Essenes.*

Diaspora Greek for "dispersion." In Hebrew, *galut.* The term refers to the whole world except Israel.

*Dreyfus, Alfred (1858–1935) French Jewish army officer who was falsely accused of being a spy. After a long legal battle that brought out deep anti-Semitism in the French government and the army, Dreyfus was cleared and freed.

E

Einstein, Albert (1879–1955) Physicist who developed the Theory of Relativity. Einstein was a Zionist, and he worked for international cooperation and world government.

*Elijah (about 875 B.C.E.) Biblical prophet who sought justice for the weak against the strong. According to the Aggadah, Elijah is still helping people in need and he will some day announce the coming of the Messiah.

Eretz Yisrael See *Israel.*

Essenes Small groups of religious Jews during the time of the Second Temple. They lived very simply, deep in the desert, far from other Jews. The Essenes wrote the Dead Sea Scrolls.

*Esther (about 475 B.C.E.). Wife of King Ahasuerus of Persia. The Book of Esther, read on Purim, tells how she saved the Jews from Haman's wicked plot.

Etrog Citron, a fruit in the lemon family, which is used in the Sukkot holiday celebration.

Exile See *Diaspora.*

F

Falashas Jews of Ethiopia.

Frank, Anne (1929–45) A young Dutch Jewish girl who kept a diary while she hid from the Nazis. Anne later died in a concentration camp, but her diary survived. The movie and plays based on the diary show a tragic picture of life under the Nazis. See *Holocaust.*

G

Galut See *Diaspora.*

Gan Eden Hebrew for "Garden of Eden" (delight). The fruitful, beautiful first home of all living creatures, as described in the Book of Genesis.

*Ghetto An area of a city where only one group lives, historically only Jews. The first ghettos were established in Europe in the twelfth century. A wall often surrounded the ghetto, with a gate that was locked at night.

*Golem A being created by magic. Legend tells of the Golem of Prague, who was brought to life by a famous rabbi in order to fight anti-Semites.

Gordon, A. D. (1856–1922) Zionist writer who urged Jews to work as farmers and laborers to build their homeland. He worked on a kibbutz in Palestine.

Goy Hebrew for "nation." The term is often used to refer to a non-Jew.

H

Haftarah Hebrew for "conclusion." The *Haftarah* is the chapter from the Prophets that concludes the Torah reading in the synagogue. It is often the section read by the bar/bat mitzvah.

Haganah Hebrew for "defense." The name of the underground army of the Jews of Palestine before the State of Israel was established.

*Haggadah Hebrew for "narration." The *Haggadah* is the slim book that tells the story of the Exodus from Egypt. It is read aloud at the Passover *seder*.

Halakhah Hebrew for "as it goes" or "tradition." *Halakhah* is Jewish law as interpreted by the rabbis from the laws of the Torah, Talmud, and later writings.

*Halutzim Hebrew for "pioneers." The *halutzim* went to Palestine and risked disease, hunger, and attack to build a modern Jewish homeland.

*Haman (about 475 B.C.E.) Evil Persian prime minister, described in the Book of Esther, who tried to destroy the Jews. There have been many "Hamans" in Jewish history. A Yiddish saying complains, "So many Hamans, but only one Purim." See *Purim*.

*Hanukkah Midwinter holiday that celebrates the Maccabees' victory over the Syrians and the rededication of the Holy Temple in Jerusalem.

Ha-Shomer Hebrew for "the watchman." An organization of guards who defended early settlements in Palestine against stealing and attack, it was the forerunner of the Haganah.

*Hasidim Groups of Orthodox Jewish followers of the ideas of the Ba'al Shem Tov. Each Hasidic group, such as the Lubavicher and the Belzer, is led by a respected rabbi and forms a close-knit community.

*Ha-Tikvah Hebrew for "the hope." *Ha-Tikvah* is the national anthem of the State of Israel.

Havdalah Hebrew for "separation." It is the name of the prayer, recited over a braided candle, wine, and spices, to conclude the Sabbath; or a prayer over wine at the end of other holidays. *Havdalah* "separates" the Sabbath or holiday from other days of the week.

Hazzan The cantor who leads the congregation in prayer at synagogue services.

*Hebrew Semitic language of the same family as Arabic and Aramaic. It was spoken in the days of the Bible, but later it was used mainly for study and prayer. Hebrew became a spoken language again with the rise of Zionism in the twentieth century.

Hebrews Early name for the Jewish people. The later term "Jews" came from "Judea," the name of one of the two Hebrew kingdoms.

*Herzl, Theodore (1860–1904) Viennese journalist and founder of modern, political Zionism. After seeing the anti-Semitism awakened by the Dreyfus case in France, Herzl de-

214

Mini-encyclopedia

An asterisk (∗) next to a word means there's more information in another chapter. Look it up in the index.

cided that Jews must have a homeland of their own. He wrote a book called *The Jewish State* and organized the First Zionist Congress in 1897.

∗**Hillel** (first century C.E.) A wise rabbi who gave us the rule: "Do not do to your fellow human being that which is hateful to you." Many of Hillel's ideas and judgments are included in the Talmud.

Histadrut Ha-Ovdim Largest labor union in Israel. Most working people and farmers belong to the Histadrut. It has cooperatives that do construction, run buses, market farm produce, and more. The Histadrut also has a health-care program and publishes books and newspapers.

∗**Holocaust** Program of murder carried out against the Jews of Europe during World War II (1939–45) by the Nazi government of Germany under Adolf Hitler. Two-thirds of the Jews of Europe, 6 million people, were killed. A Holocaust memorial called Yad Vashem was built in Jerusalem, Israel. There the names of the victims and their lost communities are inscribed. The twenty-seventh day of the Hebrew month of Nisan is Yom Ha-Sho'ah, a memorial day for those who died in the Holocaust.

Hoshana Rabba Hebrew for "great salvation." Holiday at the end of Sukkot.

I

Ingathering of the Exiles In Hebrew, *kibbutz galuyot.* The "ingathering" was the mass movement of the Jews to Israel from all countries of the world after the establishment of the state in 1948. From mid-May 1948 until the end of 1953, 718,000 new immigrants arrived.

Inquisition Special courts set up by the Catholic church in the 1400s to punish backsliders from the faith. Many Marranos (Jews who converted to Ca-

tholicism but secretly practiced Judaism) were put to death by the Inquisition. The Spanish brought the Inquisition to America and punished Jews in Mexico and Brazil until 1821.

∗**Islam** Religion founded in Arabia in 622 C.E. by Muhammad, an Arabian religious leader. Its sacred book is called the Koran. Believers in Islam are called Muslims.

∗**Israel, State of** Established on May 14, 1948, as the homeland of the Jewish people in part of the biblical Land of Israel *(Eretz Yisrael)*. The country has a democratic form of government and many political parties. Immigration and defense have been Israel's biggest challenges.

J

∗**Jerusalem** Capital of the State of Israel, in the hills of Judea. In biblical times the Holy Temple was built in Jerusalem by King Solomon. Jews would come to the Temple to worship and bring sacrifices at holiday time. Throughout the centuries Jews have continued to live in Jerusalem, and Jews in *galut* have prayed to return to their holy city. Muslims and Christians also have holy places in Jerusalem.

Jew See *Hebrew* and *Judaism.*

Jewish Agency An international Jewish organization, based in Jerusalem, that encourages and assists the immigration and settlement of Jews in Israel.

∗**Jewish National Fund** Organization known in Israel as Keren Kayemet Le-Yisrael. In 1901 the Jewish National Fund began to collect money to buy land in Palestine for the Jewish homeland. Since 1948, when the State of Israel was born, JNF money has been used to build roads, plant trees, and clear land for farms, towns, and recreation areas.

Jewish Publication Society of America Nonprofit publishing company founded in 1888 to publish Jewish books for the English-speaking world. JPS prints books of Jewish literary and religious value, including translations of the Bible, commentaries, histories, and children's books.

Judah Halevi (1075–1141) Poet and philosopher of the Spanish Golden Age. He yearned for Israel and wrote, "In the East is my heart, and I live at the end of the West." Many of his poems are included in the prayer book.

∗**Judah Maccabee** (second century B.C.E.) Jewish soldier who, with his four brothers, led the fight to free the Holy Temple in Jerusalem and drive out the Syrians. The holiday of Ḥanukkah celebrates their victory in 164 B.C.E.

Judaism Religion and way of life that is based on the teachings of the Bible, Talmud, and Commentaries and on a sense of history and tradition shared with other Jews since the time of Moses.

K

*Knesset The parliament of the State of Israel.

*Kibbutz A type of farm settlement in Israel where property and work are shared equally by all members. Kibbutzim were the first to settle the dangerous and infertile regions of the country.

Korczak, Janusz (1878–1942) Brave teacher and writer who organized an orphanage for Jewish children in Poland as a self-governing republic. Although he could have escaped, he chose to die with the orphans in a Nazi extermination camp.

*Kosher Hebrew for "fit" or "suitable." The term refers to food or sacred objects that meet the religious requirements of observant Jews.

*Kotel Ma'aravi A wall of huge stones that is the last remnant of the Holy Temple in Jerusalem. For centuries Jews came to pray at the *Kotel,* except when it was under Arab control between 1948 and 1967. It became part of Israel again when the Old City of Jerusalem was taken in the 1967 Six-Day War.

L

*Ladino Jewish language blending fifteenth-century Spanish and Hebrew, with some Arabic, Turkish, Italian, and French as well. It is spoken by Jews in the countries of the eastern Mediterranean and in North and South America.

*Lag Ba-Omer Holiday on the thirty-third day of the counting of the *Omer,* between Passover and Shavuot. Hebrew school students celebrate by having picnics, going on hikes, or playing out of doors. See *Omer.*

Landsmanshaften Associations of people who come from the same town in a faraway land. European Jews formed landsmanshaften in the United States, and today in Israel there are landsmanshaft clubs of immigrants from New York, Paris, and elsewhere.

Lulav The palm branch that is tied to willow and myrtle branches and waved during the Sukkot holiday.

M

Maccabees See *Judah Maccabee.*

Maccabiah Sports competition for Jews of the whole world, held every few years in Israel.

Magen David Hebrew for "shield of David." The term usually refers to the six-pointed star that has become a symbol of Judaism. Under Nazi rule Jews were ordered to wear a yellow *magen David* on their clothing. The flag of Israel has a blue *magen David* and two blue stripes on a white field.

*Maimonides, Moses, also called **Rambam** (1135–1204) Maimonides was a Jewish religious philosopher and doctor who lived in Egypt but whose influence spread throughout the Jewish world. He wrote a Mishnah commentary, a guide for the perplexed that combined religion and philosophy, and many letters of advice on religious matters.

*Marranos See *Inquisition.*

*Masada Fortress on top of a mountain near the Dead Sea in Israel. The Zealots, a group of Jewish patriots, made a last heroic stand against the Roman armies in Masada in 73 C.E. Today young Israelis climb to the top of that fortress to be sworn into the army.

Meir, Golda (1898–1978) Zionist leader who became Israel's first ambassador to Russia and its fourth prime minister.

*Menorah A candleholder or oil lamp with many branches. The great gold menorah at the Holy Temple in Jerusalem had seven branches. At Hanukkah an eight-branched menorah plus a lighter (*shamash*) is used.

Messiah By Jewish tradition the Messiah is God's Chosen One, a descendant of the family of King David, who will bring peace and justice to the world. Over the centuries Jews have rejoiced at the appearances of self-proclaimed Messiahs and have been disappointed as they disappeared, leaving the world even worse than before.

Mezuzah A small holder containing part of the Hebrew prayer *Shema.* The *mezuzah* is attached to the door frame of a Jewish home to remind the Jew of his or her closeness to God at all times.

An asterisk (∗) next to a word means there's more information in another chapter. Look it up in the index.

Middle East Geographical region that Israel shares with Egypt, Syria, Lebanon, Iraq, Saudi Arabia, Jordan, and other countries. The Middle East bubbles with oil and unrest.

∗Midrash Interpretations of the Bible by rabbis of the first, second, and third centuries C.E., supplying answers to the problems of their times. Scholars later collected their words into books of Midrashim.

∗Minyan The minimum number of adult Jews required to conduct a religious service. Traditionally the requirement has been for ten men, though some non-Orthodox congregations now count women.

∗Mishnah Discussions and explanations of the Torah collected for four hundred years and written down in 200 C.E.

∗Mitzvah A commandment of Jewish religious law, or a good deed. The Talmud lists 613 *mitzvot,* but the prophet Habakkuk simplified them down to one: "The righteous person shall live according to his religion."

∗Moses (thirteenth century B.C.E.) Great leader who brought the Jewish people out of slavery in Egypt. For forty years he led them through the desert and taught them how to be strong and how to follow the laws of the Torah. Moses is known as *Moshe Rabbenu* ("Moses our Teacher"), and the first five books of the Bible are called the Five Books of Moses.

N

Ner Tamid Hebrew for "eternal light." A lit lamp that burns in front of the *aron kodesh* in every synagogue. It reminds us of the great menorah that was always kept burning in the Holy Temple.

O

∗Omer Hebrew for "sheaf" (of grain). The forty-nine days between the holidays of Passover and Shavuot, when the grain is ripening in the field, are counted as days of the *Omer.* This is a time when no celebrations take place, except for Lag Ba-Omer and Israel Independence Day.

∗Oneg Shabbat Hebrew for "joy of Sabbath." A Friday evening or Saturday afternoon gathering for singing, reading, talking, and "noshing."

Organizations, American Jewish Hundreds of groups covering a wide range of interests. Some, such as American ORT, Federation of Jewish Agencies, Hadassah, and the National Conference on Soviet Jewry, work hard to raise money and build support for Jews abroad and in Israel. Some stress Jewish religious education and practices, like Agudat Israel and the Jewish Reconstructionist Foundation. The Anti-Defamation League and the American Jewish Congress fight in the courts for social justice for Jews and all Americans. Art, books, language, and other areas of Jewish culture are the special interests of members of the Jewish Book Council and the Histadrut Ivrit. You'll find a full list of all the organizations and their interests in the *American Jewish Year Book* published by the American Jewish Committee and The Jewish Publication Society of America.

Organizations, American Jewish Youth Something for everybody. Ha-Shomer Ha-Tza'ir and Habonim members go hiking, study Hebrew, and prepare to go and live on a kibbutz in Israel. Members of Ha-Shachar are staunch Zionists too. B'nai B'rith Youth Organization people have dances, weekend outings, and celebrate Jewish holidays. B'nai Akiva is for Orthodox Jewish youth, many of whom are preparing to settle in Israel. The list could go on and on, so check the *American Jewish Year Book* for more information.

∗Orthodox Judaism Branch of Judaism that holds closely to the laws and customs of the Torah. Yeshivot are day schools attended by many Orthodox young people.

P

*Palestine The Land of Israel, homeland of the Jews since biblical times. The Greeks and Romans called the country Palestine after the Philistines, who had lived along the coast. Today Arabs who live on the West Bank call the area Palestine.

*Passover (Pesah) Springtime holiday celebrating the freeing of the Jewish people from slavery in Egypt. Passover is celebrated at a gathering of family and friends called a *seder*. At the *seder* everybody reads the Passover story, sings, and shares the holiday meal. See *Haggadah*.

*Peretz, Isaac Leib (1851–1915) Writer of short stories and plays in the Yiddish language. He made the world of Hasidim and of poor working people in Polish ghettos come to life for the reader.

Pidyon Ha-Ben A traditional ceremony in which the firstborn son in a Jewish family is freed from service in the Temple by a symbolic payment to a *kohen* (a descendant of the priestly family).

*Pogrom Russian for "riot." Many attacks, riots, and massacres of Jews happened in Russia in the late 1800s and early 1900s. These pogroms caused a rush of Jewish emigration from the country.

Population, Jewish The number of Jews in the world, according to the 1992 *American Jewish Year Book:* 12,806,400. There are 5,535,000 Jews in the United States; 1,150,000 in the former Soviet Union; 3,946,700 in Israel.

Prayer Praise, thanks, and requests directed to God. Jews pray alone or in a congregation. They read from a *siddur* (prayer book for weekdays and the Sabbath) or *mahzor* (prayer book for holidays with added hymns). Congregational prayers are said in the morning (*Shaharit*), afternoon (*Minhah*), and evening (*Ma'ariv*). Some of the most important daily prayers are the *Shema* (which proclaims the unity of God), the *Shemoneh-Esreh* (the eighteen blessings), and the *Ashrei* and *Aleinu* (prayers of praise to God). Some important prayers said at home are the *Kiddush* (blessing over wine), *Birkhat ha-Mazon* (grace after meals), and *Havdalah* (to end the Sabbath).

*Prophets Religious leaders, rebels, and teachers inspired by God in the days of the Bible. Prophets such as Isaiah, Amos, and Jeremiah fought for justice to the poor and for obedience to all the laws of the Torah. Their words are still used today by reformers, rebels, and politicians.

*Purim Hebrew for "lots." The Purim holiday celebrates the victory of the Jews of Persia over a villain called Haman through the courage of a Jewish woman called Esther. It's a happy holiday of feasting and costume parties.

R

Rabbi Title given to a religious leader and teacher. Today rabbis are trained at rabbinical schools. They work as teachers, leaders of congregations, and often as scholars and community leaders too.

*Rashi (1040–1105) French rabbi, teacher, and scholar who wrote commentaries on the Talmud and Bible that are still used today. In 1475 Rashi's Bible commentary was the first Hebrew book ever to be printed.

Reconstructionism A Jewish religious movement that seeks to combine traditional values and customs with new interpretations of Jewish culture. Strong Jewish communities, good Hebrew schools, and close ties with the State of Israel are some of the Reconstructionist goals.

*Reform Judaism Branch of Judaism that has changed many religious practices in an effort to adapt them to modern life and thus make them more meaningful for its members. For example, the laws of keeping kosher and of Sabbath observance have been relaxed, and the prayer book has been shortened for use in Reform synagogues. Both Reform Judaism and Reconstructionism ordain women as rabbis.

218

Mini-encyclopedia

An asterisk (*) next to a word means there's more information in another chapter. Look it up in the index.

Refusenik Soviet (Russian) Jew who had been "refused" permission to emigrate to Israel. Many refuseniks defied Soviet laws forbidding the study of the Hebrew language and Jewish culture and denying the right of Soviet Jews to support Zionism. Those who were in prison were called "prisoners of conscience."

*Rosh Ha-Shanah Hebrew for "head of the year." This is the beginning of the Jewish calendar year, a time when people think over their way of living and pray for a good year to come.

*Rothschild Family of European Jewish bankers who became important in Germany in the 1700s. Family members moved to other large cities and set up a network of banks used by rulers and businesses all over Europe. Baron Edmond de Rothschild helped the early Zionists in Palestine with money and advice.

S

*Sabbath (Shabbat) Seventh day of the week. The Bible commands that each Jew, and his or her family, servants, and work animals must rest on the Sabbath. "The Sabbath is a foretaste of heaven," says a Jewish proverb.

Sabra Cactus fruit. Children born in Israel, who are supposed to be prickly and tough on the outside but sweet as sugar on the inside (like the cactus fruit), are known as Sabras.

*Salomon, Haym (1740–85) Polish-born Jewish financier and patriot who helped raise the money to support the American Revolutionary government and army.

Sarah (about nineteenth century B.C.E.) Wife of Abraham and "mother of the Jewish people."

*Schechter, Solomon (1847–1915) Rabbi and scholar who discovered ancient writings of the Cairo *Genizah* ("storage place") and later became a leader of Conservative Judaism.

*Seder See *Passover*.

*Senesch, Hanna (1921–44) One of a brave band of parachutists from Palestine who jumped into Nazi Europe to try to save the imprisoned Jews. She was captured and executed.

*Sephardim Hebrew for "Spanish." Sephardim are Jews whose ancestors came from Spain and Portugal as well as Jews, like those of Yemen, who have always lived in the Middle East. Today many Sephardi Jews live in North and South America, but most live in Israel.

*Shammai (first century C.E.) Strict rabbi and teacher who lived at the time of Hillel. His teachings are included in the Talmud.

*Shavuot Late spring holiday that celebrates the giving of the Torah to the Jewish people. Shavuot, Passover, and Sukkot were the three harvest holidays when Jews came to the Temple in Jerusalem to offer sacrifices to God.

Shekel Measure of money in biblical times. The Maccabees made a silver coin called a shekel. Modern Israel also uses the shekel.

Shemini Atzeret Fall holiday that ends Sukkot and precedes Simhat Torah. It is a solemn time when prayers for rain are said.

Shivah Hebrew for "seven." The *shivah* period is the seven days of mourning after the death of a close family member.

Shofar Ram's horn that was blown at important times in ancient Israel. The *shofar* is sounded during the month (Elul) before Rosh Ha-Shanah and during the holiday services to remind people to think about their lives and deeds. It is also sounded at the end of Yom Kippur.

*Sholom Aleichem (1859–1916) Yiddish writer born in Russia who wrote funny and sad-funny descriptions of small-town Jewish life in Europe. He is called the "Jewish Mark Twain."

*Siddur Prayer book for Sabbath and weekdays. See *Prayer*.

*Simhat Torah Hebrew for "rejoicing of the Torah." At Simhat Torah, which comes at the end of Sukkot, the year-long reading of the Torah is finished. The Torah scrolls are carried in a happy, singing parade around the synagogue. Then one scroll is opened and the reading begins again from the very beginning.

Singer, Isaac Bashevis (1904–1991) American Jewish author, born in Poland, who wrote novels primarily about life in Eastern Europe. Singer, who won a Nobel Prize, also wrote children's books.

Solomon (tenth century B.C.E.) Third king of Israel and builder of the Holy Temple in Jerusalem. According to tradition, he wrote the Song of Songs.

*Sukkot Hebrew word for "booths" or "small shelters." The autumn holiday that follows Yom Kippur. During this holiday, which lasts a full week, Jews eat (and sometimes even sleep) in a *sukkah* (booth) that is set up outside the house as a reminder of the time when the Jewish people wandered in the desert.

Synagogue Greek for "assembly." Jews began to study and pray in synagogues during the Babylonian exile in the sixth century B.C.E. When the Second Temple was destroyed in 70 C.E. and the Jews were forced out of Judea, the local synagogue (today also called *shul* or temple; in Hebrew, *bet ha-kenesset*) became the center of Jewish life.

Szold, Henrietta (1860–1945) American Jewish woman who was editor of the Jewish Publication Society and founder of Hadassah, a women's Zionist organization. She led the work of Youth Aliyah, which saved thousands of Jewish children from the Nazis.

T

Tablets of the Law Stone tablets on which God's Ten Commandments were engraved. Moses and the Jews carried them through the desert to Israel in the Ark of the Covenant.

*Tallit Prayer shawl that has fringes *(tzitzit)* on its four corners.

*Talmud The set of works that explain and interpret the teachings of the Torah. The Talmud contains nearly one thousand years of debates and discussions of many scholars, beginning in 200 B.C.E.

*Tefillin (Phylacteries) Two small boxes containing passages from the Torah. *Tefillin* are placed on the forehead and the left arm for daily morning prayers.

*Temple The First Temple was built in Jerusalem by King Solomon in the tenth century B.C.E. The people came there to worship and celebrate the three pilgrimage holidays each year, while the Levites *(levi'im)* and the priests *(kohanim)* made music and offered sacrifices to God. The Temple was destroyed by the Babylonians on the ninth day of Av, 586 B.C.E. The Second Temple was built seventy years later and destroyed by the Romans on the ninth day of Av, 70 C.E. Today only an outer wall remains. See *Kotel Ma'aravi.*

∗Tisha Be-Av A day of fasting (no eating) when we remember the destruction of the Holy Temple in Jerusalem.

∗Torah See *Bible.*

Trumpeldor, Joseph (1880–1920) Zionist leader and soldier. Trumpeldor lost an arm in the Russian army, but that didn't stop him. He worked as a farmer in Palestine and organized a Jewish army unit in World War I. He was killed defending an outpost in northern Palestine against Arab attack.

∗Tu Bi-Shevat Hebrew for "fifteenth day of Shevat," which the Mishnah designates as the "New Year of the Trees." This holiday comes in early springtime, when almond trees bloom in Israel. It is a time when Israeli and American Jewish children plant seeds and saplings.

U

Union of American Hebrew Congregations See *Reform Judaism.*

Union of Orthodox Jewish Congregations See *Orthodox Judaism.*

United Synagogue See *Conservative Judaism.*

W

Wald, Lillian (1867–1940) Warmhearted nurse and social worker who led the fight to end child labor. She started the Henry Street Settlement House in New York to help new immigrants.

Wallenberg, Raoul (1912–?) Swedish businessman and diplomat who risked his life to save thousands of Jews from the Nazis during World War II. He has not been seen or heard from since the end of the war, when he was arrested by the Russians.

Weizmann, Chaim (1874–1952) Famous scientist and a Zionist leader from the time of the Fifth Zionist Congress in 1901. In 1948 Weizmann became the first president of the State of Israel.

∗Western Wall See *Kotel Ma'aravi.*

World Jewish Congress Association of Jewish organizations from all over the world. It represents the Jewish people at international meetings and defends Jewish rights.

Y

Yahrzeit Yiddish for "time of the year," specifically the date of the death of a family member on the Jewish calendar. A memorial candle that burns for twenty-four hours is lit on the eve of that day, and the *Kaddish* is said.

Yeshivah A school for talmudic learning. Yeshivah study began in Judea and Babylonia in the days of the Second Temple. Today an Orthodox day school is sometimes called a yeshivah.

∗Yiddish Language spoken by European Jews that grew from a mixture of medieval German, Hebrew, and other

languages into a completely separate language with a rich and unique literature.

∗Yom Ha-Atzma'ut Israel's "independence day," commemorating the birthday of the modern state in 1948. It is celebrated with parades and parties in Israel and in Jewish communities around the world.

Yom Ha-sho'ah See *Holocaust.*

∗Yom Kippur A fast day when there is much praying and thinking about how to live according to the standards of the Torah.

∗Youth Aliyah A program that helps children immigrate to Israel and helps them and needy Israeli children to become educated and adjusted to life in Israel. Youth Aliyah was started in Germany in 1934 by Recha Freier to rescue Jewish children from the Nazis.

Z

∗Zionism A movement to build a Jewish homeland in Palestine. Jewish pioneers (halutzim) began to go to Palestine in the late 1800s and built farms and cities. Others fought for political support in the League of Nations. Jews all over the world contributed help and money. At last the State of Israel was established on May 14, 1948. Zionists still work hard to support Israel, and some go and settle there.

Index

ABOUT THE AUTHOR

Chaya M. Burstein is the author-illustrator of many books for Jewish children, including Rifka Grows Up, *winner of the 1977 National Jewish Book Award for children's literature. She writes about herself: "I was brought up with Bible stories and shtetl stories rather than with tales of Mother Goose. The goats and chickens of my mother's small town in Russia became imaginary friends. And Sarah, Deborah the Judge, and King Solomon felt like an extended family. I would sit on the milk box in front of my family's grocery store in Brooklyn and draw paper dolls to act out their troubles and adventures. There wasn't much time for writing and drawing as I grew older. I worked as a draftswoman, married, lived on a kibbutz in Israel, returned to America, and had three children. But the old stories were still tucked away in my mind. Finally, I began to write and draw about them again. I wrote two* Rifka *books about my mother's shtetl, a Jewish holiday cookbook for kids, and now this book, about the absorbing, dramatic Jewish heritage . . . about my extended family."*